Faith Alone
IN ONE HUNDRED VERSES

Robert N. Wilkin

GRACE EVANGELICAL SOCIETY
Denton, TX 76210

Faith Alone in One Hundred Verses

Copyright © 2020 Grace Evangelical Society
All rights reserved. Published 2020.

Wilkin, Robert N., 1952–

ISBN 978-1-943399-39-0

Grace Evangelical Society
P.O. Box 1308
Denton, TX 76202
www.faithalone.org
ges@faithalone.org

All rights reserved. No part of this book may be reproduced in any form without the prior permission of the publisher, except as provided by USA copyright law.

Scripture taken from the New King James Version.
Copyright © 1982 by Thomas Nelson, Inc.
Used by permission. All rights reserved.

Printed in the United States of America.

For Ken Yates and Pam Esteven,
for their help in research and editing,
and Shawn Lazar, for typesetting.

Contents

Prologue

SECTION 1: CRYSTAL CLEAR VERSES

1. Abraham Believed in the Lord for Righteousness (Genesis 15:6)
2. Lest They Should Believe and Be Saved (Luke 8:11-12)
3. Those Who Believe in His Name Are Children of God (John 1:12-13)
4. Whoever Believes in Him Will Not Perish But Has Eternal Life (John 3:14-15)
5. Whoever Believes in Him Won't Perish, But Has Eternal Life (John 3:16)
6. He Who Believes in Him Is Not Condemned (John 3:18)
7. He Who Believes in the Son Has Everlasting Life (John 3:36)
8. Whoever Drinks the Living Water Jesus Gives Has Everlasting Life (John 4:13-14)
9. The Woman Drank the Living Water and Gained Everlasting Life (John 4:25-26)
10. Samaritans Believe in Jesus and Gain Everlasting Life (John 4:39-42)
11. He Who Believes in Him Is Secure Forever (John 5:24)
12. All Who Come to Jesus Have Everlasting Life (John 5:39-40)
13. He Who Believes in Me Shall Never Thirst (John 6:35)
14. Everyone Who Believes in the Son Has Everlasting Life (John 6:40)
15. He Who Believes in Me Has Everlasting Life (John 6:47)
16. My Sheep Believe in Me, and I Give Them Eternal Life (John 10:24-30)
17. He Who Believes in Me…Shall Live (John 11:25)
18. Whoever Lives and Believes in Me Shall Never Die (John 11:26)

19. I Believe You Are the Christ, the Son of God (John 11:27)
20. Believe in the Light That You May Become Sons of Light (John 12:36)
21. He Who Believes in Me Has Everlasting Life (John 12:44-50)
22. By Believing You Have Life in His Name (John 20:30-31)
23. Whoever Believes in Him Will Receive Remission of Sins (Acts 10:43)
24. The Gift of Salvation Even for Gentiles Who Believe in Christ (Acts 11:17)
25. All Who Believe in Jesus Are Justified (Acts 13:39)
26. All Who Believe in Jesus Are Purified (Acts 15:9)
27. In the Same Manner: Salvation by Faith (Acts 15:11)
28. Believe on the Lord Jesus Christ, and You Will Be Saved (Acts 16:31)
29. Positional Sanctification by Faith in Jesus (Acts 26:18)
30. The Just by Faith (Romans 1:17)
31. The Righteousness of God through Faith (Romans 3:22)
32. Justified Freely by His Grace through Faith (Romans 3:24-25)
33. The Justifier of the One Who Has Faith in Jesus (Romans 3:26)
34. Boasting Excluded Because of the Law of Faith (Romans 3:27)
35. Justified by Faith Apart from the Deeds of the Law (Romans 3:28)
36. Jews and Gentiles Justified by Faith (Romans 3:30)
37. The Prime Example of Justification by Faith Alone: Abraham (Romans 4:3)
38. Justification by Faith Is for Him Who Does Not Work (Romans 4:5)
39. The Blessing of Justification Is for All Who Believe in Christ (Romans 4:9)
40. Circumcision Is a Seal of Righteousness by Faith (Romans 4:11)
41. The Promise Came Through the Righteousness of Faith (Romans 4:13)
42. All Who Are of the Faith of Abraham (Romans 4:16)
43. Therefore, It Was Accounted to Him for Righteousness (Romans 4:22)
44. Justification by Faith Alone Is for Us Too (Romans 4:23-24)
45. Having Been Justified by Faith, We Have Peace with God (Romans 5:1)
46. The Righteousness of Faith (Romans 9:30)
47. Do Not Be Ashamed of Being Justified by Faith in Christ (Romans 9:32-33)
48. Christ Is the End of the Law for Righteousness for the Believer (Romans 10:4)
49. With the Heart One Believes unto Righteousness (Romans 10:9-10)

50. To Save Those Who Believe (1 Corinthians 1:21)
51. By Faith We Know We Will Have Glorious Eternal Bodies (2 Corinthians 5:1, 7)
52. By Faith We Know That to Be Absent from the Body Is to Be Present with the Lord (2 Corinthians 5:8)
53. Triply Justified by Faith, Not Works (Galatians 2:16)
54. Receiving the Spirit by Faith, Not Works (Galatians 3:2)
55. Supply of the Spirit and Working of Miracles by Faith, Not by Works (Galatians 3:5)
56. Abraham's Justification by Faith in Messiah (Galatians 3:6)
57. Only Believers Are Sons of Abraham (Galatians 3:7)
58. The Old Testament Foresaw Justification by Faith for Gentiles (Galatians 3:8)
59. Those Who Are of Faith (Galatians 3:9)
60. Receiving the Promise of the Spirit Through Faith (Galatians 3:14)
61. The Promise by Faith to Those Who Believe (Galatians 3:22)
62. Saved and Sealed (Ephesians 1:13)
63. Salvation by Grace Through Faith, Apart from Works (Ephesians 2:8-9)
64. Righteousness Through Faith in Christ (Philippians 3:9)
65. Believing on Him for Everlasting Life (1 Timothy 1:16)
66. I Know Whom I Have Believed (2 Timothy 1:12)
67. Salvation Through Faith in Christ Jesus (2 Timothy 3:15)
68. Salvation by Grace Through Faith in Christ (Titus 3:5-8)
69. Whoever Believes That Jesus Is the Christ Is Born of God (1 John 5:1)
70. He Who Has the Son Has Life (1 John 5:9-12)
71. That You May Know That You Have Eternal Life (1 John 5:13)
72. The Free Water of Life to Him Who Thirsts (Revelation 21:6)
73. Take the Water of Life Freely (Revelation 22:17)

SECTION 2: CONTEXTUALLY CLEAR VERSES

74. Rejoice Because Your Names Are Written in Heaven (Luke 10:20)
75. Slay Those Enemies of Mine (Luke 19:24-27)
76. John the Baptist Led People to Believe in Christ (John 1:7)
77. Many Believed in His Name (John 2:23)
78. Believe in Him Whom He Sent (John 6:27-29)
79. If You Do Not Believe That I Am He (John 8:24)
80. If You Abide in His Word, the Truth Shall Make You Free (John 8:30-32)

81. I Am the Way, the Truth, and the Life (John 14:6)
82. No Other Name by Which We Must Be Saved (Acts 4:12)
83. They Believed Concerning the Name of Jesus Christ (Acts 8:12-13)
84. Words by Which You Will Be Saved (Acts 11:14)
85. Rejecting the Words of Everlasting Life (Acts 13:46)
86. As Many as Had Been Attracted to Eternal Life Believed (Acts 13:48)
87. Hearing the Gospel and Believing in Christ for Salvation (Acts 15:7)
88. The Gift of God Is Eternal Life in Christ (Romans 6:23)
89. If It Is by Grace, It Is No Longer of Works (Romans 11:6)
90. Now Our Salvation Is Nearer Than When We First Believed (Romans 13:11)
91. Whose Names Are in the Book of Life (Philippians 4:3)
92. Eternal Security for All Believers Who Have Died (1 Thessalonians 4:14)
93. Even Morally Lethargic Believers Will Live Forever with Him (1 Thessalonians 5:10)
94. Sanctified by Faith Once for All (Hebrews 10:10)
95. Perfected Forever (Hebrews 10:14)
96. He Brought Us Forth by the Word of Truth (James 1:18)
97. Faith Was Accounted to Abraham for Righteousness (James 2:23)
98. Born Again Through the Word of God (1 Peter 1:23)
99. The Promise of Life (1 John 2:25)
100. Having One's Name in the Book of Life (Revelation 20:15)

Epilogue
Subject Index
Scripture Index

Prologue

I came to believe the faith-alone message through two verses (Eph 2:8-9) that a friend shared with me. What a joy it was to me when I saw that the Bible teaches that all who simply believe in Jesus for their eternal destiny have everlasting life that can never be lost.

Each chapter in this book can be read in a few minutes. Most chapters are just two pages in length.

While most people do not read footnotes, I hope you will. I have placed a lot of helpful information in the notes.

I should warn you that when I suggest that the Bible teaches that salvation is by faith-alone, apart from works, I mean just that. I do not mean that we are eternally saved if we have faith in Christ combined with a lifetime characterized by good works.

The Bible does not guarantee that once a person believes in Christ, then he is guaranteed to live a victorious life. Of course, that *should* happen and that *can* happen but that is not guaranteed. What is guaranteed to the believer is everlasting life that can never be lost.

If, like me, you grew up in a group that taught that once-saved, always-saved is heresy and dangerous, I hope you will prayerfully read this book. My experience is that when I became sure of my eternal destiny, it helped, rather than hurt, my ability to live a victorious life.

Over a hundred verses in the Bible teach that the sole condition of everlasting life that can never be lost is faith-alone in the Lord Jesus Christ. Apart from works. That message is the heart of the Christian faith. It produces an attitude of gratitude in those who believe and reflect on it.

SECTION 1

Crystal Clear Verses

ONE

Abraham Believed in the Lord for Righteousness (Genesis 15:6)

And he [Abraham] believed in the Lord, and He accounted it to him for righteousness.

A Promise-Based Hope

My parents had lost hope for a boy. Though their first child, a daughter, came after just a few years of trying, the second child, another daughter, did not come until nearly eight years later. Seven years after that, when my mom was thirty-nine and well past hope, they found out they were expecting again. When I was born, they learned they finally had a boy. I imagine that is what Abraham felt when Isaac was born. But unlike my parents, Abraham had a promise from God Almighty that he and Sarah would indeed have a son. That promise from God came long after it was reasonable for them to have a child.

The Accounting of Righteousness Refers to Justification before God (Romans 4; Galatians 3)

Paul quotes Gen 15:6 in Rom 4:3 and Gal 3:6. In both those contexts, Paul was clearly defending justification before God by faith in Christ, apart from works (see Rom 4:1-8; Gal 3:6-14, esp. vv 8, 11). Genesis 15:6 tells us that God declared Abraham righteous because he had faith in the Lord. But was Paul stretching things to suggest that Abraham is an example of one who believed in the Messiah for his justification before God?

Abraham Believed in the Lord Jesus Christ for Everlasting Life (John 8:56; Heb 11:10)

If all we had was the Book of Genesis, we would have to do some guesswork about what Moses meant when he said, "And he believed in the Lord." Without other OT and NT books, we would not know that he believed in the Lord Jesus Christ for everlasting life.

But it is clear from Gen 15:1-6 that Abraham believed the Lord was going to provide an heir who would be from him and Sarah. Considering Gen 12:1-3, we know that Abraham believed this coming heir would be the source of worldwide blessing. As Ross puts it, the promises given in Genesis 12 were primarily for the benefit of Abraham but would "ultimately benefit all the families of the world."[1] In light of the land promises of the Lord to Abraham, we also know that Abraham believed this coming heir would rule in the Promised Land, and Abraham believed that he himself would be resurrected and would gain the land which was promised to him.

If we go outside Genesis, we know that the Lord in whom Abraham believed is the Messiah, the pre-incarnate Lord Jesus Christ. Indeed, the Lord Jesus Himself said, "Abraham rejoiced to see My day" (John 8:56). That is, Abraham was happy to realize that the Lord Jesus was coming to establish His kingdom in the Promised Land. Compare Heb 11:10, which says that Abraham was looking for the New Jerusalem.

Paul quotes Gen 15:6 in both Romans 4 and Galatians 3. In both cases he uses that verse to prove that justification is by faith alone in the Lord Jesus Christ. Moo maintains that Paul sees a "Christological focus" in Gen 15:6 and that this focus is both "fair and appropriate."[2] If Gen 15:6 is not about justification by faith in Christ, then Paul has deceived us. But that is impossible, for God's Word is true.

---

[1] Allen P. Ross, *Creation and Blessing: A Guide to the Study and Exposition of Genesis* (Grand Rapids, MI: Baker, 1996), 262.

[2] Douglas Moo, *Romans 1–8* (Chicago, IL: Moody Press, 1991), 265.

Abraham Actually Met the Lord Jesus Christ and Spoke with Him on Many Occasions (Genesis 12-18, 21-22)

We tend to think of Abraham as someone who knew little or nothing about the Lord Jesus. But that is not true. He met the pre-incarnate Lord Jesus Christ on many occasions. Face to face. See especially the dialogue Abraham had with the Lord Jesus in Genesis 18 as Abraham comically tried to negotiate for the saving of Sodom (50…45…40…30…20…10). You and I have never seen Him. But Abraham met with Him often. Neyrey takes this position. While God the Father is invisible, Christ is the visible God who appeared to Abraham.[3]

Remember that the Lord Jesus said, "Abraham rejoiced to see My day." He saw, that is, anticipated, Jesus' day, His coming kingdom, while he was meeting with Him. Now, we do not know if Abraham knew that His name is Jesus. But he knew that He was the Lord. And he believed that by faith in Him he would spend eternity in His coming kingdom in the Promised Land.[4]

---

[3] Jerome Neyrey, *The Gospel of John in Cultural and Rhetorical Perspective* (Grand Rapids, MI: Eerdmans, 2009), 442-43.
[4] Faith is simple and uncomplicated. To have faith is be convinced or persuaded that something is true. For more discussion see Robert N. Wilkin, *The Ten Most Misunderstood Words in the Bible* (Denton, TX: Grace Evangelical Society, 2012), 7-22.

TWO

Lest They Should Believe and Be Saved (Luke 8:11-12)

"Now the parable is this: The seed is the word of God. Those by the wayside are the ones who hear; then the devil comes and takes away the word out of their hearts, lest they should believe and be saved."

When a Believer Falls

Billy Graham and Charles Templeton were two major crusade-style evangelists in the 1950s. Both spoke nightly to stadiums filled with 25,000 or more people wanting to hear about Christ. Graham went on to become the leading evangelist of the second half of the twentieth century. In 1957, Templeton left the ministry, declaring himself an agnostic. In 1995, he wrote a book entitled, *Farewell to God: My Reasons for Rejecting the Christian Faith*. He died in 2001. If Templeton believed in Christ before he fell away, is he with the Lord now?

Salvation from Eternal Condemnation Is in View

No other type of deliverance makes sense in this context. Commenting on v 12, Bock says that the "spiritual condition of this first seed is clearly a picture of the unsaved."[1] The devil wants to keep people from being born again. So he works hard to take the word out of the hearts of people. Satan knows that if they believe in the Lord Jesus Christ, then they will be irrevocably saved.

---

[1] Darrell L. Bock, *Luke 1:1–9:50* (Grand Rapids, MI: Baker, 1994), 733.

He puts a lot of effort into keeping people from coming to faith in Christ.

The Sole Condition Is Faith

The Lord does not mention repentance, turning from sins, commitment, obedience, or anything other than faith. While He does not specify that the faith is *in Him*, it would be obvious to Theophilus, the believing reader of Luke-Acts, or to any believing reader, that the Lord was speaking about faith in Himself.

Luke is not an evangelistic book. But there is enough in Luke 8:12 to show that salvation from eternal condemnation is by faith alone in Christ alone.

The Lord Then Illustrates Three Types of Believers (Luke 8:13-15)

Verses 13-15 illustrate three types of people who believe and are saved.

Only in v 13 with the rocky soil do we specifically read "who believe." We know from v 12 that what they believe is the saving message. So they are saved. Yet the Lord said that after they believe "for a time," "in time of temptation [they] fall away." The first type of believer is one who falls away. Green points out that this parable of the Lord clearly teaches that there is "the possibility" that those who have believed will not finish the course.[2] If Templeton believed the faith-alone message before his departure, then he is indeed with the Lord now.

Verse 14 tells us of a type of believer whose fruitfulness is choked out by "cares, riches, and the pleasures of life." Cares are not sinful. Nor are riches. Nor are the pleasures of life (hunting, fishing, golf, tennis, reading, talking, etc.). But all of them have the potential of robbing a believer of his devotion to Christ. Ironside says that these kinds of things are "innocent," but if they occupy the mind of the believer, he will be "sorry through eternity" that

---

[2] Joel B. Green, *The Gospel of Luke* (Grand Rapids, MI: Eerdmans, 1997), 329.

he put these things before devotion to the Lord.[3] Though this sort of believer does not fall away, he fails to bring "fruit to maturity."

The third type of believer (v 15) is the one who endures in faithfulness to Christ. The Lord calls him "the good soil."

Make no mistake. Soils 2, 3, and 4 all "sprang up" (Luke 8:6, 7, 8). The Word of God germinated in their lives. They believed in Christ and were born again.

Some believers fall away. Some believers are distracted and only halfhearted in their service for Christ. And some believers are wholehearted in their service. But all believers are born again.

---

[3] H. A. Ironside, *Addresses on the Gospel of Luke* (Neptune, NJ: Loizeaux Brothers, 1947), 245.

THREE

Those Who Believe in His Name Are Children of God (John 1:12-13)

But as many as received Him, to them He gave the right to become children of God, to those who believe in His name: who were born, not of blood, nor of the will of the flesh, nor of the will of man, but of God.

It's Good to Be King

Prince Charles and Diana, Princess of Wales, were overjoyed to have a son, William, who would likely one day become the king of England. Prince William is a child of royalty. He is tremendously blessed. An even greater blessing is being a child of God, the Almighty.

The Prologue Lays Out the Faith-Alone Message

John 1:1-18 is the prologue of the book. In the prologue, the Apostle John whets the unbelieving readers' appetite (John 20:31) for the saving message. He tells them a bit of who Jesus is.

John 1:12-13 May Be the Pinnacle of the Prologue

Various chiastic structures (e.g., ABCDC'B'A') have been suggested for the prologue. Many of these show John 1:12-13 as the very center of the prologue.

Most in Israel rejected Jesus and His message (John 1:11). Bruce states that Jesus "came in the form of special revelation to the people of Israel," but this revelation was repeatedly ignored.[1] However, some received Him and His message. That is, some "believed in His name." Those who believed in His name "become children of God" (John 1:12) and hence have been "born of God" (John 1:13).

Faith. Alone.

The Issue Is Faith in Christ for Everlasting Life

John 1:12-13 clearly states that whoever believes in the Lord Jesus Christ has become a child of God and has been born of God. Brodie says that the main idea of these two verses is that "belief generates birth, a supernatural birth."[2] The sole issue is faith in Christ for the life He promises.

---

[1] F. F. Bruce, *The Gospel of John* (Grand Rapids, MI: Eerdmans, 1983), 37.
[2] Thomas L. Brodie, *The Gospel According to John: A Literary and Theological Commentary* (New York, NY: Oxford University Press, 1993), 140.

FOUR

Whoever Believes in Him Will Not Perish But Has Eternal Life (John 3:14-15)

"And as Moses lifted up the serpent in the wilderness, even so must the Son of Man be lifted up, that whoever believes in Him should not perish but have eternal life."

Snakes on a Staff

Have you ever wondered about the odd symbol of the American Medical Association? It is two snakes wrapped around a staff or pole. In Greek mythology snakes on a staff are associated with healing. However, that myth goes back to an actual historical account of how dying Israelite people were healed by looking upon an uplifted bronze serpent. The Lord Jesus referred to that account to teach people that He saves all who look to Him in faith.

The Bronze Serpent Moses Lifted Up (John 3:14; Numbers 21:4-9)

The Lord here recalled a famous event in Israel's history. During the forty years of wilderness wandering, the people often complained and rebelled. On one of those occasions the Lord sent venomous snakes through the camp. As a result, "many of the people of Israel died" (Num 21:6).

After the people confessed their sins, Moses prayed for them. God told Moses to make a serpent and set it on a pole "that everyone who is bitten, when he looks at it, shall live."

Look and live.

This deliverance from physical death was not of works. Barnhouse says that the Israelites "were to cease from human remedies and turn to a divine remedy."[1] The people did nothing for this healing other than look to the uplifted serpent as God had said.

The Cross and the Gift of Life Are the Antitype (John 3:15)

This incident was a type of "the Son of Man be[ing] lifted up on the cross" and of faith in Him for eternal life ("that whoever believes in Him should not perish but have eternal life"). Boice rightly says that we can only understand the point of Numbers 21 here in John 3 when we see that it is "intended to prefigure the raising up of the Lord Jesus Christ on the cross."[2]

A type is a literal historical event which has prophetic significance. Abraham offering up his only son Isaac foreshadows God the Father offering up His only Son on the cross for our sins. Likewise, Moses lifting up the bronze serpent on a pole for healing to all who look upon it foreshadows Jesus being lifted up on the cross for salvation to all who look to Him for that salvation.

By looking in faith to the uplifted Messiah, we live. That is, we gain everlasting life which can never be lost. The Israelites in Numbers 21 "received a prolongation of mortal life, but it is eternal life that the Son of Man ensures to those who look to him."[3]

Look and live.

The sole condition is faith in the Lord Jesus Christ.

---

[1] Donald G. Barnhouse, *God's Remedy* (Grand Rapids, MI: Eerdmans, 1954), 219.
[2] James Montgomery Boice, *The Gospel of John: The Coming of the Light* (Grand Rapids, MI: Baker, 1985), 221.
[3] F. F. Bruce, *The Gospel of John* (Grand Rapids, MI: Eerdmans, 1983), 89.

FIVE

Whoever Believes in Him Won't Perish, But Has Eternal Life (John 3:16)

"For God so loved the world that He gave His only begotten Son, that whoever believes in Him should not perish but have everlasting life."

Known and Unknown

John 3:16 stands out as one of the best known verses in the Bible. Many people memorized it during childhood. Sadly, however, it is one of the most misunderstood verses in the Bible, not because it is difficult to understand, but because it is hard to believe.

The Manner in Which God Loved the World

The little word *so* in "For God so loved the world..." is a Greek word (*houtōs*) which means "in this manner."[1] The Lord Jesus is not talking about the magnitude of God the Father's love for the world, though it is obviously implied in what follows. Instead, He is speaking of the way in which He demonstrated His love for the world. Lincoln phrases it in this way: "The greatness of the divine love is not simply an inspiring theological concept but is demonstrated in its gift, that of the only Son."[2]

---

[1] See Bauer, Danker, Arndt, and Gingrich, *A Greek-English Lexicon of the New Testament and Other Early Christian Literature*, 3rd ed. (Chicago, IL: University of Chicago Press, 2000), 742: "in this way, as follows... John 3:16."

[2] Andrew T. Lincoln, *The Gospel According to Saint John* (Peabody, MA: Hendrickson Publishers, 2005), 154.

When Abraham was about to take Isaac's life, he demonstrated his love for God. When the Father gave His only Son, the Lord Jesus Christ, to die on the cross for our sins, He demonstrated His love for us.

The word *world* here refers to humanity, all of it. The Father loved Adam and Eve and all their descendants in such an amazing way that He gave His one and only Son. Carson agrees and says that this means Christ did not die just for Israel, but for all of "sinful humanity."[3]

Whoever Believes in Him

Most people who call themselves Christians today do not believe John 3:16. Most think that in order to avoid eternal condemnation and in order to have everlasting life one must not only believe in Jesus, but must also turn from his sins, commit his life to Christ, and obediently follow Christ until death.

But the sole condition the Lord Jesus Christ Himself gives is believing in Him. If we reject that, we are rejecting the only way in which we can be saved from eternal condemnation.

Won't Perish but Has Everlasting Life

It does not seem fair or right to most people today that a person who simply believes in Jesus should escape eternal condemnation and should have eternal salvation. We know that Jesus is talking about eternal condemnation and eternal salvation in John 3:16 because in John 3:17 He elaborates: "For God did not send His Son into the world to condemn the world, but that the world through Him might be saved." Perishing is explained as being condemned. Everlasting life is explained as being saved. Köstenberger correctly notes that even though the word *perish* can mean different things, in this context it is the "antithesis of 'have eternal life.'"[4]

---

[3] D. A. Carson, *The Gospel According to John* (Grand Rapids, MI: Eerdmans, 1991), 204.

[4] Andreas J. Köstenberger, *John* (Grand Rapids, MI: Baker, 2004), 129.

A little slogan found in many churches is: "God said it. I believe it. That settles it." I think the middle line, "I believe it," is not needed for the statement to be true. "God said it. That settles it." Whether I believe it or not, it is a settled matter. Of course, whether or not I believe the promise of John 3:16 has eternal significance for me. But it does not change the truth of John 3:16. It is true no matter how few or how many people believe it.

SIX

He Who Believes in Him Is Not Condemned (John 3:18)

"He who believes in Him is not condemned; but he who does not believe is condemned already, because he has not believed in the name of the only begotten Son of God."

A Failure to Confess

Nicodemus came to faith in Christ sometime between John 3:14 and John 3:18. What follows in John 3:19-21 is a call for Nicodemus to come out of the darkness, out of the night, and openly confess his faith in Christ. Nicodemus is mentioned two more times in John. Both times John mentions that he came to Jesus by night (John 7:50; 19:39; compare John 3:2). Both times Nicodemus fails to confess his faith in Christ, though when he helps claim the body of Jesus for burial, he is at least hinting that he believes in Jesus.

Condemned or Not Condemned

John 3:16 and John 3:17 speak of two options: perishing (= condemnation) versus everlasting life (= salvation). But in v 18, the Lord only discusses condemnation. He does not speak of everlasting life, though it is obvious that the one who is not condemned is the one who has everlasting life. They go hand in hand.

In v 18, the Lord tells us something new about the condemnation of the unbeliever. The unbeliever "is condemned already." We tend to think that eternal condemnation will occur at the Great

White Throne Judgment (Rev 20:11-15). That is true. But what the Lord says here is also true. How do we reconcile the two?

The unbeliever lives in a state of condemnation before God. That is, the one who lacks everlasting life is one who is already condemned. Fortunately that state is reversible as long as one is alive. That is, the one who is already condemned can be saved by believing on the Lord Jesus Christ during his lifetime. As Borchert puts it, the unbeliever faces "the necessity of escaping an already existing condemnation."[1] The Lord's point in v 18 is that people are on the clock. They only have one lifetime in order to believe in Him. If a person believes in Jesus, he "is not condemned." That is, he has passed from death into life (John 5:24). Bruce comments that, "the believer does not need to wait for the last day to hear the judge's favorable verdict; it has been pronounced already."[2] Condemnation is no longer possible for the believer. But for the unbeliever, condemnation is a very real possibility, so much so that Jesus can say that the unbeliever is condemned already.

The Issue Is Whether One Believes in Him (= in His Name)

One condition only is given for escaping condemnation. But it is stated in two slightly different ways. First, "He who believes in Him is not condemned." Second, failure to "believe in the name of the only begotten Son of God" means that one is "condemned already." Ridderbos points out that these verses (vv 12-18) obviously teach that mankind has the responsibility to believe in Christ for life.[3]

In the Bible, a person's *name* stands for the person. So to believe in the name of the only begotten Son of God is to believe in

---

[1] Gerald L. Borchert, *John 1–11* (Nashville, TN: Broadman & Holman, 1996), 185.
[2] F. F. Bruce, *The Gospel of John* (Grand Rapids, MI: Eerdmans, 1983), 131.
[3] Herman N. Ridderbos, *The Gospel According to John,* trans. John Vriend (Grand Rapids, MI: Eerdmans, 1997), 140.

His character. It is to believe that He is trustworthy. His promise of everlasting life to the believer is true because He is true.

In John 3:18, faith in Christ clearly stands out as the sole condition of escaping eternal condemnation.

SEVEN

He Who Believes in the Son Has Everlasting Life (John 3:36)

"He who believes in the Son has everlasting life; and he who does not believe *the Son shall not see life, but the wrath of God abides on him" (NKJV, emphasis added; see also YLT, HCSB).*

Whoever believes in the Son has eternal life, but whoever rejects *the Son will not see life, for God's wrath remains on them (NIV, emphasis added; see also NET, CEV).*

"He who believes in the Son has eternal life; but he who does not obey *the Son will not see life, but the wrath of God abides on him" (NASB, emphasis added; see also LEB, RSV, NRSV).*

Open Confession

Though some commentators and translations (e.g., NET Bible, HCSB, NIV, ESV, CEV, RSV) suggest that John 3:36 are the words of the Apostle John (and that the words of John the Baptist end in v 30), the evidence is strong that these are the words of John the Baptist. John 3:22-36 gives the reader the last look at John the Baptist's ministry in the Fourth Gospel, with the exception of a passing note found in John 4:1. He is the prime example of someone who openly confesses his faith in Christ.

The Baptist's words start in John 3:27 and run all the way to John 3:36 (KJV, NKJV, NASB).

He Who Believes in the Son Has Everlasting Life

This is simple. There is one condition only. Believing in the Son of God, the Lord Jesus Christ. Anyone who believes in Him *has* (present tense) everlasting life. Köstenberger correctly points out that the present tense here "indicates that eternal life is not merely a future expectation but already a present experience."[1]

It is easy to see why some think these are the words of the Apostle John. They sound exactly like what the Lord Jesus said in John 3:14-18 and what He said throughout His ministry (e.g., John 5:24, 39-40; 6:35, 47; 11:25-27). Morris maintains that Jesus' teaching on this subject opposed the Jewish idea that one attained eternal life on the future day of judgment.[2]

However, it is not surprising that John the Baptist preached the same evangelistic faith-alone message that his Lord proclaimed.

He Who Does Not Believe (or Rejects or Does Not Obey) the Son Shall Not See Life

As you will notice above (see the emphasized portions of quotes), there are three different ways in which translators render *ho apeithōn*: *he who does not believe, whoever rejects,* and *he who does not obey*. All three are legitimate translations. The literal sense is *the one who does not obey*. However, in this context *ho apeithōn* is set in opposition to *ho pisteuōn* ("he who believes"). Therefore, all three translations convey the same idea in the context. As Bruce puts it, "[to] disobey is used here as the antithesis to 'believe.'"[3] The second edition of the leading dictionary for NT Greek explains:

---

[1] Andreas J. Köstenberger, *John* (Grand Rapids, MI: Baker, 2004), 140.
[2] Leon Morris, *The Gospel According to John* (Grand Rapids, MI: Eerdmans, 1995), 280.
[3] F. F. Bruce, *The Gospel of John* (Grand Rapids, MI: Eerdmans, 1983), 98.

> Since, in the view of the early Christians, the supreme disobedience was a refusal to believe their gospel, *apeitheō* may be restricted in some passages to the meaning *disbelieve, be an unbeliever*…This sense, though greatly disputed (it is not found outside our literature), seems most probable in John 3:36.[4]

John the Baptist was not contradicting himself. He had just said that the one who believes in Jesus has everlasting life. Now he repeats himself by saying the opposite: the one who does not believe in Him shall not see everlasting life, but the wrath of God abides on him. Compare John 3:14-18.

The opposite of believing in Christ is not believing in Him. The opposite of not having eternal life is being under God's wrath in the state of condemnation.

John the Baptist was not saying that one must obey God's commands to avoid eternal condemnation. He was saying that one must believe in Christ to avoid condemnation.

John the Baptist Proclaimed the Faith-Alone Message

John 3:36 is one of the great faith-alone verses for two reasons. First, these are the words of the Lord's forerunner, John the Baptist. This is an independent witness to what Jesus preached (cf. John 5:32-36). On the testimony of two or three witnesses, a matter is confirmed (cf. John 5:31-47). Second, the words are crystal clear. One condition only. Believe in the Son, and you have everlasting life.

---

[4] Bauer, Arndt, Gingrich, and Danker, *A Greek-English Lexicon of the New Testament and Other Early Christian Literature,* 2nd ed. (Chicago, IL: University of Chicago Press, 1957, 1979), 82. Surprisingly, the third edition does not include these sentences.

EIGHT

Whoever Drinks the Living Water Jesus Gives Has Everlasting Life (John 4:13-14)

Jesus answered and said to her, "Whoever drinks of this water will thirst again, but whoever drinks of the water that I shall give him will never thirst. But the water that I shall give him will become in him a fountain of water springing up into everlasting life."

Interactive Evangelism

The Lord's evangelism was extremely interactive. If you read through the entire narrative of Jesus and the woman at the well (John 4:7-26), you see that He spoke seven times, and she spoke six times.

It starts out with Jesus asking her to give Him a drink. But He wasn't really interested in receiving water *from* her; He wanted to give water *to* her. But not the water from the well. He wanted to give her *living water*. Living water is water which, if drunk, gives the recipient everlasting life.

Asking for What?

What did Jesus mean when He said, "If you knew the gift of God [everlasting life] and who it is [Jesus the Messiah] who says to you, 'Give Me a drink,' you would have asked Him, and He would have given you living water" (John 4:10).

What would she have asked Him for?

The answer is obvious. He asked her for well water, and she should have asked Him for living water.[1]

But what is living water? Living water is not everlasting life. We see that clearly in John 4:14: "whoever drinks of the water that I shall give him will never thirst. But the water that I shall give him will become in him a fountain of water springing up into everlasting life." Instead, living water is *the message* which results in everlasting life to all who believe it.

Drinking Illustrates Faith Alone

When the Lord said that if she drank this water, she would never thirst again, she asked for the water so that she would not have to come back to the well to draw water and to keep on drinking (John 4:15). Like Nicodemus in John 3 ("How can a man be born when he is old? Can he enter a second time into his mother's womb and be born?" John 3:4), she is thinking initially in physical terms. McGee correctly points out that at the very beginning of the conversation "[the woman's] thinking could get no higher than the water level down in the well."[2]

The Lord will get her to the truth with further discussion. But at this point, He has laid out the issue: receive the living water, that is, believe in Jesus, and you have everlasting life. In John 6:35, He came back to this theme again, but this time with only half of the figure. He said, "He who believes in Me shall never thirst." Morris says that in both John 6:35 and John 4:10-14, the Lord says that the one who receives eternal life can "never, not at any time" thirst for it again.[3]

---

[1] By the end of the conversation, she does ask Him for that water in a roundabout way. After He revealed He knew things about her that He could not possibly know, she said, "I know that Messiah is coming" (who is called Christ). "When He comes, He will tell us all things." Jesus responds by giving her the living water: "I who speak to you am *He*." See chap. 9 for more details.

[2] J. Vernon McGee, *John: Chapters 1–10* (Nashville, TN: Thomas Nelson, 1991), 168.

[3] Leon Morris, *Reflections on the Gospel of John* (Peabody, MA: Hendrickson Publishers, 2000), 229.

One drink. Thirst quenched forever. That means that when a person believes in Christ, he has everlasting life which can never be lost. Faith in the Lord Jesus is all that is required to quench one's thirst forever. Boice says about the spring of water Jesus offers: "The spring will never cease but will continue to bubble away forever."[4]

---

[4] James Montgomery Boice, *The Gospel of John: The Coming of the Light* (Grand Rapids, MI: Baker, 1985), 280.

NINE

The Woman Drank the Living Water and Gained Everlasting Life (John 4:25-26)

The woman said to Him, "I know that Messiah is coming" (who is called Christ). "When He comes, He will tell us all things." Jesus said to her, "I who speak to you am He."

I Know That Messiah Is Coming (John 4:25)

The Lord skillfully guided the conversation. The unnamed woman was wondering if Jesus might be the Messiah. She said, "I know that Messiah is coming. When He comes, He will tell us all things" (John 4:25).

Notice the words, "He will tell us all things." These are key words in the narrative. Remember that He told her to "Go, call your husband, and come here" (John 4:17). When she said she did not have a husband, He said, "You have had five husbands, and the one whom you now have is not your husband" (John 4:18).

This had led to the immediate comment, "Sir, I perceive that You are a prophet" (v 19).

Almost there.

After a discussion of worship, she wonders aloud if He might be the Messiah: "I know that Messiah is coming." This One who had told her all about herself sounds like the Messiah who "will tell us all things." Bowman suggests that the Samaritans were looking for a teaching Messiah, based upon Deut 18:15-18.[1]

Jesus Gives Her the Living Water (John 4:26)

His response must have been quite dramatic: "I who speak to you am *He*" (John 4:26). Literally the Greek is quite emphatic: "I am [*egō eimi*], the One who is speaking to you." Köstenberger says, "In a momentous self-disclosure that is unique to any Gospel narrative prior to Jesus' trials, Jesus now acknowledges frankly that he is the Messiah."[2] He has now given her the living water.

She Drank the Living Water (John 4:27-29)

What did she do at that point?

She received the living water. That is, she believed in Him for everlasting life.

We know that in two ways.

First, she left the waterpot (John 4:28). Why leave it when she had come here to draw the water? Clearly something life-altering has happened.

The waterpot contained the old water. It may be that it symbolizes the old religion, the works-salvation thinking she had before. In any case, she is on a new mission, and the waterpot is not part of that mission.

Second, she goes to the city and witnesses to the men of the village: "Come, see a man who told me all things that I ever did [compare v 25]. Could this be the Christ?" (John 4:29). Why not come right out and say, "I found the Christ!"? Probably the reason she chose this approach is because she was a woman of low reputation. McGee suggests that not only had she come to faith, she went to the men because she was "not on speaking terms"

---

[1] J. Bowman, *Samaritan Studies* (Manchester: Manchester University Press, 1958), 298ff.
[2] Andreas J. Köstenberger, *John* (Grand Rapids, MI: Baker, 2004), 158.

with the women in her town.[3] Her witness would be stronger if she asked a question. She was baiting the hook.

What did she do to get everlasting life? She simply believed in Jesus for it. No more. No less. And she was calling for the men of the village to believe in Him as well. The faith-alone message was indeed received by them as we see in the next chapter.

---

[3] J. Vernon McGee, *John: Chapters 1–10* (Nashville, TN: Thomas Nelson, 1991), 73.

TEN

Samaritans Believe in Jesus and Gain Everlasting Life (John 4:39-42)

And many of the Samaritans of that city believed in Him because of the word of the woman who testified, "He told me all that I ever did." So when the Samaritans had come to Him, they urged Him to stay with them; and He stayed there two days. And many more believed because of His own word. Then they said to the woman, "Now we believe, not because of what you said, for we ourselves have heard Him and we know that this is indeed the Christ, the Savior of the world."

The Woman's Witness Was Received

The Apostle John tells us that "many of the Samaritans of that city *believed in Him* because of the word of the woman who testified, 'He told me all that I ever did'" (John 4:39, emphasis added). He then adds, "And many more believed because of His own word" (John 4:41). Lincoln gives the woman high praise when he says that she becomes "a witness who bears testimony to Jesus and, like John the Baptist and the Beloved Disciple (cf. 1:7; 19:35), the purpose of her witness is to lead others to belief."[1]

Notice the words *believed in Him*. Those are the famous words of John 3:16. Whoever believes in Him has everlasting life.

---

[1] Andrew T. Lincoln, *The Gospel According to Saint John* (Peabody, MA: Hendrickson, 2006), 180-81.

John says nothing about commitment of life, turning from sins, praying a prayer, or good works. Faith alone is the message.

What started this revival? It started because the Lord Jesus talked to a woman at a well about living water that would forever quench her spiritual thirst.

The Samaritans Testify Concerning Jesus (John 4:42)

They now speak to the woman, "Now we believe, not because of what you said, for we ourselves have heard Him and we know that this is indeed the Christ, the Savior of the world" (John 4:42).

Here we find the only use of the word *Savior* in the entirety of John's Gospel. And it is not on the lips of Jesus or one of His disciples. It is not even Jews who are saying this. It is Samaritans who make this amazing declaration.

Notice, too, that the words *the Savior of the world* modify *the Christ*. The men now believe that Jesus is the Christ. In their understanding, the Christ is the Savior of the world. Koester adds that the "Samaritans accept that salvation may be from the Jews, but it is ultimately for all people."[2]

We know that some came to faith through the witness of the woman (v 39). Others believed in Him when they heard Him speak (v 41).

Are the people speaking in v 42 the ones who came to faith through Jesus' own words? Probably. It is a group saying this ("we believe"). It could even include a few people who came to faith at least in part because of what the woman said but who wanted to be able to say that Jesus Himself led them to faith.

What they testify to is the faith-alone message. They know that salvation comes from faith in Jesus, apart from works.

It is not clear what they understand by the words *the Savior of the world*. Maybe the Lord explained to them about His coming death, and they understood what He was saying—something the

---

[2] C. R. Koester, "The Savior of the World," *Journal of Biblical Literature* 109 (1990): 668.

disciples did not understand when He explained it to them (e.g., Matt 16:21-28). Possibly the Samaritans did not yet understand about His coming death. Maybe they simply meant that He is the Savior in the sense that whoever believes in Him is saved once and for all. Whatever the case, Van Doren suggests that Jesus probably gave the Samaritans this knowledge about Himself. He asks, "Whence, then, did these despised dwellers in Sychar obtain it?"[3]

Faith Alone in Jesus as Messiah

In Biblical terms, to believe that Jesus is the Christ, the Messiah, is to believe that He guarantees everlasting life which can never be lost to all who simply believe in Him. We saw that in John 4:10-26. It is also evident in John 11:25-27 in Jesus' dialogue with Martha. There He promised resurrection and life to the one who believes in Him. She said she believed that because, "You are the Christ, the Son of God." The Christ, that is, the Messiah, means that He guarantees everlasting life to all who believe in Him.

We will see the same thing when we come to John 20:30-31 and to 1 John 5:1.

Faith alone. No more. No less.

---

[3] W. H. Van Doren, *Gospel of John: Expository and Homiletical* (Grand Rapids, MI: Kregel Publications, 1981), 393.

ELEVEN

He Who Believes in Him Is Secure Forever (John 5:24)

"Most assuredly, I say to you, he who hears My word and believes in Him who sent Me has everlasting life, and shall not come into judgment, but has passed from death into life."

Normally in John's Gospel, the Lord Jesus simply calls for faith in Himself. Here He calls for faith in Himself by saying that to believe in Him (i.e., to hear His word) is to believe in God the Father who sent Him.

Most of Israel rejected Jesus (John 1:11). But those who rejected Jesus still claimed to believe in God and in the coming Messiah. But that cannot be. Jesus is the promised Messiah. To reject Him is to reject the Father who sent Him. To accept Him, that is, to believe in Him (John 1:12), is to accept the Father who sent Him. Jesus' Jewish opponents needed to wake up.

Three Tenses of Salvation

Theologians often speak of the believer having been saved from the penalty of sin, currently being saved from the power of sin, and finally being saved from the presence of sin. While there is truth in that trilogy, the Lord Jesus lays out a different past, present, and future salvation in John 5:24.

Present Tense

The one who believes in Jesus "has everlasting life." Present tense. That means that anyone who believes in Jesus, no matter how long he has been a believer, has everlasting life. We do not get everlasting life after we die. As Ironside commented, "it is not that you may *hope* to have it, providing that you continue faithful… every believer, here and now, possesses life, eternal life."[1] We get it at the moment of faith, and since everlasting life is ever-lasting life, once a person has it, he is secure forever.

Future Tense

The Lord covered all the bases. What about the day of judgment? Isn't there a coming day when all unbelievers will be judged by Christ? Yes, Jesus spoke of "the day of judgment" often (Matt 10:15; 11:22, 24; 12:36; Mark 6:11; Luke 10:14; 11:31; John 5:22; 16:8-11). Theologians now call this *final judgment*, although that expression is not found in the Bible.

The Lord Jesus promises that the believer "shall not come into judgment." In discussing these words, Carson says that "the believer does not come to the final judgment, but leaves the court already acquitted."[2] The believer will not be judged concerning everlasting life. Everlasting life is mentioned in the previous phrase and in the following one (passing from death into *life*). The believer will not be judged to determine his eternal destiny. That is a settled matter. He will not be judged at the Great White Throne Judgment (Rev 20:11-15). That's a promise.

Now we know from many other texts that believers will be judged at the Judgment Seat of Christ *to determine their eternal rewards* (Matt 16:24-27; Luke 19:16-26; Rom 14:10-12; 1 Cor 3:10-15; 9:24-27; 2 Cor 5:9-11; Gal 6:7-9; 2 Tim 4:6-8; Jas 2:13; 3:1; 5:9; 1 John 2:28; 4:17-19; Rev 22:12-14). But eternal rewards are not under discussion in John 5:24. Eternal destiny is.

There will be no *final judgment* for the believer. That is good news.

---

[1] H. A. Ironside, *Addresses on the Gospel of John* (New York, NY: Loizeaux Brothers, 1942), 198.
[2] D. A. Carson, *The Gospel According to John* (Grand Rapids, MI: Eerdmans, 1991), 256.

Past Tense

The Lord ends with a past tense. The believer "has passed from death into life." We speak of someone who has died as having *passed*.[3] But the Lord says that living believers have already passed from death into life.

Biblically, the believer has already "passed" in the sense that he is eternally alive *now*. Before faith in Christ, he was spiritually dead. He lacked God's life. But when he believed in Christ, he passed from spiritual death into spiritual life, everlasting life. Bruce relates this to the resurrection, when he says that the believer does not have to wait until the last day to experience the essence of the resurrection. He has already passed from death into eternal life.[4]

So, anyone who is a believer has already passed from death into life. And it is a one-way only journey. Once you gain everlasting life, there is no going back. You have everlasting life forever. You cannot undo the new birth. God guarantees it.

If your friends are unbelievers and you are a believer, you better get busy and pray for them to come to faith. Seek opportunities to tell them about the promise of everlasting life for all who simply believe in Jesus. It is not too late for them to go with you into Jesus' kingdom. But it is too late for you to join them in the place where they are currently bound, the lake of fire.

---

[3] It is a bit misleading to refer to dying as *passing* since it might give the impression the deceased person is not conscious now, or that he already has a glorified body. Believers who have died have departed from the body and are in the presence of the Lord, but they do not yet have their glorified bodies. They look forward, as we do, to His soon return. All believers should look forward with great anticipation to "the life...that is to come" (1 Tim 4:8), when we will gain our immortal, glorified bodies (cf. 2 Cor 5:1-8).

[4] F. F. Bruce, *The Gospel of John* (Grand Rapids, MI: Eerdmans, 1983), 131.

Faith Plus Nothing

The Lord says nothing about turning from sins, commitment of life, obedience, perseverance, good works, or anything other than believing in Him whom the Father sent. Faith plus nothing.

The Lord Jesus taught the faith-alone message. To add anything to faith-alone is to pervert the promise of everlasting life to the believer (Gal 1:6-9).

TWELVE

All Who Come to Jesus Have Everlasting Life (John 5:39-40)

"You search the Scriptures, for in them you think you have eternal life; and these are they which testify of Me. But you are not willing to come to Me that you may have life."

Law Keeping Won't Result in Everlasting Life

The expression *searching the Scriptures* is found in the Bible only twice, here and in Acts 17:11, the famous Berean passage. In Acts 17:11 it is a good thing to search the Scriptures to find the truth. Here it is a bad thing to search the Scriptures merely to seek justification for your works-salvation thinking.

The Jewish leaders believed in salvation by law keeping. They searched the Scriptures so that they might make sure they understood all of the commandments and that they might know which were the most important. You will recall that Jesus was asked what the greatest commandments were. This was asked so that the listeners could feel better about themselves.

The Jewish religious teachers thought that "in them [the OT Scriptures] you think you have eternal life." They did not believe the faith-alone message. They believed that faith in the one true God was necessary. But that alone would not save anyone. They believed that faith in God must be wedded with a life of good works. Sound familiar? Many people in Christianity believe that today.

The Old Testament Testifies That Jesus Is the Messiah

The words "and these are they which testify of Me" are meant to draw the audience to faith in Christ. They should have been searching the Scriptures, but not to make sure they were doing enough. They should search the Scriptures to see if what Jesus is saying is true (cf. Acts 17:11).

The Messiah was to be born in Bethlehem. Jesus was born there. He was to spend time in Egypt. Jesus was in Egypt while he was a toddler. Messiah was to be born of a virgin. His was a virgin birth according to the testimony of angels and of His parents. He was to heal the sick. Jesus did that. The Christ was to teach with authority. Jesus did that too.

Though Jesus' death, burial, resurrection, Second Coming, and kingdom were yet future when He spoke these words, He would soon go to the cross and then rise from the dead, in fulfillment of Scripture (1 Cor 15:3-4). And His prophesied Second Coming and kingdom have been imminent since His ascension.

Being Willing to Come to Jesus for Life

Legalists typically are not open to the faith-alone message. I was raised in a sinless-perfection group and became an extreme legalist. I was closed to the faith-alone message until a few weeks before the start of my senior year in college. A friend from the group came to faith in Christ and said to me, "Bob, is it possible your view of the gospel is wrong?" That shook me up. I suddenly became willing to believe something different from what I'd been taught. I was afraid. But I prayed for God to show me the truth, and I went with my friend to a Campus Crusade for Christ meeting, and a month later I came to faith.

The Lord lamented, "But you are not willing to come to Me that you may have life." The long-awaited Messiah was in Israel. Yet most of Israel was unwilling to believe in Him. Commenting on Jesus' audience, Morris notes that, "The fundamental trouble was that they did not want to see."[1]

The sad result of being unwilling to believe in Jesus is the failure to gain what they wanted, everlasting life: "You search the Scriptures, for in them you think you have eternal life." Though they were religious and read the Bible, they were not born again. Godet put it succinctly when he said concerning the Jews in John 5: "They seek life, and they reject Him who brings it!"[2]

When the Lord Jesus said *he who comes to Me* in John's Gospel, He was referring to believing in Him for everlasting life. For example, in John 6:35 He said, "He who comes to Me shall never hunger, and he who believes in Me shall never thirst." Brown correctly states that in this verse *coming to Jesus* and *believing in Him* are parallel statements that mean the same thing.[3]

Faith Alone, Apart from Works

The answer is in the Bible for those who are willing to accept it. The million-dollar question is not which are the two greatest commands in the Bible. It is instead: *who did Jesus say has everlasting life?* He said that one who has everlasting life is the one who believes in Him (John 3:16; 5:24; 6:35, 47). It is that simple. Faith in Jesus, plus nothing.

If you've been unwilling to believe the faith-alone message, why not pray about this? Ask God to show you if the faith-alone message is true.

---

[1] Leon Morris, *Reflections on the Gospel of John* (Peabody, MA: Hendrickson Publishers, 2000), 200.
[2] Frederick L. Godet, *Commentary on John's Gospel* (Grand Rapids, MI: Kregel, 1978), 487.
[3] Raymond E. Brown, *The Gospel According to John I–XII* (Garden City, NY: Doubleday, 1966), 269.

THIRTEEN

He Who Believes in Me Shall Never Thirst (John 6:35)

And Jesus said to them, "I am the bread of life. He who comes to Me shall never hunger, and he who believes in Me shall never thirst."

Partaking of the Bread of Life

After feeding 5,000 men, plus women and children, with a small boy's lunch, the Lord offered spiritual food to those who had followed Him to the other side of the Sea of Galilee. He offered them everlasting life.

He surely got their attention when He said, "I am the bread of life." He did not point to someone else. He made one of His amazing "I am" statements.

What would *the bread of life* be?

It is spiritual food which, once received, results in never hungering again: "He who comes to Me shall never hunger."

What is that spiritual food? It is the message that Jesus is the Christ, the Son of God, who gives everlasting life to all who believe in Him (cf. John 4:14, 26; 5:24; 11:26; 20:31). Everlasting life is a present possession and it guarantees physical resurrection.[1]

Never hungering is a figure of speech for eternal security. Once someone partakes of the bread of life (= believes in Him), then he will never lack that life again. One reception of this bread, and one is secure forever. Ironside laments that this wonderful

---

[1] Andrew T. Lincoln, *The Gospel According to Saint John* (Peabody, MA: Hendrickson, 2006), 324.

news is not believed by most people: "But sad it is that no matter how clearly the message is given, very few believe."[2]

Drinking the Living Water

The second half of John 6:35 reminds the reader of John 4 and Jesus' offer of living water to the woman at the well (see esp. John 4:10-14). There drinking the living water was a figure of speech for believing in Jesus for everlasting life. Lenski says that in these two passages, eating and drinking are metaphors for faith in Christ that leads to unending life.[3]

The Lord repeats the John 4 image: "He who believes in Me [= drinks the living water] shall never thirst." Never thirsting is another figure representing eternal security: "whoever drinks of this water [from Jacob's well] will thirst again, but whoever drinks of the water that I shall give him will never thirst. But the water that I shall give him will become in him a fountain of living water springing up into everlasting life" (John 4:13-14).

Believing in Jesus Is the Sole Condition for Everlasting Life

Eating the bread of life and drinking the water of life are figures of speech for believing in Jesus. The Lord makes this crystal clear in John 6:35b when He says, "he who believes in Me shall never thirst." Drinking is believing. Eating is believing.

That's it. John 6:35 says nothing about commitment, surrender, confession, obedience, or perseverance. Only believe.

---

[2] H. A. Ironside, *Addresses on the Gospel of John* (New York, NY: Loizeaux Brothers, 1942), 251.

[3] R. C. H. Lenski, *The Interpretation of St. John's Gospel* (Columbus, OH: Lutheran Book Concern, 1942), 460-62.

FOURTEEN

Everyone Who Believes in the Son Has Everlasting Life (John 6:40)

"And this is the will of Him who sent Me, that everyone who sees the Son and believes in Him may have everlasting life; and I will raise him up at the last day."

Everlasting Life Is the Will of the Father

The will of God the Father is that whoever sees the Son and believes in Him has everlasting life. A subjunctive mood is used, and hence many translations say that the believer "may have everlasting life." But the point is that the one who believes in the Son has everlasting life now. Several English translations bring this out (e.g., NET, WYC, NIV, CSB, and CEB read "shall [or will] have" and LEB reads "would have"). As Godet notes, the promise of the Lord that He *will* raise the believer from the dead makes it clear that the subjunctive here does not introduce the idea of doubt.[1]

In Addition to Everlasting Life Now, the Believer Will Be Raised Up

John 6:40 is parallel to John 11:25-26. In both places the Lord promises the one who believes in Him two things: everlasting life now and future bodily resurrection on the last day. Lincoln notes that here in 6:40, Jesus emphasizes these same truths

---

[1] Frederick L. Godet, *Commentary on John's Gospel* (Grand Rapids, MI: Kregel, 1978), 588.

in the previous verse when He says that He will lose nothing that His Father has given Him.[2]

The raising up of the believer refers to glorification, when the believer is given a glorified body. Even unbelievers will be raised from the dead before they are judged at the Great White Throne Judgment (Rev 20:11-15). But the Lord is not merely speaking of resurrection here. He is speaking of the resurrection of those who are righteous by faith, which the Lord earlier called "the resurrection of life" (cf. John 5:29). Barrett describes the resurrection of believers as a resurrection that shares "the life of the age to come," while unbelievers rise to "come under the adverse judgment that believers escape."[3]

Faith Plus Nothing Is Required

In John 6:40, no other condition is mentioned besides seeing the Son and believing in Him. Obviously, seeing Him is not required to be born again. Remember that Jesus later said to Thomas, "Blessed are those who have not seen, and yet have believed" (John 20:29). The point is that merely seeing, or hearing, Jesus is not enough. To have everlasting life one must believe in Him for the life which He promises.

If there were other conditions, like commitment, obedience, or endurance, then the Lord would have said so.

---

[2] Andrew T. Lincoln, *The Gospel According to Saint John,* (Peabody, MA: Hendrickson, 2006), 229.
[3] C. K. Barrett, *The Gospel According to St. John* (London: SPCK, 1955), 263.

FIFTEEN

He Who Believes in Me Has Everlasting Life (John 6:47)

"Most assuredly, I say to you, he who believes in Me has everlasting life."

He Who Believes in Jesus

Most manuscripts include the words *in Me*. Many modern English translations omit those words (e.g., NIV, NASB, ESV, HCSB, NET, LEB, RSV, NRSV). However, since they are included in most Greek manuscripts, translations like the KJV, NKJV, CEV, MEV, YLT, NTE, and WEB are right to include them. Borchert says that even if the words "in Me" were not in the original, Jesus clearly meant that He Himself was the implied object.[1]

Of course, whether or not an English translation includes the words *in Me*, it is clear based on the context of John 6 (cf. 6:35, 37, 39, 40) that the Lord promised that whoever believes *in Him* has everlasting life. He did not leave the object of saving faith unstated.

The Present Tense of the Verb *to Have*

I came to faith at the start of my senior year in college through the ministry of Campus Crusade for Christ (Cru). A few months later I was doing personal Bible study, using one of the *Ten Transferable Concepts* booklets. I came to this question: "What is the significance of the verb tense of *has* in John 6:47?"

---

[1] Gerald L. Borchert, *John 1–11* (Nashville, TN: B&H Publishing, 1996), 269.

I wrote something like this in the booklet, "*Has* is present tense. The Lord promises that whoever believes in Him has everlasting life *right now*. We do not get it when we die. We get it the moment we believe in Him." Bruce said that in John 6:47, the Lord declares that the believer in Jesus "has eternal life here and now, without waiting for the last day: he already anticipates the conditions of the coming resurrection age."[2]

Everlasting Life

The Lord was not vague about what we believe in Him *for*. We only have everlasting life if we believe in Him for that life (compare 1 Tim 1:16). I've met people who believed in Him for prosperity, health, a happy marriage, and peace of mind. The Lord does not promise those things to the one who believes in Him. What He promises is everlasting life. But we must believe in Him for that. Unless and until we believe that by faith in Him we have life which can never be lost (or the equivalent, like once saved always saved, an eternal relationship, irrevocable justification before God, a guaranteed home with Him forever), we've not yet *believed in Him* for what He promises. As Hodges points out, "the offer of eternal life [is] central to [the] message of eternal salvation:...[it is] the core of that message."[3]

Faith in Him Is the Only Condition

No other condition is mentioned in John 6:47. Faith in Christ is the only condition of everlasting life.

---

[2] F. F. Bruce, *The Gospel of John* (Grand Rapids, MI: Eerdmans, 1983), 157.
[3] Zane C. Hodges, "The Promise of Everlasting Life in Paul's First Recorded Sermon (Acts 13:14-41)," *JOTGES* 29 (Autumn 2016): 75-76.

SIXTEEN

My Sheep Believe in Me, and I Give Them Eternal Life (John 10:24-30)

Then the Jews surrounded Him and said to Him, "How long do You keep us in doubt? If You are the Christ, tell us plainly." Jesus answered them, "I told you, and you do not believe. The works that I do in My Father's name, they bear witness of Me. But you do not believe, because you are not of My sheep, as I said to you. My sheep hear My voice, and I know them, and they follow Me. And I give them eternal life, and they shall never perish; neither shall anyone snatch them out of My hand. My Father, who has given them to Me, is greater than all; and no one is able to snatch them out of My Father's hand. I and My Father are one."

Believing in Jesus Is the Implicit Condition

The unbelieving crowd asked Him to tell them plainly if He was the Christ. He did. But He was a bit veiled in the way He said it.

The Lord told them, "I told you, and you do not believe." In other words, I told you that I am the Christ, and you do not believe that. Then He added, "But you do not believe, because you are not of My sheep."

The point is that Jesus' sheep believe that He is the Christ, the Messiah. Within John's Gospel, *the Christ* means the One who guarantees the eternal destiny of all who believe in Him (John 6:68-69; 11:25-27; 20:30-31).

Here the Lord does not explicitly say that His sheep believe in Him. It is clear that is what He is saying, however, when He states,

"But you do not believe, because you are not of My sheep." His sheep believe in Him. As Lenski explains, Jesus says to the crowd that the evidence is plain: "Since you are not my sheep, you do not believe."[1]

I Give Them [My Sheep] Eternal Life

The promise of eternal security for Jesus' sheep runs all through Jesus' teachings in John 10. The sheepfold in v 1 refers to the security of the sheep. The salvation of v 9 is eternal salvation, as v 10 makes clear, "that they may have life…"

Eternal life is given to all who believe in Him: "I give them eternal life, and they shall never perish…" Carson says that this verse clearly teaches eternal security. The fact that they have eternal life means, by definition, that they cannot perish. "It could not be otherwise."[2]

No Other Condition Is Given

Some are confused by the Lord's words in v 27: "My sheep hear My voice, and I know them, and they follow Me." They think that following Jesus is an additional condition of eternal life besides believing in Him. Morris takes this position when he says that people who are "really" Christ's sheep will not only respond in faith but "will follow Him as the disciples had done."[3]

However, the words *My sheep…follow Me* do not refer to discipleship in John 10. At the start of the chapter the Lord said, "And when he brings out his own sheep, he goes before them; and the sheep follow him, for they know his voice."[4]

---

[1] R. C. H. Lenski, *The Interpretation of St. John's Gospel* (Columbus, OH: Lutheran Book Concern, 1942), 752-53.
[2] D. A. Carson, *The Gospel According to John* (Grand Rapids, MI: Eerdmans, 1991), 393.
[3] Leon Morris, *Reflections on the Gospel of John* (Peabody, MA: Hendrickson, 2000), 389.
[4] One of the editors, Pam Esteven, commented: "Totally agree. If *follow* means to imitate (as in discipleship), then sheep are the wrong image. Sheep are not known for imitating or copying the behavior of their shepherd."

Some have suggested that the figure of sheep following their shepherd illustrates faith in him.[5] That may be. However, I think it more likely that the Good Shepherd is here promising what He promises in John 14:3. The Good Shepherd laid His life down for the sheep (v 15) and then He went to be with the Father until He returns (John 14:1-4). His sheep will be where He is. That is, they will follow Him to the third heaven if they die before He returns, then they will follow Him back to earth for the Millennium, then on to the new earth after that (Revelation 21-22). His promise that His sheep follow Him is a promise of eternal security.

---

[5] See, for example, Zane C. Hodges, *The Gospel Under Siege* (Dallas, TX: Redencion Viva, 1981), 44.

SEVENTEEN

He Who Believes in Me... Shall Live (John 11:25)

Jesus said to her, "I am the resurrection and the life. He who believes in Me, though he may die, he shall live."

Jesus Promises to Raise Believers Who Die

The Lord gave seven "I am" statements in John's Gospel. This one, like the one in John 14:6, is a compound statement. The Lord says that He is 1) the resurrection and 2) the life.

In v 25 He explains what He means by "I am the resurrection." He promises that "He who believes in Me, though he may die, he shall live." The death here is clearly physical, though I've found that most believers seem to think this is a promise of spiritual life (everlasting life).

The words "he shall live" are connected with "I am the resurrection," not with "I am the life." The latter is explained in John 11:26. C. H. Dodd agrees and says that the two statements by Jesus in 11:25-26 are not synonymous, but parallel.[1]

The promise "he shall live" is a promise of bodily resurrection. As "the resurrection," the Lord promises to raise from the dead all who simply believe in Him. Godet says that the raising of Lazarus is an example of what Jesus will do for the believer: "In virtue of the new life which they have received by faith, they continue living," and "at the moment when Jesus wills," they will be recalled to corporeal existence.[2]

---

[1] C. H. Dodd, *The Interpretation of the Fourth Gospel* (Cambridge: Cambridge University Press, 1965), 365.
[2] Frederick L. Godet, *Commentary on John's Gospel* (Grand Rapids, MI: Kregel, 1978), 740.

The Resurrection of Life Is Certain

We know from other texts in John (John 5:29) and in the rest of the NT (1 Thess 4:16; Rev 20:12-13) that the Lord will raise both believers and unbelievers from the dead. However, the promise here concerns the resurrection *of believers*. In John 5:29, He calls this coming event "the resurrection of life."

Here is a promise that everyone who believes in Him will be raised from the dead in order to participate in His coming kingdom. The future glorious resurrection, also called *glorification*, is certain for the believer.

The Only Condition of Resurrection Life is Believing in Jesus

John 11:25 is a faith-alone verse. The sole condition for glorification is believing in Christ. When Martha says that she believes that Jesus is the Christ, this includes the fact that what Jesus said must be true because of who He is.[3]

If there were additional conditions for glorification, then the Lord misled Martha and all who read John's Gospel. Of course, since God and His Word are true, that is impossible. We can be certain that all who believe in Jesus will experience the resurrection of life.

---

[3] H. A. Ironside, *Addresses on the Gospel of John* (New York, NY: Loizeaux Brothers, 1942), 462.

EIGHTEEN

Whoever Lives and Believes in Me Shall Never Die (John 11:26)

"And whoever lives and believes in Me shall never die. Do you believe this?"

Promising a Positive by Denying a Negative

In this verse the Lord is explaining the second part of the "I am" statement He made in the previous verse. As "the life" ("I am... the life"), Jesus promises that "whoever lives and believes in Me shall never die." Remember, He is explaining "I am the life." He does so by denying the opposite.

He guarantees that the one who believes in Him will never die spiritually. We know He cannot be talking about a guarantee of no *physical death* because He just said in the previous verse that believers do die physically.

What is future *spiritual death*? Revelation 20:14 explains: "Then Death and Hades were cast into the lake of fire. This is the second death." The first death is physical death. Both believers and unbelievers experience the first death. But only unbelievers experience the second death. Peterson summarizes the meaning here as it relates to a bodily resurrection. Unbelievers will "receive resurrection bodies that are different from their former mortal bodies."[1] One difference is that they will be indestructible as they are tormented forever in the lake of fire.

The believer "shall never die" in this second sense.

---

[1] Robert A. Peterson, "A Traditionalist Response to John Stott's Arguments for Annihilationism," *JETS* 37:4 (December 1994): 553-68.

Faith Alone Is the Sole Condition, But There Is a Time Limit

Only here in John's Gospel do we read about an additional condition besides believing in Jesus: "whoever *lives and* believes in Me shall never die." The reason why this condition is added is because the Lord is making it clear that only in this life can people believe and be born again. It is certainly not superfluous to state that only those who are alive can be born again.[2]

The new birth occurs in this life or not at all.[3] We do not have eternity to be born again.

There will be no post-mortem new births. Likely many people will come to believe the saving message after they die. I imagine that eventually most, if not all, in the lake of fire will believe the truth, that is, that all who in this life believed in Jesus were given everlasting life and were not cast into the lake of fire. They will believe that they could have avoided the lake of fire if they had believed in Jesus while they were alive. But it will be too late.

Studies show that most who come to faith in Christ do so before age eighteen. However, there is no age restriction. People can be

---

[2] Contra Andrew T. Lincoln, *The Gospel According to Saint John* (Peabody, MA: Hendrickson, 2006), 324. It is Lincoln's position that v 26a is superfluous, even though he mentions that others disagree.

[3] I am not including the case of those who die before the age of accountability or those who die who were never able to believe due to low mental capacity. Some or all of these people will indeed gain everlasting life before or during the Millennium. Most Evangelicals believe they will all be given everlasting life and glorified bodies at some time between their death and the start of the Millennium. While I think that is possible, I consider it more likely that all such people will be brought back to life and will live during the Millennium *in natural bodies* with full mental and physical abilities and that those of them who come to faith in Christ during that thousand years will be born again. In that case, John 11:26a would still apply. There have been dozens of people in the history of the world who were raised from the dead and who had more years to live before they died a second time (e.g., Lazarus in John 11). The idea that people who died who were unable to believe could be given a chance to live out this life with the possibility of believing in Christ seems quite reasonable. If so, it would mean that all who will have everlasting life will be people who actually believed in Jesus Christ in this life.

born again at any age *prior to death*. Ironside calls it a "wonderful revelation" that everyone living on earth can be born again.[4] Some have even come to faith in Christ on their deathbeds. But only those who live and believe in Jesus will never die spiritually.

---

[4] H. A. Ironside, *Addresses on the Gospel of John* (New York, NY: Loizeaux Brothers, 1942), 461.

NINETEEN

I Believe You Are the Christ, the Son of God (John 11:27)

She said to Him, "Yes, Lord, I believe that You are the Christ, the Son of God, who is to come into the world."

Martha Was Assured

The Lord has just asked, "Do you believe this?" (John 11:26b). That is as close as we get in the NT to an evangelistic appeal. And even that question is not an evangelistic appeal since the Lord already knows that Martha believes. He wants her to express her faith to Him.

"Yes" was a clear answer. "Yes, Lord" was both clear and worshipful. Martha did not have to check her works or her feelings to see if she believed. She knew she did. We should too. Barrett points out that Martha's words here show that she believed what Jesus had told her even if she did not believe Jesus was going to raise Lazarus from the dead at that time.[1]

Why then add, "I believe that You are the Christ, the Son of God, who is to come into the world"? Jesus did not ask if she believed that. He asked if she believed He guarantees glorification and everlasting life to all who believe in Him. She was stating *why* she knew what He said was true. The Christ, the Son of God is the one who guarantees glorification and life to the believer. Of course, this fits perfectly with the purpose statement of John's

---
[1] C. K. Barrett, *The Gospel According to St. John* (London: SPCK, 1955), 396.

Gospel (John 20:30-31). It also is nearly identical to what Peter said in John 6:69 (in most manuscripts).

A proper understanding of the OT (note her words "who is to come into the world") produces such faith. Martha believed both because of the OT witness and because of the words and works of Jesus. She knew that He was the promised Messiah whom the OT said would come and that He would do what He promised to her about eternal life.[2]

She Was Assured That She Would Be Glorified and That She Would Never Die Spiritually

There is no ambiguity about what she believed. The Lord had promised glorification and everlasting life to the believer. She affirmed that she believed that. Martha was certain that she (and her brother Lazarus, see John 11:24) would be glorified at the end of the age ("at the last day," v 24). And she knew that she was secure in her salvation now. She was convinced that she would never die spiritually.

Was this hubris on Martha's part? Was she saying she knew she would persevere in faith and good works? No. Perseverance is not in the passage. She knew she had everlasting life and that she would be glorified at the end of the age.

Constable accurately explains the importance of Martha's confession in the Gospel of John:

> Martha's confession of faith is a high point in the fourth Gospel... This is the clearest expression of saving faith thus far in this book. Doubtless John recorded it because it advances his major purpose of convincing his readers that Jesus is the Christ, the Son of God, so they might obtain eternal life by believing in Him.[3]

---

[2] R. C. H. Lenski, *The Interpretation of St. John's Gospel* (Columbus, OH: Lutheran Book Concern, 1942), 804.

[3] Thomas L. Constable, "John." See https://netbible.org/bible/John+1.

It is a sad fact that most Evangelicals, whether Calvinist or Arminian, cannot answer the Lord's question affirmatively. Most Evangelicals think that perseverance in faith and good works is required in order to have what they call *final salvation*. The Lord, however, promised that our salvation is final the very moment we believe in Him for it.

TWENTY

Believe in the Light That You May Become Sons of Light (John 12:36)

"While you have the light, believe in the light, that you may become sons of light." These things Jesus spoke, and departed, and was hidden from them.

Jesus Is the Light

Jesus is called *the Light* in John 1:4, 5, 7, 9. The Lord calls Himself *the Light* in one of his "I am" sayings: "I am the light of the world. He who follows Me shall not walk in darkness, but have the light of life" (John 8:12). Again, in John 9:5, He said, "As long as I am in the world, I am the light of the world." See also John 12:35, 46.

Jesus is *the Light* in both a salvific and discipleship sense. He revealed what people must do to have everlasting life: believe in Him. He told them to believe in Him *while He was there*. His public ministry was almost over.[1] It would be more difficult, on a human level, to believe after He ascended to heaven.

He also reveals what one must do to have abundant life: follow Him. Light reveals the truth. Of course, Jesus is both *the Light* and *the truth* (John 1:4, 5, 7, 9; 8:12; 9:5; 14:6). He used many metaphors to call people to faith in Him.

---

[1] Edwin A. Blum, "John," in *The Bible Knowledge Commentary*, New Testament Edition, ed. by John F. Walvoord and Roy B. Zuck (Wheaton, IL: Victor Books, 1983), 318. Another way to understand it is that the unbeliever should believe when he is confronted with the truth.

To Become Children of God, We Must Believe in Jesus

What the Lord says in John 12:36 is out of step with modern evangelistic approaches. He does not speak of commitment, surrender, allegiance, repentance, or any of the terms commonly associated with the condition of everlasting life. Instead He simply says, "Believe in the light, that you may become sons of light." Since Jesus is God and the Light, He is saying that if you believe in Him, then you become sons of God. Borchert maintains that this verse is a simple call to believe in Christ. By nature, children of God do not belong to the night or darkness.[2]

The idea that believers are sons of light was picked up by the Apostle Paul in 1 Thess 5:5, probably from this statement by Christ. See also Eph 5:8. When we combine this with 1 Thessalonians 5, we understand that those who believe in the Light are sons of light in their position, even though their experience may or may not be described as walking in the light.[3]

While John 12:36 does not *directly* mention everlasting life, it does so indirectly since sons of light are sons of God, part of His forever family.

The sole condition of being a son of light is believing in the Light, the Lord Jesus Christ.

---

[2] Gerald L. Borchert, *John 12–21* (Nashville, TN: Broadman & Holman, 2002), 61.

[3] Robert N. Wilkin, "The Gospel According to John," in *The Grace New Testament Commentary*, vol. 1, ed. by Robert N. Wilkin (Denton, TX: Grace Evangelical Society, 2010), 435.

TWENTY-ONE

He Who Believes in Me Has Everlasting Life (John 12:44-50)

*Then Jesus cried out and said, **"He who believes in Me,** believes not in Me but in Him who sent Me. And he who sees Me sees Him who sent Me. I have come as a light into the world, that whoever believes in Me should not abide in darkness. And if anyone hears My words and does not believe, I do not judge him; for I did not come to judge the world but to save the world. He who rejects Me, and does not receive My words, has that which judges him—the word that I have spoken will judge him in the last day. For I have not spoken on My own authority; but the Father who sent Me gave Me a command, what I should say and what I should speak. And I know that **His command is everlasting life.** Therefore, whatever I speak, just as the Father has told Me, so I speak" (emphasis added).*

Jesus Came to Save the World

When speaking to Nicodemus, Jesus also said that "God did not send His Son into the world to condemn the world, but that the world through Him should be saved" (John 3:17). Here He repeats that idea: "I did not come to judge the world but to save the world."

Lest there be any doubt about what type of salvation He has in mind, the Lord makes it clear here in v 50 ("His command is everlasting life") as well as in His remarks to Nicodemus (compare John 3:16 and 3:17) that He is talking about everlasting life.

Whoever Believes in Jesus Is Saved/
Has Everlasting Life

While He is not as direct in this passage as He was in other texts we've looked at, He is still clear that the one who does not believe is the one who will be condemned, and it is the one who believes in Him who will be saved (i.e., have everlasting life). He is saying that the one who does not believe will be judged (i.e., condemned), and the one who does believe will not be judged, but will be saved. As Blum comments, "Condemnation at the last day is the penalty for rejecting the One whom the Father sent."[1]

In this section Christ speaks of rejecting Him. This is the same thing as not believing in Him. In this regard, to reject Him is to reject the offer of eternal life and place oneself under a sure judgment.[2]

Whoever Believes in Him Should
Not Abide in Darkness

As He does in other texts, the Lord not only talks about being saved, but He also says, "I have come as a light into the world, that whoever believes in Me should not abide in darkness." The point is that the believer is able to abide (i.e., dwell) in the sphere of light. He is able to live a godly life. So, the Lord not only gives the believer everlasting life, but He offers him the opportunity to experience life more abundantly (cf. John 10:10). Wiersbe points out that when we believe in Jesus, we go through "the Door" and are saved. As we continue to go "in and out" in our relationship with Him, we "enjoy abundant life in the rich pastures of the Lord."[3]

---

[1] Edwin A. Blum, "John," in *The Bible Knowledge Commentary*, New Testament Edition, ed. by John F. Walvoord and Roy B. Zuck (Wheaton, IL: Victor Books, 1985), 319.
[2] Lawrence O. Richards, *The Teacher's Commentary* (Wheaton, IL: Victor Books, 1987), 736.
[3] Warren W. Wiersbe, *The Bible Exposition Commentary,* vol. 1 (Wheaton, IL: Victor Books, 1996), 330.

While it is possible for a believer to abide in the sphere of darkness, that is not what the Lord wants. That is not good for the believer or for the Lord. The Lord is glorified when believers walk in the light. That is, God is lifted up when children of light live like who they are in the core of their being.

TWENTY-TWO

By Believing You Have Life in His Name (John 20:30-31)

And truly Jesus did many other signs in the presence of His disciples, which are not written in this book; but these are written that you may believe that Jesus is the Christ, the Son of God, and that believing you may have life in His name.

The Purpose of the Book Is to Lead the Readers to Believe in Christ

John presents eight named signs in his Gospel. Each of those signs was "written that you may believe that Jesus is the Christ, the Son of God." He is indicating that his readers do not believe that Jesus is the Christ, the Son of God. But John hopes to convince them that He is. The purpose of the Gospel of John is given here. *The Holman Bible Handbook* says that John wanted the readers to know the reason for his "carefully detailed narrative of the life and teaching of Jesus."[1]

The expression "the Christ, the Son of God" occurs on only two other occasions in John's Gospel: 6:69 and 11:27. The reference in John 11:27 is crucial since Martha is answering the question, "Do you believe this?" (John 11:26b). Jesus had just promised that all who believe in Him will be raised from the dead (11:25b) and will never die spiritually (11:26a). See chaps. 17-18.

---

[1] David S. Dockery, ed., *Holman Bible Handbook* (Nashville, TN: Holman Bible Publishers, 1992), 630.

When Martha answers, "Yes, Lord, I believe that you are the Christ, the Son of God, who is to come into the world" (John 11:27), she was saying why she knew what Jesus had just said is true. The Christ, the Son of God guarantees to give glorified bodies and keep eternally secure all who believe in Him.

To believe *that* Jesus is the Christ, the Son of God, is to believe *in Him* for everlasting life. In John there is no difference between *believing in* (*pisteuō eis*) and *believing that* (*pisteuō hoti*).

While Martha does not explain what she means by "the Christ, the Son of God," the context of the entire book makes it clear. In John's Gospel "the Christ" is explained as "the Messiah," that is, God's Anointed One who is coming to rule over Israel and the world. The appositional expression *the Son of God* is a Messianic title in John. Compare John 1:49 in which Nathanael says, "Rabbi, You are the Son of God! You are the King of Israel!" Son of God equals King of Israel equals Messiah. Borchert agrees and says that Nathanael equates the title "Son of God" with the coming King of Israel promised in the OT.[2]

Morris comments, "Here he singles out two things in faith's content. The one is that Jesus is the Christ, that is, the Messiah, the long-expected one. The other is that he is the Son of God. We take these two as more or less identical, but the Jews of the day did not."[3]

In other words, Martha was convinced that Jesus is the long-awaited Messiah, the King of Israel, and that as such what He promises is true. Since He promises that all who believe in Him will live again and will never die spiritually, then she is certain that is true. The readers can and should believe that as well.

---

[2] Gerald L. Borchert, *John 1–11* (Nashville, TN: Broadman & Holman, 1996), 148.
[3] Leon Morris, *The Gospel According to John* (Grand Rapids, MI: Eerdmans, 1995), 756.

Whenever Anyone Believes in Christ, He Has Everlasting Life

The ending of the purpose statement is powerful: "that believing you may have life in His name." The Greek verb translated as *believing* in the NKJV is a participle. It conveys the means by which one gains everlasting life: *that by means of believing, you may have life in His name.*

Many English translations bring out the sense of means. The NIV, ESV, HCSB, NET, and LEB all read "by believing…" The NRSV has "through believing…"

Of course, the life spoken of in John 20:31 is everlasting life, the life mentioned throughout the Gospel. All who believe in Jesus, that is, all who believe that He is the Christ, the Son of God, have everlasting life in His name.

The sole condition of everlasting life, according to the purpose statement of John's Gospel, is believing that Jesus is the Christ, the Son of God. Nothing else is required. Niemelä points out that this object of faith is sufficient: "John does not say that 99% of those who believe that Jesus is the Christ are born again. He asserts that 100% of the people who believe this content are regenerate."[4] If a person thinks that believing in Jesus is not enough, then he does not believe the saving message.

---

[4] John H. Niemelä, "The Message of Life in the Gospel of John," *Chafer Theological Seminary Journal* (July-September 2001): 11.

TWENTY-THREE

Whoever Believes in Him Will Receive Remission of Sins (Acts 10:43)

"To Him all the prophets witness that, through His name, whoever believes in Him will receive remission of sins."

The First Evangelistic Outreach to a Group of Gentiles

Earlier in Acts, Philip the Evangelist led many Samaritans to faith in Christ (Acts 8:4-13), and then he also led an Ethiopian eunuch to faith (Acts 8:26-39). The Ethiopian was most likely a Jew. However, even if he were a Gentile, this was not seen in Acts as bringing the message to Gentiles. Compare Acts 15:7.

Peter was not prepared to go into a Gentile home and eat with them and speak with them. But God gave him a vision three times, and Peter understood that God wanted him to put aside his previous tradition.

We know that Peter was giving the saving message because in Acts 11:14 Luke tells us that Cornelius had been told by an angel that Peter "will tell you words by which you and your household will be saved."

The message was a simple faith-alone message.

Whoever Believes in Him

Peter's reference to "whoever believes in Him" is taken directly from the ministry of the Lord Jesus (cf. John 3:16).

We learn from v 44 that "while Peter was still speaking these words, the Holy Spirit fell upon all those who heard the word." Cornelius and his household believed in Jesus even before Peter had finished his message. Surely, he meant to say more than "whoever believes in Him will receive remission of sins." But that was enough since Cornelius had been told in advance that this would be a salvation message.

This message was not unique to Peter or even the Apostles. "All the prophets witness that, through His name, whoever believes in Him will receive remission of sins." Peter probably has in mind both the OT prophets and the prophets in the early church. Marshall comments, "We cannot be sure what prophecies Peter may have had in mind, but possible texts include Isaiah 33:24; 53:4-6, 11; Jeremiah 31:34; Daniel 9:24."[1] Bruce adds, "Peter's reference to 'all the prophets' was doubtless supported by relevant quotations from their writings, including the prophecy of the suffering Servant who was to 'justify many' and 'bear their iniquities' (Isa. 53:11)."[2] Of course, Peter could also have in mind OT speaking prophets whose messages were not recorded in Scripture.

The Remission of Sins

The word translated *remission* is *aphesis*. It has a range of meanings including *remission, forgiveness, release*, and *pardon*. The leading dictionary for NT Greek lists Acts 10:43 usage under the heading "the act of freeing from an obligation, guilt, or punishment, *pardon, cancellation*."[3]

The Greek has an aorist infinitive (to receive), not a future tense. Though many translations render this as a future tense (NKJV, KJV, HCSB, MEV), many others show it as a present tense: "everyone who believes in Him *receives* forgiveness of sins"

---

[1] I. Howard Marshall, *Acts* (Grand Rapids, MI: Eerdmans, 1980), 193.
[2] F. F. Bruce, *Commentary on the Book of the Acts* (Grand Rapids, MI: Eerdmans, 1988), 228-29.
[3] Bauer, Danker, Arndt, and Gingrich, *A Greek-English Lexicon of the New Testament and Other Early Christian Literature*, 3rd ed. (Chicago, IL: University of Chicago Press, 2000), s.v. "aphesis," 155.

(NASB, NIV, ESV, LEB, NET). Either way, Peter's point is that when a person believes in Christ, he receives the forgiveness of sins.

This is the only evangelistic text in the NT in which what the believer is said to receive is the remission or pardon of sins.[4] However, Peter intended to say more. He undoubtedly would have followed his Lord's example and spoken of the gift of everlasting life. But since the Spirit fell on them as he was speaking, he knew they had already believed the promise of everlasting life (cf. vv 45-48).

When Peter mentioned the cancellation of sins, he was likely speaking of positional forgiveness as in Col 2:13-14 ("having wiped out the handwriting of requirements that was against us… having nailed it to the cross").[5] Cornelius and his household understood that Peter was speaking of irrevocable pardon and salvation. Compare Acts 11:14 and Acts 15:7-11. And they knew that the sole condition for this secure salvation is faith in Christ.

---

[4] John's Gospel never says that the one who believes in Jesus has the forgiveness of sins. In fact, the forgiveness of sins is not mentioned at all in John's Gospel prior to chap. 13, and then only twice. Once forgiveness is implicitly found in the foot washing example in John 13:1-17 (an example of fellowship forgiveness; compare 1 John 1:9). And once forgiveness is explicitly mentioned when Jesus told His Apostles after His resurrection, "If you forgive the sins of any, they are forgiven them; if you retain the sins of any, they are retained" (John 20:23). The latter reference is understood by many commentators to refer to positional forgiveness of sins, granted through the preaching of the gospel. But it might instead refer to fellowship forgiveness and church discipline.

[5] It is possible that Peter might have been saying that at the start of one's Christian life, he is in fellowship with God and has fellowship forgiveness of all the sins he had ever committed. However, it is more likely that he is speaking of positional forgiveness, not fellowship forgiveness.

TWENTY-FOUR

The Gift of Salvation Even for Gentiles Who Believe in Christ (Acts 11:17)

"If therefore God gave them the same gift as He gave us when we believed on the Lord Jesus Christ, who was I that I could withstand God?"

The Gift of Salvation Includes RIBS

Prior to Acts 10 and the promise of life going to the Gentiles, when a Jew or Samaritan believed in Christ, he would be regenerated and sealed by the Holy Spirit, but no indwelt and placed into the church. Before this incident, the indwelling and baptizing ministries of the Holy Spirit did not occur when one believed in Christ (cf. Acts 2:1-13, 38; 8:14-17). In the case of the Samaritans in Acts 8, Polhill says that there was a delay in receiving the Holy Spirit because through Peter and John's later participation, "the Samaritan mission was given the stamp of approval of the mother church in Jerusalem."[1] That is why Peter and the Jewish believers with him were shocked when the Spirit fell upon these Gentiles when they believed, not later via the laying on of hands. Toussaint comments that in this event God had "made no distinction between Jew and Gentile."[2]

The situation which is well known to us today did not begin until the first Gentiles came to faith. Today, whenever a person believes in Christ, he is regenerated, indwelt, baptized into the

---

[1] John B. Polhill, *Acts* (Nashville, TN: Broadman & Holman, 1992), 218.
[2] Stanley D. Toussaint, "Acts," in *The Bible Knowledge Commentary,* New Testament Edition, ed. by John F. Walvoord and Roy B. Zuck (Wheaton, IL: Victor Books, 1983), 382.

Body of Christ, and sealed forever by the Holy Spirit. When Peter speaks of "the same gift as He gave us," he was speaking principally of the indwelling of the Holy Spirit, but essentially he was alluding to the entire package of everlasting life, i.e., regeneration (R), permanent indwelling (I), becoming part of the Church (Spirit baptism, B), and being sealed forever (S).

Bruce comments,

> There is no explicit mention of faith in the immediate context, but it is certainly implied; it is suggested more definitely in 11:17, where Peter's words "when we believed on the Lord Jesus Christ" clearly mean that the Gentiles received the Spirit when they believed, while in 15:7–9 Peter expressly links the Gentiles' reception of the Spirit with their believing and having their hearts cleansed by faith. Only after the manifest descent of the Spirit on these believing Gentiles were they baptized in water. As for the imposition of apostolic hands (whatever inferences may be drawn from the silence on this subject in ch. 2), nothing of the kind took place before the Gentiles received the Spirit, and nothing is said about its taking place subsequently.[3]

When They Believed

Peter and John had earlier gone to Samaria to lay hands on Samaritans who had come to faith in Christ and been born again days earlier (Acts 8:14-17). Only then were they baptized by the Spirit into the Body of Christ and permanently indwelt by Him. But here the Spirit fell on Cornelius and his household "when they believed." Not later.

Why did God choose to start the fourfold RIBS ministry of the Spirit with Gentiles? While Luke does not tell us, he implies it is because God wanted to make it clear that Gentiles were not second-class members of the Body of Christ. All are one in the

---

[3] F. F. Bruce, *The Book of the Acts* (Grand Rapids, MI: Eerdmans, 1988), 217.

Church (cf. Gal 3:28). Osborne comments that in the Body of Christ "every people group stands equal in the eyes of God."[4]

The sole condition for the gift of salvation is believing in Christ. That is the way all people gain everlasting life, whether Jew or Gentile, slave or free, male or female, or young or old.

---

[4] Grant R. Osborne, *Acts* (Bellingham, WA: Lexham Press, 2019), 214.

TWENTY-FIVE

All Who Believe in Jesus Are Justified (Acts 13:39)

"...and by Him everyone who believes is justified from all things from which you could not be justified by the law of Moses."

Everyone Who Believes

The start of this verse is reminiscent of the Lord's words in John 3:16, "whoever believes in Him." The Greek is identical in both verses: *pas ho pisteuōn*. The words *by Him* (*en toutō*) can also be translated *in Him*. Some translations read, "everyone who believes in Him..." (HCSB, CEV, GNT, NLT; CEV says "everyone who has faith in Jesus," Phillips says "through faith in Him," and GW says "everyone who believes in Jesus"). Paul is saying that the sole condition of justification is faith in Jesus Christ (see Acts 13:16-38).

Robertson says, "the kind of righteousness that God demands is...made possible in and by Christ alone...on the basis of faith."[1]

Is Justified

In the portion of this message that Luke reports, Paul spoke of justification, being declared righteous by God. While justification and regeneration are separate ministries, the former by God the Father and the latter by God the Holy Spirit, both occur when one believes in Christ and indicate that the believer is now secure.

---
[1] A. T. Robertson, *Word Pictures in the New Testament* (Nashville, TN: Broadman, 1933), s.v. Acts 13:39.

A week later, in Paul's follow-up sermon, he spoke of regeneration, everlasting life (Acts 13:46).

The sole condition for justification and regeneration is faith in Christ.

You Can't Be Justified by the Law of Moses

As Paul often did (see, for example, Gal 2:16), he made it clear that the Law of Moses cannot justify anyone. He was not implying that some other law can justify. His point is that there is no justification apart from faith in Christ. Lange says, "[Paul's] words contain a negative and a positive declaration; the negative is: the law is insufficient with respect to our justification; the positive: in Christ, every one that believeth is justified."[2] Polhill says that the statement about justification by believing in Christ "could hardly be more Pauline."[3] He adds,

> "Everyone who believes" is reminiscent of Paul's constant emphasis on the sole necessity of faith in Christ. Justification was his favorite term for describing the saving work of Christ. It is a law-court term and carries the idea of being acceptable to God. Through faith in Christ, one is "put right with God" and becomes acceptable to him. The idea is that the law of Moses could never serve as a basis for acceptability to God. Only in Christ is one truly "justified," forgiven of sin, and acceptable to God.[4]

Bruce agrees:

> Grammatically, the words could indeed be taken to mean that Christ provides for everyone who believes justification from all those things from which Moses' law provides no justification—namely, most deliberate sins. But quite certainly they mean that believers in Christ are

---

[2] John P. Lange, et al., *A Commentary on the Holy Scriptures: Acts* (Bellingham, WA: Logos Bible Software, 2008), 253.
[3] John B. Polhill, *Acts* (Nashville, TN: Broadman & Holman, 1992), 305.
[4] Ibid.

completely justified ("justified from all things")—something which Moses' law could never achieve for anyone. In other words, Moses' law does not justify; faith in Christ does.[5]

The Lord Jesus taught the same thing in reference to regeneration (cf. John 5:39-40; 6:28-29).

---

[5] F. F. Bruce, *The Book of the Acts* (Grand Rapids, MI: Eerdmans, 1988), 262.

TWENTY-SIX

All Who Believe in Jesus Are Purified (Acts 15:9)

"...[God] made no distinction between us [Jews] and them [Gentiles], purifying their hearts by faith."

There Is No Distinction Between Jews and Gentiles

Acts 15 reports on what has been called *the Jerusalem Council.* The evangelistic message that Paul and Barnabas preached to Gentiles was being discussed (cf. Acts 15:1-6).

Peter was the first of the apostles to bring the gospel to the Gentiles (Acts 10). Therefore, Peter stands up at the Council and reminds all present that God sent him to Cornelius to tell him that all people cleansed by God by faith. Toussaint writes:

> The issue of whether to accept Gentiles was settled then and there. This was evidenced, Peter said, because God gave the Holy Spirit to them (10:44–46) just as He did to the Jews (2:4; 11:15). So, God made no distinction between believing Jews and Gentiles. All are accepted by faith.[1]

Purifying Their Hearts

While this is not a common NT way of referring to justification, it is used several other times in the NT in this way

---

[1] Stanley D. Toussaint, "Acts," *The Bible Knowledge Commentary,* New Testament Edition, ed. by John F. Walvoord and Roy B. Zuck (Wheaton, IL: Victor Books, 1983), 393.

(Titus 2:14; Heb 10:2; 1 Pet 1:22, though using a different Greek word). This may hearken back to the Lord's words to Peter and the other justified disciples when He said, "You are clean, but not all of you" (John 13:10, 11; 15:3). Peter may also be thinking about what God said to him before he went to Cornelius' home: "Do not call anything impure that God has made clean" (10:15).[2]

Gentiles too have purified hearts when they fulfill God's condition, which Peter next states.

By Faith

God purified the hearts of Cornelius and his household "by faith," that is, when they believed (Acts 10:43; 15:7). That is the sole condition. Polhill comments:

> In the account of Cornelius in chap. 10, his faith is never explicitly mentioned but is certainly evidenced in his following without question every direction God gave him. Here Peter made explicit what was implicit there: Cornelius had been accepted by God on the basis of his faith.[3]

Unbelieving Jews had caused the need for the Jerusalem Council when they came to Antioch and said, "Unless you are circumcised according to the custom of Moses, you cannot be saved" (15:1). These men did not believe in salvation by faith alone. It is not an accident that Luke does not call them believers.[4]

Peter rejected salvation by circumcision and law keeping. The sole condition, he said, was faith in Christ.

---

[2] John B. Polhill, *Acts* (Nashville, TN: Broadman & Holman, 1992), 326.
[3] Ibid., 327.
[4] Alberto S. Valdés, "The Acts of the Apostles," in *The Grace New Testament Commentary,* vol. 1, ed. by Robert N. Wilkin (Denton, TX: Grace Evangelical Society, 2010), 560.

TWENTY-SEVEN

In the Same Manner: Salvation by Faith (Acts 15:11)

"But we believe that through the grace of the Lord Jesus Christ we shall be saved in the same manner as they."

The Manner of Salvation Is the Same

Peter had just said that purification is by faith, apart from works (Acts 15:9-10). To make that clear he says that Jews are saved "in the same manner as they [Gentiles]." As is often seen in Acts, the Apostles make it clear that whoever believes in Jesus, whether Jew or Gentile, is born again, justified, and purified. Peter here is repeating that theme. Lenski comments, "Even in the old covenant the saving means was the Old Testament gospel and promise of the Messiah and not the law."[1]

Faith Is Either Explicitly or Implicitly the Condition in 15:11

Many translations have something like the NKJV, cited at the start of this chapter. In this sort of translation, the words *we believe* do not refer to the condition of everlasting life, but to the fact that Jews and Gentiles are saved in the same manner. Of course, faith in Christ as the means of salvation would be implicit in this translation since Peter mentioned purification by faith in Christ just two verses before. We might paraphrase that

---

[1] R. C. H. Lenski, *The Interpretation of the Acts of the Apostles* (Minneapolis, MN: Augsburg Publishing House, 1961), 604–605.

translation: *We believe that through the grace of the Lord Jesus we will be saved in the same manner as they, that is, by faith in Christ.*

The Greek, however, does not have a future tense of the verb *save* here. That has led some translations to put: "that we are saved in the same way as they" (NASB, NIV, HCSB, CEB, NLT, GNT). Instead of a verb in the indicative, the Greek has an aorist passive infinitive. That has led to a much different translation by some. Young's Literal Translation reads, "but, through the grace of the Lord Jesus, we believe to be saved, even as they also." The Wycliffe translation also reads "we believe to be saved…" J. B. Phillips translates it: "Surely the fact is that it is by the grace of the Lord Jesus that we are saved by faith, just as they are!" In translations like this, faith is understood to be explicitly stated as the condition.

I think it should be translated as, "But we believe that we are saved in the same manner as they, through the grace of the Lord Jesus."[2] Polhill is correct when he says that in the verse, the emphasis is on grace. He states: "There is only *one* way of salvation—'through the grace of our Lord Jesus.'"[3]

But in any of the translations, salvation is by grace through faith, whether the faith is understood from the context or is explicit. Constable summarized it in a succinct way: "Salvation is by grace (v. 11) through faith (v. 9) plus nothing."[4]

---

[2] The NET Bible, commenting on this verse, addresses how radical an idea this was for the Jewish religious mind: "Here is an interesting reversal of the argument. Jews are saved by grace (without law), as Gentiles are."
[3] John B. Polhill, *Acts* (Nashville, TN: B&H Publishing, 1992), 327.
[4] Thomas Constable, "Constable Notes," s.v. Acts 15:11: https://netbible.org/bible/Acts+15.

TWENTY-EIGHT

Believe on the Lord Jesus Christ, and You Will Be Saved (Acts 16:31)

And he brought them out and said, "Sirs, what must I do to be saved?" So they said, "Believe on the Lord Jesus Christ, and you will be saved, you and your household. Then they spoke the word of the Lord to him and to all who were in his house" (Acts 16:30-32).

The Question: What Must I Do to Be Saved?

Some have speculated that the jailer was concerned about *physical salvation* from Rome. After all, Rome would kill jailers if prisoners escaped. But since no prisoners escaped, that type of salvation is not relevant here. His physical life had already been saved when all teh prisoners stayed in their cells (Acts 16:27-28). Polhill says that the salvation here deals with salvation in the "full religious sense."[1]

Believing in Jesus would not save someone from the judgment of Rome.

The jailer was asking what he must do to have everlasting life. Evidently he heard Paul and Silas praying and singing to God (Acts 16:25). He knew enough to know that they were ministers who proclaimed the way of salvation from eternal condemnation. But he did not yet know what he must do to have that salvation.

Wouldn't we all like someone to ask us this question? Wiersbe says that this is the cry of people around the world who do not have eternal life, and "we better be able to give them the right

---

[1] John B. Polhill, *Acts* (Nashville, TN: Broadman & Holman, 1992), 355.

answer" if they ask.[2] But if they did, would we give the simple answer that Paul gives?

The Answer: "Believe on the Lord Jesus Christ"

The answer Paul gave—*"Believe on the Lord Jesus Christ and you will be saved"*—was a sufficient answer. However, it would be hard for the jailer to believe that is true without some additional information. Who is Jesus? Why can He guarantee eternal salvation to those who believe in Him?

Paul did what many rarely, if ever, do in evangelism. He stated the condition accurately and simply *before* he got into details proving that assertion.

Luke reports in the very next verse, "Then they spoke the word of the Lord to him and to all who were in his house" (Acts 16:32). Luke does not tell us what he said. Whatever he said (surely about Jesus' death for our sins on the cross, His resurrection from the dead, His post-resurrection appearances, etc.) was enough to convince the jailer and his family and servants that they were eternally saved simply by believing in Jesus ("having believed in God with his whole household," v 34).

The Promise Is for All, Not Just for the Jailer

The Philippian jailer was likely a very rough man. Unlike Lydia who came to faith earlier in the chapter when she was at the place of prayer (Acts 16:14), he was not a God-fearing Gentile. He was about to kill himself when Paul told him not to harm himself since none of the prisoners had escaped (Acts 16:27-28).

If the condition for an unrepentant man like the jailer was simply to believe on the Lord Jesus Christ, then it stands to reason that anyone else in his family would certainly be faced with the same condition. But we do not need to wonder, for Paul says that. Paul was not saying, as some mistakenly think, that if the jailer believed and was saved, then his whole household would be

---

[2] Warren W. Wiersbe, *The Bible Exposition Commentary* (Wheaton, IL: Victor Books, 1996), 468.

saved too. As Gangel correctly notes: "Luke carefully reminds us that the faith of the jailer would not automatically transfer to the rest of the household."[3] Paul's point is that the promise is for his whole household too. If they too believe in the Lord Jesus Christ, then they too will be saved.

Believe on the Lord Jesus Christ, and you will be saved. Simple. Clear. One condition only. Faith alone. Nothing else required.

---

[3] Kenneth O. Gangel, *Acts* (Nashville, TN: Broadman & Holman, 1998), 273.

TWENTY-NINE

Positional Sanctification by Faith in Jesus (Acts 26:18)

"I will deliver you from the Jewish people, as well as from the Gentiles, to whom I now send you, to open their eyes, in order to turn them from darkness to light, and from the power of Satan to God, that they may receive forgiveness of sins and an inheritance among those who are sanctified by faith in Me" *(vv 17-18, emphasis added).*

What Is Positional Sanctification?

The basic meaning of the word *sanctification* is *being set apart*. It can refer to things or people.[1] There are three types of sanctification spoken of in the NT.

Past sanctification, also called *positional sanctification*, is what occurs the moment a person believes in Jesus for everlasting life. At that time, he is set apart once and for all into God's forever family (cf. Heb 10:10, 14). That is the type of sanctification that the risen Lord Jesus Christ was talking about when He spoke these words to Paul on the road to Damascus. Toussaint says that those who are sanctified by faith in Christ are those who "are positionally set apart to God by His redeeming work."[2]

---

[1] Bauer, Danker, Arndt, and Gingrich, *A Greek-English Lexicon of the New Testament and Other Early Christian Literature*, 3rd ed. (Chicago, IL: University of Chicago Press, 2000), s.v. "*hagiazō*," 9-10.
[2] Stanley D. Toussaint, "Acts," in *The Bible Knowledge Commentary*, New Testament Edition, ed. by John F. Walvoord and Roy B. Zuck (Wheaton, IL: Victor Books, 1985), 424.

Present sanctification, also called *progressive sanctification*, refers to the process whereby God is moving believers to be more and more set apart from the world and its thinking and practices. This type of sanctification is not instantaneous, and it is not guaranteed. A believer might progress for a time and then backslide. A believer might even fall away. This process is facilitated by hearing the Word of God taught regularly in the local church (Rom 12:2; 2 Cor 3:18; Heb 10:23-25).

Future sanctification, also called *glorification*, refers to when believers will be changed in the twinkling of an eye (1 Cor 15:52; 1 Thess 4:17). We will be forever set apart from our old bodies, old thinking, and old ways. The moment we are glorified, we will never sin again. We will never suffer again. We will have perfect bodies, and we will live forever without aging or decay.

The Condition of Positional Sanctification: Faith in Jesus

Of course, Paul had heard this message many times before from Christians whom he had arrested. But he had not believed it until this day when he met the risen Lord Jesus Christ. Then he knew that all who believe in Jesus indeed are forever set apart into God's family. Polhill says that the one who has been positionally sanctified has an "assurance of a place, a portion among the saints in God's eternal kingdom."[3] With this message from the Risen Lord, Paul went from being Christ's greatest human enemy to being His greatest proclaimer.

As with John 3:16 and 6:47, here the Lord says that whoever has "faith in Me" is secure forever. No other condition. No other way.

---

[3] John B. Polhill, *Acts* (Nashville, TN: Broadman & Holman, 1992), 504.

THIRTY

The Just by Faith (Romans 1:17)

For in it the righteousness of God is revealed from faith to faith; as it is written, "The just shall live by faith."

God's Righteousness Revealed from Faith to Faith

The noun *righteousness* (*dikaiosunē*) here refers to God's righteousness. When someone believes in the Lord Jesus Christ, God declares that person to have right standing with Him. To be justified (*dikaioō*) is to be declared *righteous* by God.

Moo suggests that God's righteousness refers to three things: 1) "an attribute of God...God's justice, or rectitude,"[1] 2) "a status given by God...a new standing imparted to the sinner who believes,"[2] and 3) "God's salvific intervention."[3]

Lenski comments:

> This saving revelation never occurs except *ek pisteōs*, 'out of faith.' When the heart hardens itself, prevents faith from being kindled, all remains dark, no revelation takes place, no righteousness is pronounced by God, no salvation is obtained, no life enters. All these come about only "out of faith."[4]

---

[1] Douglas Moo, *The Epistle to the Romans* (Grand Rapids, MI: Eerdmans, 1996), 70.
[2] Ibid., 71.
[3] Ibid., 72.
[4] R. C. H. Lenski, *The Interpretation of St. Paul's Epistle to the Romans* (Columbus, OH: Lutheran Book Concern, 1936), 82.

Justification Is by Faith

The words *justify* (*dikaioō*), *righteousness* (*dikaiosunē*), and *just* (*dikaios*) are used in two different senses in Romans and in the NT.

The first sense refers to someone's being *declared righteous*. This is often called a *positional truth*. That is, in our position in Christ, we are righteous. Our experience is not necessarily righteous. But if we are believers, then our standing is. It is like a legal verdict in a human court. Witmer says that in Romans 1, "to justify a person is to declare him forensically (legally) righteous."[5]

The second sense refers to being *righteous in one's experience*. The verb *dikaioō* has the sense of *being vindicated* when used in this way. For example, Abraham was justified, or vindicated, by works before men when he offered up Isaac (Rom 4:2a,b). But not before God (Rom 4:2c).

Romans 1:17 is a quotation of Hab 2:4.

Some understand Rom 1:17 to explain how those who are justified shall live. The just shall live by faith. If that view is correct, then Rom 1:17 does not deal with how one is justified.

However, there is good reason to believe that Rom 1:17 does say how one is justified. In this case it means that those who have been justified by faith are called to live for God in this life. Hodges agrees and translates the last part of v 17 this way: "Now, the one who is righteous by faith shall live."[6]

The Place of Romans 1:17 in the Letter

I am convinced that the latter understanding is correct. However, in light of the teaching of the entire letter of Paul to the churches in Rome, even those taking the first interpretation see justification by faith as implicit in Rom 1:17. I put it in the explicit

---

[5] John A. Witmer, "Romans," in *The Bible Knowledge Commentary*, New Testament Edition, ed. by John F. Walvoord and Roy B. Zuck (Wheaton, IL: Victor Books, 1983), 441.
[6] Zane C. Hodges, *Romans: Deliverance from Wrath* (Corinth, TX: Grace Evangelical Society, 2013), 35.

category because I see the flow of Romans as first discussing justification by faith (Rom 3:21–4:25) and then discussing how the just by faith should live (Romans 5–8).

There are many references to the life which the justified are called to live in Romans 5–8. We are called to "walk in newness of life" (Rom 6:4). "Those who live according to the Spirit [set their minds on] the things of the Spirit" (Rom 8:5b). "For to be carnally minded is death, but to be spiritually minded is life and peace" (Rom 8:6). "For if you live according to the flesh you will die; but if by the Spirit you put to death the deeds of the body, you will live" (Rom 8:13). López speaks of this glorious possibility: "Believers now have the power to live the resurrection life which expresses a new, superior quality…Christians need not, and should not, live in the old realm."[7]

Those who are just by faith shall *or should* live, which in Romans refers to being spiritually minded and living according to the Spirit. (A future tense can have the force of a command, which is the case in Rom 1:17.)

Romans 1:17 affirms justification by faith alone, and it calls upon the justified to live the abundant life God desires for each of us.

---

[7] René A. López, "The Epistle of Paul the Apostle to the Romans," in *The Grace New Testament Commentary*, vol. 2, ed. by Robert N. Wilkin (Denton, TX: Grace Evangelical Society, 2010), 652.

THIRTY-ONE

The Righteousness of God through Faith (Romans 3:22)

But now the righteousness of God apart from the law is revealed, being witnessed by the Law and the Prophets, even the righteousness of God, through faith in Jesus Christ, to all and on all who believe. For there is no difference... (Rom 3:21-22).

God's Righteousness Is True Righteousness

The expression *the righteousness of God* (*dikaiosunē Theou*) refers to the righteousness which He imputes to humans who beliece in Christ. We might think of this righteousness not as a commodity like silver or gold, but as a standing, a position. Newell says it refers to how God reckons us because of our faith.[1] Ultimately, of course, this standing, this righteousness, is a Person, the Lord Jesus Christ. He is righteous, and He imputes righteousness to all who meet a simple condition. Anyone who has God's righteousness has right standing with God.

Paul says that "the righteousness of God [is]...to all and on all who believe."

Apart from the Law

God's righteousness, Paul says, is revealed "apart from the law." No one can be justified by God, that is, declared righteous before Him, based on works. In the very next verse Paul says,

---

[1] William R. Newell, *Romans: Verse-by-Verse* (Grand Rapids, MI: Kregel, 1994), 110.

"For all have sinned and fall short of the glory of God" (Rom 3:23). This means that not only has everyone sinned in the past, but all continue to sin even in the present.[2]

The Lord Jesus indicated that the only *work* someone could do in order to obtain right standing with God was "to believe in Him whom He [God the Father] sent" (John 6:29). Borchert suggests that in that verse Jesus was saying that the unbeliever should not be engaged in "working works" but instead should be "believing in him—the one who was on a mission from God (6:29)."[3]

In Gal 2:16 Paul wrote, "knowing that a man is not justified by the works of the law but by faith in Jesus Christ, even we have believed in Jesus Christ, that we might be justified by faith in Christ and not by the works of the law; for by the works of the law no flesh shall be justified." See chap. 53 for more discussion of Gal 2:16.

Through Faith in Jesus Christ

His righteousness comes "through faith in Jesus Christ, to all and on all who believe." Notice the noun *faith* (*pistis*) and the related verb *believe* (*pisteuō*). Paul is not merely in passing mentioning justification by faith alone. He is emphasizing it.

In the remainder of the third and fourth chapters of Romans, Paul proclaims justification by faith alone, apart from works.

---

[2] John A. Witmer, "Romans," in *The Bible Knowledge Commentary*, New Testament Edition, ed. by John F. Walvoord and Roy B. Zuck (Wheaton, IL: Victor Books, 1983), 450.

[3] Gerald L. Borchert, *John 1–11* (Nashville, TN: Broadman & Holman, 1996), 262.

THIRTY-TWO

Justified Freely by His Grace through Faith (Romans 3:24-25)

...being justified freely by His grace through the redemption that is in Christ Jesus, whom God set forth as a propitiation by His blood, through faith, to demonstrate His righteousness, because in His forbearance God had passed over the sins that were previously committed...

Justified Freely

The word translated *freely* is the Greek word *dōrean*, which has a basic meaning of "as a gift, without payment, gratis."[1] Being declared righteous (justified) by God the Father is not something we can purchase by work done. It is a gift (cf. John 4:10; Eph 2:8-9).

By His Grace

The word *grace* (*charis*) means "a beneficent disposition toward someone, favor, grace, gracious care/help, goodwill."[2] God showered His favor on mankind by sending His Son to die on the cross in our place (redemption...propitiation/mercy seat) so that all who believe in Him have right standing with Him.

---

[1] Bauer, Danker, Arndt, and Gingrich, *A Greek-English Lexicon of the New Testament and Other Early Christian Literature*, 3rd ed. (Chicago, IL: University of Chicago Press, 2000), s.v. "*dōrean*," 266.
[2] Ibid., 1079.

Through the Redemption in Christ Jesus

Jesus removed the sin barrier when He died on the cross in our place (cf. John 1:29). The result was "propitiation [better, *mercy seat*] by His blood." Just as the mercy seat in the tabernacle and temple was the place where the priest could meet with God, so the blood of Christ is the mercy seat that allows us to draw near to God. Apart from Jesus' shed blood, there would be no justification of humans possible (cf. Rom 3:23).

Through Faith in Christ

Some translations mistakenly render this expression as "through faith in His blood." See, for example, the KJV, LEB, HCSB, YLT, NCV, and GNV. However, the phrase *through faith* (*dia tēs pisteōs*) is more naturally linked to *mercy seat* (and ultimately to *justified freely* in the previous verse). The following translations take it that way: NET, NASB, RSV, ESV, and CEV. Hodges writes, "His role is to be a 'meeting place' between God and man *whenever* man exercises faith in God's Son."[3] The NET Bible has this footnote: "The prepositional phrase *dia pisteōs* here modifies the noun *hilastērion*. As such it forms a complete noun phrase and could be written as 'mercy-seat-accessible-through-faith' to emphasize the singular idea."[4] The mercy seat is Christ, and the mercy seat alludes to justification by faith *in Christ* (cf. Rom 3:26, "that He might be just and the justifier of the one who has faith in Jesus").

He Passed Over the Pre-Cross Sins

Not only does the shed blood of Christ remove the sin barrier for people born *after the cross*, it also removed the sin barrier for everyone born *before the cross*. That is why Jesus could give

---

[3] Zane C. Hodges, *Romans: Deliverance from Wrath* (Corinth, TX: Grace Evangelical Society, 2013), 100.
[4] *The NET Bible, New English Translation* (NP: Biblical Studies Press, 1996), 2167 note F.

everlasting life to all who believed in Him during His earthly ministry (e.g., John 3:14-18; 11:25-27), even though He had not yet died on the cross. God was able to anticipate the blood of Christ and apply it even to those who lived and died pre-cross.

Justification and regeneration have always been by grace through faith and apart from works.

THIRTY-THREE

The Justifier of the One Who Has Faith in Jesus (Romans 3:26)

...to demonstrate at the present time His righteousness, that He might be just and the justifier of the one who has faith in Jesus.

That He Might Be Just

Since God is just, He always acts in accordance with justice. One of God's attributes is that He is just (e.g., Deut 32:4; Ps 9:7-8; Acts 17:31; Rom 3:26; Col 3:25). He cannot be unjust. Thus, God sent His Son to die on the cross for our sins so that He might justly be able to justify humans. *He could not justify all humans, regardless of their response to His Son.* That would be unjust. Boa and Kruidenier accurately say, "If he had forgiven sin without a sacrifice, the charge of injustice would be valid."[1] But He could act justly by justifying the one who has faith in Jesus. Mounce comments, "The good news is good only to those who receive [i.e., believe] it."[2]

That He Might Be the Justifier of the Believer

A "justifier" is one who justifies. Divine justification is the act whereby God the Father declares a person righteous, once and for all. God does not justify everyone. He justifies specific people,

---
[1] Kenneth Boa and William Kruidenier, *Romans* (Nashville, TN: Broadman & Holman, 2000), 112.
[2] Robert H. Mounce, *Romans* (Nashville, TN: Broadman & Holman, 1995), 118.

the ones who have faith in Jesus: "that He might be just and the justifier of the one who has faith in Jesus."

God does not justify those who keep the law since there are no such people (cf. Rom 3:23). Paul previously said that both Jews and Gentiles are guilty before God, and thus there is universal guilt before Him (Rom 3:9-20). Moo comments:

> Paul's point is that God can maintain his righteous character ('his righteousness' in vv. 25 and 26) even while he acts to justify sinful people ('God's righteousness' in vv. 21 and 22) because Christ, in his propitiatory sacrifice, provides full satisfaction of the demands of God's impartial, invariable justice.[3]

He then added, "Luther called this paragraph 'the chief point … of the whole Bible'…because it focuses on what Luther thought was the heart of the Bible: justification by faith."[4]

God does not justify those who feel love toward Him or those who are trying hard to please Him. He only justifies those who believe in His Son.

Jesus removed the sin barrier (John 1:29). He lived a sinless life. A righteous life. When we believe in Him, God justifies us because He counts our faith in the Righteous One as righteousness (Gen 15:6; Rom 4:3).

There is no other condition. There is no other way to be justified by God other than faith in Jesus. Justification is by faith in Christ, plus nothing else.

---

[3] Douglas J. Moo, *The Epistle to the Romans* (Grand Rapids, MI: Eerdmans, 1996), 242.
[4] Ibid.

THIRTY-FOUR

Boasting Excluded Because of the Law of Faith (Romans 3:27)

Where is boasting then? It is excluded. By what law? Of works? No, but by the law of faith.

Boasting Is Excluded

People boast in relation to their performance, whether in athletics, academics, work, politics, or religion. But since forensic justification by God is not based on our performance, boasting is excluded.

I came to faith in Christ through the message of Eph 2:8-9. There too Paul speaks of the exclusion of boasting. He says that our salvation is "not of works, lest anyone should boast." If our salvation and justification were "of works," then we would have a ground for boasting. When it comes to that salvation, as Hoehner points out, all boasting is "in the Lord."[1] Likewise, Morris comments:

> In any religion of law the worshipper may legitimately feel satisfaction in his personal achievement, but this is a satisfaction that can lead to pride. For those saved by grace, however, that is impossible. Grace leaves no place for satisfaction in one's own achievement, for salvation is all of God.[2]

---

[1] Harold W. Hoehner, "Ephesians" in *The Bible Knowledge Commentary*, New Testament Edition, ed. by John F. Walvoord and Roy B. Zuck (Wheaton, IL: Victor Books, 1983), 624.

[2] Leon Morris, *The Epistle to the Romans* (Grand Rapids, MI: Eerdmans, 1988), 185.

By the Law of Faith

The expression *law of faith* is found only here in the Bible. Paul is using the word *law* (*nomos*) in the sense of a *principle, teaching,* or *rule*.³ But there were other Greek words Paul could have used to convey that idea (e.g., *logos, axiōma, archē, didachē*). Paul was clearly contrasting the law of works with the principle of faith in Christ. By using *law* in both places, *the law of faith* has an ironic sense. This is quite like Jesus' use of the word *work* in John 6:29. He was asked what works, plural, constitute the works that satisfy God's requirement for eternal salvation. His answer was, "This is the work of God [i.e., the act which meets God's requirement for everlasting life], that you believe in Him whom He sent."

The only way to be justified before God is by faith in Christ. Works will not produce justification no matter how sincere and dedicated. Saul of Tarsus was example one. See Paul's comments in 1 Tim 1:16 (chap. 65).

Longenecker puts it well: "It is the 'law of faith' that reigns supreme in biblical religion, and particularly so in the 'good news' of the Christian proclamation—not any kind of 'law of works.'"⁴

---

³ Richard N. Longenecker, *The Epistle to the Romans* (Grand Rapids, MI: Eerdmans, 2016), 444; Zane C. Hodges, *Romans: Deliverance from Wrath* (Corinth, TX: Grace Evangelical Society, 2013), 105; John Murray, *The Epistle to the Romans*, vol. 1 (Grand Rapids, MI: Eerdmans, 1959), 122-23.

⁴ Longenecker, *Romans,* 444.

THIRTY-FIVE

Justified by Faith Apart from the Deeds of the Law (Romans 3:28)

Therefore we conclude that a man is justified by faith apart from the deeds of the law.

Therefore We Conclude

Though Paul will proceed in Romans 4 to defend his thesis with the examples of Abraham and David, here in vv 28-31 he concludes the point he has been making in Rom 3:21-27. We cannot be saved from eternal condemnation by doing good works, even good works found in the OT Law. Witmer comments, "Doing works (i.e., observing the Law) is no basis for boasting for the Law cannot justify. It was not given for that purpose (v. 20)."[1] If we do not believe in the faith-alone message, that is, that justification is by faith in Christ apart from works, then we are rejecting the teachings of Paul, as well as the teachings of the Lord Jesus Christ and His other apostles.

The letters QED stand for the Latin "*Quod erat demonstrandum,*" which means "that which was to be demonstrated" or "it has been proven." QED is often put at the end of mathematical proofs to indicate that the matter is now settled. It has been proven.

---

[1] John A. Witmer, "Romans," *The Bible Knowledge Commentary,* New Testament Edition, ed. by John F. Walvoord and Roy B. Zuck (Wheaton, IL: Victor Books, 1983), 452.

Verse 28 is Paul's QED. Mounce says, "Verse 28 states in summary form Paul's basic premise—by faith we are justified quite apart from keeping the law (cf. Gal 2:16)."[2]

A Man Is Justified by Faith

The importance of a subject is often shown by how often it is repeated. Justification by faith alone is repeated frequently in Romans 3-4 and in the Bible. It is important.

The word translated *a man* is *anthrōpos*, the word that refers to humans generically. Morris comments,

> A man is any member of the human race; the term is quite general. Justification is brought about in the same way for all, by faith. We can do nothing to merit it, and the insistence on faith emphasizes that we simply receive it as God's good gift. Apart from observing the law, more literally "apart from works of law," is virtually equivalent to "apart from law" (v. 21).[3]

For any human to be declared righteous by God, he must believe in Christ. Period. Nothing added.

Apart from the Deeds of the Law

Paul is clear that our deeds have no part in our justification. Lenski comments,

> Since all "works of law" are barred out, "faith" alone is left. Luther so translated, and since his time Sola Fide [by faith alone] has become a slogan... "Alone" is not found in the Greek text and yet is there. The vocable[4]

---

[2] Robert H. Mounce, *Romans* (Nashville, TN: Broadman & Holman, 1995), 119.
[3] Leon Morris, *The Epistle to the Romans* (Grand Rapids, MI: Eerdmans, 1988), 187.
[4] *Vocable* means *a word or expression*. Lenski's point is that although the word *alone* is not present, the sense is.

is not there, the sense is. If faith alone is not the sense, what else goes with it? Anything else that has ever been or can be named belongs in the category of "works of law," the very thing which Paul shuts out here and everywhere. Thus faith alone is left, and Paul himself places it in this lone position.[5]

However, while working on this chapter and the preceding ones, I came across a popular commentary on Romans that argues that while faith alone is the condition of justification, we need *true faith* in order to be justified. The commentator then went on for four pages to give nine different "reliable evidences of saving faith." He said that the evidences of saving faith include "love for God," "repentance from sin and hatred of it," "genuine humility," "devotion to God's glory," "prayer," "selfless love," "separation from the world," "spiritual growth," and "obedient living."[6]

Many commentators and theologians today affirm justification by faith alone, apart from works, yet they backload the message by saying that the only way you know that you *truly believe* is by examining your works. While that approach is well intentioned, it is inconsistent with the faith-alone teaching of the Lord Jesus and of His apostles.

---

[5] R. C. H. Lenski, *The Interpretation of St. Paul's Epistle to the Romans* (Columbus, OH: Lutheran Book Concern, 1936), 271.
[6] John F. MacArthur, *Romans 1–8* (Chicago, IL: Moody, 1991), 323-26.

THIRTY-SIX

Jews and Gentiles Justified by Faith (Romans 3:30)

...since there is one God who will justify the circumcised by faith and the uncircumcised through faith.

Jews Justified by Faith

Verse 30 is Paul's summary of what he has said in Rom 3:21-29. He wishes to make it clear that both Jews and Gentiles are justified by (or through) faith in Christ.

Why does Paul use a future tense in v 30? He says, "God *will justify* the circumcised by faith." Until this point, Paul has spoken of justification in the present tense (vv 24, 26, 28). God instantly justifies once and for all anyone at the moment he believes in Jesus for his justification.

The future tense here does not mean that Jews and Gentiles *will be justified after this life is over*. The timing of justification conforms to the timing of believing in Jesus. The sense here is gnomic, meaning that when faith occurs, God declares the person righteous.[1] Alternately, it could be understood as a logical future, again indicating that when belief occurs, God justifies.[2]

Concerning Jews, Paul says they are justified "by [*ek*] faith." *Ek* (or *ex* before words beginning with a vowel) is the preposition

---

[1] Daniel B. Wallace, *Greek Grammar Beyond the Basics* (Grand Rapids, MI: Zondervan, 1996), 571. Wallace discusses the gnomic use of the future.
[2] C. E. B. Cranfield, *The Epistle to the Romans,* vol. 1 (New York, NY: T&T Clark, 1975), 222.

Paul has used several times already in his discussion of justification. In v 20 he said, "**by** the deeds of the law [*ex ergōn nomou*] no flesh will be justified in His sight..." In v 26 Paul spoke of God as "the justifier of the one who **has** faith in Jesus [*ton ek pisteōs Iēsou*]." Hodges suggests that "the *ek* phrase…retains its usual force expressing an operating principle (the 'by-faith way')."[3] A slightly different preposition is used when Paul speaks of the justification of Gentiles.

Gentiles Justified Through Faith

The shift in prepositions is probably largely, if not completely, a matter of stylistic variation, with the meaning either essentially the same or the same as the by-faith justification of Jews.

Literally, Paul speaks of Gentiles being justified *through the faith* (*dia tēs pisteōs*). Hodges suggests that the definite article "is almost an article of previous reference," meaning that "the thought is more that they [Gentiles] are justified *through* the very thing just referred to, i.e., *faith* [in the first half of verse 30]."[4]

Faith is the only way that anyone, Jew or Gentile, will be justified by God. When a person believes in Jesus for everlasting life, then not only does the Holy Spirit regenerate him (John 3:16), but at the same time God the Father justifies him (Rom 3:30).

Faith is the sole condition. Nothing else.

---

[3] Zane C. Hodges, *Romans: Deliverance from Wrath* (Corinth, TX: Grace Evangelical Society, 2013), 107.
[4] Ibid.

THIRTY-SEVEN

The Prime Example of Justification by Faith Alone: Abraham (Romans 4:3)

For what does the Scripture say? "Abraham believed God, and it was accounted to him for righteousness."

What Does the Scripture Say?

At the end of Romans 3 (vv 21-31), Paul asserted that justification by God is by faith, apart from works of the law. Now in chap. 4 he is going to prove from the OT that it is true.

The patriarch of both Judaism and Christianity (as well as Islam) is Abraham. By citing Abraham, Paul is appealing to both Jews and Gentiles.

He begins with the telling words, "What does the Scripture say?" That is the question, isn't it? The question is not, what does our tradition say? What did the Church Fathers say? Or what did the Reformers say?

By *the Scripture*, Paul refers to what we call *the Hebrew Scriptures* or the OT. (With the possible exception of Luke, every book in the entire Bible was written by a Jew. I think we could call the entire Bible *the Hebrew Scriptures*. Christianity is not some new religion. It is the fulfillment of Biblical Judaism.)

While many people think the OT had nothing to say about justification or regeneration, Paul disagrees. He sees in Abraham proof of justification by faith in Christ, apart from works.

Abraham Believed God

Paul is quoting from Gen 15:6. While Paul does not say *explicitly* what Abraham believed God *for*, he clearly implies that Abraham believed in the coming Messiah *for his eternal destiny in the Messiah's kingdom*. If Abraham merely believed that God existed—and if he did not believe in justification by faith in Messiah—he would in no way prove Paul's point. To do that, Abraham had to believe in the Messiah for his eternal destiny. The whole context of Gen 15:6 shows that Abraham believed in a coming Messiah that would bless the whole world.[1]

Of course, the Lord Jesus had already said that Abraham believed in Him: "Abraham rejoiced to see My day" (John 8:56). The author of Hebrews said that Abraham was looking forward to the New Jerusalem, meaning he believed he would be raised from the dead and would return to live in the Promised Land in Messiah's kingdom (Heb 11:10, 16).

A careful reading of Gen 15:1-6 shows that what God promised Abraham was an heir through himself and Sarah. In light of Gal 3:8, in which Paul says that Gen 12:3 referred to the promise of justification by faith, it is clear that when Abraham heard the words of Gen 15:1-5, he believed in the coming Messiah for his justification before God; hence he became "believing Abraham" (Gal 3:9). Abraham's promised son, Isaac, would be in the line of Messiah.

It seems likely that Abraham met face to face with the pre-incarnate Messiah in Genesis 12 and again in Genesis 15. Abraham later met with Him on many other occasions (e.g., Gen 17:1-22; 18:1-33; 21:12-13; 22:1-2, 11-12, 15-18).

---

[1] René A. López, "The Epistle of Paul the Apostle to the Romans," in *The Grace New Testament Commentary,* vol. 2, ed. by Robert N. Wilkin (Denton, TX: Grace Evangelical Society, 2010), 642.

Abraham's Faith Was Accounted to Him for Righteousness

The patriarch Abraham is a prime example of one who was justified by faith, apart from works. His faith was accounted to Him for righteousness. Longenecker writes,

> God's reckoning or crediting Abraham as righteous meant that what was bestowed on Abraham was *the status of God's own righteousness* in response to Abraham's expression of faith, and not that God declared Abraham's faith as expressing *a quality of his own righteousness* that was in some manner intrinsic in him already...[2]

Hodges agrees, saying, "The perfect righteousness that God gives is nothing less than His accepting faith as a wholly adequate righteousness in and of itself...Abraham's faith became a substitute for the righteousness he otherwise lacked."[3]

---

[2] Richard N. Longenecker, *The Epistle to the Romans* (Grand Rapids, MI: Eerdmans, 2016), 496.
[3] Zane C. Hodges, *Romans: Deliverance from Wrath* (Corinth, TX: Grace Evangelical Society, 2013), 114.

THIRTY-EIGHT

Justification by Faith Is for Him Who Does Not Work (Romans 4:5)

But to him who does not work but believes on Him who justifies the ungodly, his faith is accounted for righteousness...

To Him Who Does Not Work

Paul is explaining the meaning of Gen 15:6, which he quoted in v 3. When God accounted Abraham's faith for righteousness, He was not doing so based on Abraham's works. Abraham is the prime example of "him who does not work but believes." Mounce says,

> The verses constitute a general statement that compares believing with working as the basis for justification. When people work, their wages come not as gifts but because they have earned them. The spiritual realm, however, is different. In this case those who do not work but believe are regarded by God as righteous. Rather than attempting to earn God's favor by meritorious deeds, they simply trust. They are accepted by God as righteous because of their faith. God is under no obligation to pronounce righteous those who would earn his favor by working. Righteousness is a gift. God freely gives it to those who believe. The disparity between legalism and grace is seen most clearly in the way God grants a right standing to people of faith.[1]

---
[1] Robert H. Mounce, *Romans* (Nashville, TN: Broadman & Holman, 1995), 123.

While some theologians are uncomfortable with this language, since they think it presents a license to sin with impunity, we should embrace it. If this were not true, then we would all be eternally condemned (cf. Rom 2:13; 3:23). The truth of Paul's words in no way promotes sin or even suggests that there are no consequences for sinful behavior (cf. Rom 6:1ff).

To Him Who Believes on Him

Faith and works are antithetical methods of justification before God. In v 2 Paul had said that Abraham was justified by works *before men*, but *not before God*. Abraham's justification *before God* was by faith alone (vv 3, 5).

God Justifies the Ungodly

Talk about a startling statement! Paul says the justification before God is "to him who believes on Him who justifies *the ungodly*." The ungodly. Not the godly. Of course, Paul has already said that we are all ungodly in terms of God's perfect holiness (Rom 3:23). But for him to come right out and say that God justifies the ungodly is a bit strong. Well, maybe strong is the wrong word. Refreshing. Amazing. Encouraging. Motivating. Liberating. Assuring.

To qualify for justification, you need to be an ungodly person who believes in the God who justifies the ungodly by faith, apart from works. Mickelsen nicely puts it, "Here in a nutshell is the Pauline doctrine of justification by faith."[2]

Faith Is Accounted for Righteousness

Paul now works back to the statement of Gen 15:6, which he quoted in v 3: "his faith is accounted for righteousness." That is, the faith in Christ for justification by the ungodly person is

---

[2] A. Berkeley Mickelsen, "The Epistle to the Romans," in *The Wycliffe Bible Commentary*, ed. by Charles F. Pfeiffer and Everett F. Harrison (Chicago, IL: Moody, 1962), 1193.

what is credited to him for righteousness. Longenecker says that God's justification of the wicked is "simply on the basis of their trust in him and apart from any consideration of such matters as payment, wage, or reward."[3]

Moo comments, "Paul's purpose in vv. 4–5, then, is to show that the faith that justifies is 'faith alone,' faith 'apart from works.'"[4]

---

[3] Richard N. Longenecker, *The Epistle to the Romans* (Grand Rapids, MI: Eerdmans, 2016), 497.

[4] Douglas Moo, *The Epistle to the Romans* (Grand Rapids, MI: Eerdmans, 1996), 265.

THIRTY-NINE

The Blessing of Justification Is for All Who Believe in Christ (Romans 4:9)

Does this blessedness then come upon the circumcised only, or upon the uncircumcised also? For we say that faith was accounted to Abraham for righteousness.

Blessedness for Jews and Gentiles

The words *this blessedness* look back to vv 7 and 8 in which the word *blessed* is found twice in the quotation from David from Ps 32:1-2. The first blessing concerns forgiveness, not justification. But the second blessing concerns justification: "Blessed is the man to whom the Lord shall not impute sin." Hodges writes, "In terms of justification God charges the justified man with nothing at all (see 8:33). That man's faith, as Paul has already shown, is 'imputed as righteousness.'"[1]

The blessing of justification comes not only upon the circumcised (Jews), but also upon the uncircumcised (Gentiles). The fact that today both Jews and Gentiles are justified by faith alone, apart from works, did not begin with Acts 2 and the birth of the church. It began in the Garden of Eden, though Paul only goes back to Abraham and David to prove his point.

Faith Was Accounted for Righteousness

Repetition is emphatic. The fact that faith is accounted for righteousness is found in vv 3, 5, and here in v 9. In finances,

---

[1] Zane C. Hodges, *Romans: Deliverance from Wrath* (Corinth, TX: Grace Evangelical Society, 2013), 117.

accounting refers to computations which are made to determine the financial health of a business or individual. In forensic justification by God, accounting refers to God's computing or counting faith in Christ as righteousness or right standing with Him. Longenecker writes, "God credits righteousness to anyone who has faith."[2] The person who believes in Christ is righteous in his standing. The one who does not believe in Him is not righteous in his position. Faith alone is the condition of justification before God.

Fitzmyer says, "We maintain that 'faith was credited to Abraham as uprightness.' Faith, and only faith, was the operative element. Again Paul cites Gen 15:6, introducing it with the emphatic *legomen*, 'we say,' repeating what he said in v 3."[3]

Hodges concurs, "The question now is no longer whether such righteousness can be bestowed since that is proved by Paul's two proof texts. The question rather is whether such a blessing can come only upon the circumcised or whether it can come also upon the uncircumcised."[4] Paul's answer is that faith is accounted for righteousness for all, Jews and Gentiles.

---

[2] Richard N. Longenecker, *The Epistle to the Romans* (Grand Rapids, MI: Eerdmans, 2016), 503.
[3] Joseph A. Fitzmyer, *Romans* (New Haven, CT: Yale University Press, 2008), 380.
[4] Hodges, *Romans*, 118.

FORTY

Circumcision Is a Seal of Righteousness by Faith (Romans 4:11)

And he received the sign of circumcision, a seal of the righteousness of the faith which he had while still uncircumcised, that he might be the father of all those who believe, though they are uncircumcised, that righteousness might be imputed to them also...

Circumcision, a Seal of Righteousness

While Jewish believers rightly regard Abraham as the father of the nation and the Jewish people, they may forget that when Abraham was justified, he was yet uncircumcised. Years after Abraham was justified (Gen 15:6), God commanded him and all the males in his house to be circumcised (Gen 17:1-14). Paul here sees circumcision as a sign (Gen 17:11) and "a seal of the righteousness of the faith which he had while still uncircumcised." In other words, Paul is suggesting that the true understanding of circumcision is that it confirms the truth of justification by faith alone, apart from works. Longenecker says that Paul here speaks of "circumcision as a sign or seal that functioned to confirm God's previous gift of righteousness to Abraham."[1]

The Righteousness of Faith

Paul has already established that righteousness is sourced in God who accounts faith in Christ as righteousness. All of that

---

[1] Richard N. Longenecker, *The Epistle to the Romans* (Grand Rapids, MI: Eerdmans, 2016), 506.

can be nicely summarized as *the righteousness of the faith* which Abraham had while still uncircumcised. Morris comments,

> This righteousness was of faith (cf. Phil. 3:9). It is important to see that the whole point of circumcision is its relation to righteousness and to faith, that faith which Abraham had while he was still uncircumcised. This is the point Paul is concerned to emphasize. Circumcision had nothing to do with Abraham's acceptance by God (cf. Gal. 5:6). It was while he was still uncircumcised that God accepted him.[2]

The Father of All Who Believe

Abraham was thought of as the father of Israel, which he was and is. But Paul's point is that he is also "the father of all those who believe." Hodges points out that Paul's argument is that if Abraham had submitted to circumcision first and then later had been justified, he "could hardly have been perceived as in any sense a true spiritual *father* to uncircumcised believers."[3] But since his justification preceded his circumcision, Gentile believers can rightly view Abraham as their spiritual father.

That Righteousness Might Be Imputed to Them Also

Longenecker comments on the definite article in the Greek text[4] before *righteousness* at the end of v 11: "The article *tēn* should be understood as pointing back to the previous use of *dikaiosunē* in 4:11…'the righteousness that we have spoken about

---

[2] Leon Morris, *The Epistle to the Romans* (Grand Rapids, MI: Eerdmans, 1988), 203.
[3] Zane C. Hodges, *Romans: Deliverance from Wrath* (Corinth, TX: Grace Evangelical Society, 2010), 119.
[4] The NKJV chose not to translate the Greek definite article here.

previously,' or, more colloquially, 'the righteousness of which we speak.'"[5]

Abraham's justification and subsequent circumcision should lead Gentiles to believe in Jesus and thereby have imputed to them the righteousness of which Paul had been speaking. Hodges comments, "Paul conveys that Abraham was intended as more than a mere prototypical figure exemplifying justification. His case is actually presented in Scripture to encourage Gentiles to believe *in order that* they too might receive *righteousness* in the same way."[6]

---

[5] Longenecker, *Romans*, 507.
[6] Hodges, *Romans*, 120.

FORTY-ONE

The Promise Came Through the Righteousness of Faith (Romans 4:13)

For the promise that he would be the heir of the world was not to Abraham or to his seed through the law, but through the righteousness of faith.

The Promise That He Would Be Heir of the World

Paul has in mind here the promise of worldwide blessing made to Abraham in Gen 12:1-4 and the promise of heirship in Gen 15:1-6. The word *heir* is found in Gen 15:2, 3, 4, and again in Gen 21:10. The exact expression "the heir of the world" is found only here in the Bible (though see Heb 1:2, "heir of all things," in reference to Christ). It combines the heirship of Genesis 15 with the promise of worldwide blessing in Gen 12:1-4. Compare also Gal 3:18, in which Paul speaks of "the inheritance...of promise" that God gave to Abraham.

Paul will now focus on what Abraham and his seed (Gen 26:4; 28:14) did in order to receive this promise of an inheritance.

Not Through the Law

The basis of this promised inheritance was not the Law of Moses. That law did not come into existence until centuries after Abraham was justified and given the promise of an inheritance. The promised inheritance was based on something else entirely—faith.

But Through the Righteousness of Faith

The basis of the promised inheritance is "through the righteousness of faith." In other words, Abraham was promised a future in the Messiah's kingdom, a kingdom in which He will rule over the whole world, through the righteousness which comes by faith in Christ.

Hodges comments, "Since the world to come will be composed exclusively of those who receive the Abrahamic blessing of justification, Abraham thereby becomes the *heir of the world*."[1] He continues, "The eternal world to come will therefore be populated and possessed by Abraham's *spiritual* descendants, both Jewish and Gentile, all of whom will be recipients of the Abrahamic blessing of *the righteousness of faith*."[2]

Concerning the expression "the righteousness of faith," Longenecker writes, "which expression had become in Paul's vocabulary a rather clipped way of speaking about 'the righteousness credited by God to those who receive it by faith.'"[3]

---

[1] Zane C. Hodges, *Romans: Deliverance from Wrath* (Corinth, TX: Grace Evangelical Society, 2013), 121.
[2] Ibid.
[3] Richard N. Longenecker, *The Epistle to the Romans* (Grand Rapids, MI: Eerdmans, 2016), 511.

FORTY-TWO

All Who Are of the Faith of Abraham (Romans 4:16)

Therefore it is of faith that it might be according to grace, so that the promise might be sure to all the seed, not only to those who are of the law, but also to those who are of the faith of Abraham, who is the father of us all...

It Is of Faith That It Might Be According to Grace

Paul has already linked faith and grace in Rom 4:4-5. If justification before God is by faith, then it is in keeping with (according to) God's grace, His merciful favor. He did all the work at Calvary. All we can do to be justified before God is to believe in the Lord Jesus Christ.

Witmer says, "If the promise were fulfilled for those who keep the Law, then no Gentiles (or Jews either) could be saved! But this cannot be, because Abraham...is the father of us all, that is, all who believe."[1]

So That the Promise Might Be Sure

What sure promise is Paul talking about? He began speaking of *the promise* in Rom 4:13-14. This is the promise to Abraham of being an heir of the world to come. That is, Abraham was promised that he would be a part of the Messiah's eternal kingdom

---

[1] John Witmer, "Romans," in *The Bible Knowledge Commentary*, New Testament Edition, ed. by John F. Walvoord and Roy B. Zuck (Wheaton, IL: Victor Books, 2013), 454.

if he believed in the Messiah for his eternal destiny. That same promise is sure to all, Jews and Gentiles, who believe in the Lord Jesus Christ.

Longenecker writes, "Paul joins the triumvirate of 'promise' (*epangelia*), 'faith' (*pistis*), and 'grace' (*charis*) in this verse, which themes constitute the three-legged platform or 'stool' on which the structure of all true religion [i.e., Christianity] rests."[2]

Regarding the word *sure*, Longenecker, in agreement with Deissmann, thinks the "nuance of the word that seems most applicable here [is] 'legally guaranteed security.'"[3]

To All Who Are of the Faith of Abraham, Father of Us All

Since Abraham believed in Messiah before he was circumcised, yet afterward became the father of all Jews, he can be the father of Jews and Gentiles who believe in the Lord Jesus Christ for their eternal destiny. While Abraham was but a man, he is the spiritual father of us all, that is, of Jewish and Gentile believers.

The *Faithlife Study Bible* says:

> In the same way that God offered Abraham the gift of land through faith, He now offers the gift of righteousness through faith to all people. This means that both Jews and Gentiles should have the same response to God's promise of righteousness apart from the law."[4]

---

[2] Richard N. Longenecker, *The Epistle to the Romans* (Grand Rapids, MI: Eerdmans, 2016), 514.
[3] Ibid.
[4] Barry, Mangum, Brown, Heiser, Custis, Ritzema, and Bomar, *Faithlife Study Bible* (Bellingham, WA: Lexham Press, 2012, 2016), s.v. Rom 4:16.

FORTY-THREE

Therefore, It Was Accounted to Him for Righteousness (Romans 4:22)

And therefore "it was accounted to him for righteousness."

What Does *Therefore* Refer to?

A famous interpretive question all first-year hermeneutics (Bible interpretation) students learn is "What is the *therefore* there for?" It clearly looks back to something in the preceding discussion. In this case, Paul is looking back primarily to the three preceding verses, Rom 4:19-21.

Abraham received the promise of an heir through Sarah when he was seventy-five, and she was sixty-five. God did fulfill that promise, but not quickly. Guess how long it was before Sarah became pregnant and had a son? Twenty-five years! That is a long time, especially if you are well beyond child-bearing years in the first place.

Paul says that Abraham "did not consider his own body, already dead (since he was about a hundred years old), and the deadness of Sarah's womb." While in v 19 Paul is looking at Abraham's faith in the days leading up to Sarah's becoming pregnant, his point covers the entire quarter century: "He did not waver at the promise of God through unbelief, but was strengthened in faith, giving glory to God, being fully convinced that what He had promised, He was also able to perform."

The issue, of course, was far more than believing in the miraculous birth of a son, as wonderful as that was. But Paul's main point is that despite logical reasons to doubt God's promise of justification by faith alone in the coming Messiah, Abraham believed that promise and was justified by God. Witmer accurately comments: "Abraham's response of faith to God and God's promise to him was the human requirement for God's justifying Abraham."[1] López says, "Abraham was certain that He (God) would perform the incredible promise of supplying a Savior."[2]

Why Quote Genesis 15:6 Again?

Paul already quoted Gen 15:6 earlier in the chapter (Rom 4:3). He also alluded to Gen 15:6 in all the verses prior to v 22 (see Rom 4:4-5, 6-8, 9-12, 13-21). Romans 4 is Paul's commentary on Gen 15:6. In v 22 Paul focuses on the last seven words of Gen 15:6 (the last four words in the Greek text).

While Cranfield is quite vague on what Abraham believed God for, his comment on v 22 is very helpful:

> The preceding verses have drawn out the meaning of the first five words of the LXX [the Greek OT] Gen 15:6, and now the *dio* [*therefore*], with which Paul introduces his quotation of the last part of that verse, makes the point that it was because Abraham's faith in God referred to in the first part of the verse was the sort of thing that Paul has just shown it to have been that God counted it to him *eis dikaiosunēn* [*for righteousness*]."[3]

There are several reasons why Paul quotes Gen 15:6 again. First, repetition is a wonderful teaching tool. At a time when people did not have copies of the OT (or of those portions of the NT available when the letter to the Romans arrived), this repetition

---

[1] John A. Witmer, "Romans," in *The Bible Knowledge Commentary,* New Testament Edition, ed. by John F. Walvoord and Roy B. Zuck (Wheaton, IL: Victor Books, 1985), 455.
[2] René A. López, "The Epistle of Paul the Apostle to the Romans," in *The Grace New Testament Commentary,* vol. 2, ed. by Robert N. Wilkin (Denton, TX: Grace Evangelical Society, 2010), 646.
[3] C. E. B. Cranfield, *The Epistle to the Romans,* vol. 1 (New York, NY: T&T Clark, 1975), 250.

during the oral reading of this passage would make it easy for the listeners to memorize Gen 15:6, if they hadn't already.

Second, if this were a trial, Abraham would be the first witness for the defense. Justification by faith alone is powerfully proven by Abraham. Evangelicals are likely to be impressed by some quotation from or about Calvin, Luther, John Nelson Darby, Billy Graham, Lewis Sperry Chafer, R. B. Thieme, Charles Ryrie, or some other popular teacher today. But while we should recognize and consider the writings of people in history and in our day, the writings of Scripture are the basis for our faith. The writings of men and women since the close of the canon of Scripture are only as valuable as they are faithful to the meaning of the Word of God on which they comment.

Third, by using a verse written around 1440 BC, Paul shows that justification has always been by faith, apart from the works of the law. Many mistakenly think that people in the OT were saved or justified by works and that only after the birth of the Church (or some might say after the baptism of Jesus by John the Baptist) did the message change to justification by faith alone. Justification has always been by faith alone, apart from works. This repeated attention to Gen 15:6 underscores that truth.

FORTY-FOUR

Justification by Faith Alone Is for Us Too (Romans 4:23-24)

Now it was not written for his sake alone that it was imputed to him, but also for us. It shall be imputed to us who believe in Him who raised up Jesus our Lord from the dead...

Genesis 15:6 Was Not for Abraham Alone

Longenecker calls vv 23-24, "a postscript that applies what he has been saying about the nature and structure of Abraham's faith specifically to his Christian addresses at Rome."[1] While surely true, he leaves unanswered a perplexing question.

The opening words, "Now it was not written for his sake alone that it was imputed to him," are puzzling. Abraham died many centuries before Gen 15:6 was written. So, what does Paul mean?

Cranfield has a helpful answer. After saying that the words *it was accounted to him* "is probably intended to call to mind the whole of Gen 15:6," he then adds that, "[Gen 15:6]…was not recorded just for his sake—that is, as a memorial to him, that he live on in men's remembrance—but for our sakes too, because his faith in God and its being reckoned *eis dikaiosunēn* [*for righteousness*] have direct relevance for us."[2] Hodges similarly writes, "Abraham himself was not the sole concern of the declaration

---

[1] Richard N. Longenecker, *The Epistle to the Romans* (Grand Rapids, MI: Eerdmans, 2016), 522.
[2] C. E. B. Cranfield, *The Epistle to the Romans,* vol. 1 (New York, NY: T&T Clark, 1975), 250.

of Gen 15:6, although the record of his faith surely commends him."³ Not only was Abraham justified by faith in Messiah, but so are all who exercise faith in Him. That is the point of Gen 15:6.

Righteousness Is Imputed to All Who Believe in Him Who Raised Jesus

At first glance, believing in God the Father, not Jesus, for justification seems wrong. No generic faith in God the Father leads to justification. However, upon further reflection, it is easy to see how faith in Jesus and faith "in Him who raised up Jesus our Lord from the dead" are one and the same. Compare Jesus' words in John 5:24 and John 6:28-29. One cannot believe in God the Father without believing in His Son whom He sent to preach and to die and whom He raised from the dead.

Hodges comments, "As Paul has just shown in vv 19-22, the faith by which Abraham was justified was *implicitly* a confidence in God's resurrecting power. The God in whom he believed could overcome his own 'dead' body as well as the 'deadness of Sarah's womb.'"⁴ Of course, Abraham's faith in the God who raised Jesus also extended to his belief that God was going to raise him and all believers from the dead one day so that they would forever be a part of Messiah's kingdom (cf. John 8:56; 11:25; Heb 11:9, 19).

Anders Nygren's extended comment on Rom 4:23-24 is outstanding:

> Thus, faith in Christ does not mean only that we believe in Him as risen from the dead. We also believe that through Him we are removed from the dominion of sin and death and received into the age of righteousness and life. God has dealt with us through Christ; He has made us, who were dead, alive in Christ. Concisely put, that is the meaning of justification. Justification is the revelation of the new righteousness of God. The sinner, who stood

---
³ Zane C. Hodges, *Romans: Deliverance from Wrath* (Corinth, TX: Grace Evangelical Society, 2013), 127.
⁴ Ibid.

under the wrath of God, is through Christ incorporated into the new reality which gets its character from "the righteousness of God." Now we see clearly why, according to Paul, justification must indeed be justification of the *sinner*. It is he who is dead, whom God raised to life. "Even when we were dead through our trespasses, he made us alive together with Christ" (Eph. 2:5).[5]

Genesis 15:6 reports that Abraham believed God *about the coming Messiah*. He believed that the coming Messiah guaranteed that he, and all who believe in the Messiah for their eternal destiny, would be resurrected and would live in His kingdom forever. Paul's message of justification by faith in Christ, apart from works, is proven by the justification of Abraham.

---

[5] Anders Nygren, *Commentary on Romans* (Minneapolis, MN: Augsburg Fortress, 1978), 183.

FORTY-FIVE

Having Been Justified by Faith, We Have Peace with God (Romans 5:1)

Therefore, having been justified by faith, we have peace with God through our Lord Jesus Christ...

Having Been Justified by Faith

Romans 3:21–4:25 deals with justification by faith alone. Romans 5:1-11 are hinge verses, reviewing justification by faith alone (5:1a), describing its triumphant results (5:1b-5), explaining how this triumph was accomplished (5:6-11), and, in the process, introducing the next section of the book, sanctification by having a Biblical mindset. The word "therefore" points to the transition from chaps. 4 and 5. Constable says that, "'Therefore' signals that what follows rests on what has preceded. Paul now put [sic] the question of whether justification is by faith or by works behind him. He had proved that it comes to us by faith."[1]

Commenting on Rom 5:1-11, Newell says: "In the first eleven verses we have the blessed results of justification by faith, along with the most comprehensive statement in the Bible of the pure love and grace of God, in giving Christ for us sinners."[2]

The words translated as *having been justified* reflect one Greek word, *dikaiōthentes*. It is an aorist passive participle, which might express the *cause* of having peace with God (*since*, or *because*, we have been justified) or simply the fact of justification that results in peace with God (having been justified). Most translations adopt

---
[1] Thomas Constable, https://netbible.org/bible/Romans+5.
[2] William R. Newell, *Romans Verse-by-Verse* (Chicago, IL: Moody, 1970), 162.

the causal understanding (e.g., NIV, NET, HCSB, RSV, NRSV, LEB, ESV).

As he starts the sanctification section of Romans (chaps. 5–8), Paul begins by describing one of the major benefits that accrues to the justified person, the one declared righteous by God.

We Have Peace with God

The first benefit mentioned is "peace with God." Paul is not speaking here of a feeling. A believer may or may not *feel that he has peace with God*. But he has it in any case.

However, Paul does not mean that every believer *is currently experiencing* peace with God. If a believer is a friend of the world, then he is at enmity with God in his experience (Jas 4:4).

Paul is speaking *of the position* of the justified person. Hodges writes, "The nature of this *peace* is of course *judicial*, since justification is the act of God as our Judge. As a result, no charge can be brought against the justified person before God's bar of justice (see Rom 8:33-34)."[3]

(The majority of Greek manuscripts are evenly divided between *echomen* [*we have*] and *echōmen* [*let us have*]. The context [i.e., internal evidence] supports *we have*, as evidenced in most translations. However, if a hortatory subjunctive were used, then instead of speaking about our *positional peace*, Paul would be urging justified people *to experience the peace of God*.)

Through Our Lord Jesus Christ

Peace with God is the standing of all justified people because of the work of the Lord Jesus Christ. Paul has already said that Jesus is our *Mercy Seat* (Rom 3:25). We can meet with God and be at peace with Him because of the shed blood of our Lord and Savior, which serves as a sort of spiritual mercy seat.

---

[3] Zane C. Hodges, *Romans: Deliverance from Wrath* (Corinth, TX: Grace Evangelical Society, 2013), 133.

We have this standing of peace with God because we have been justified by faith in Christ. Romans 5:1 is yet another faith-alone verse. The sole condition of being justified by God is faith in His Son.

FORTY-SIX

The Righteousness of Faith (Romans 9:30)

What shall we say then? That Gentiles, who did not pursue righteousness, have attained to righteousness, even the righteousness of faith; but Israel, pursuing the law of righteousness, has not attained to the law of righteousness.

Gentiles Did Not Pursue Righteousness, Yet Attained It

In Romans 9–11 Paul shifts his discussion from sanctification (Romans 5–8) to the spiritual condition of Israel, both now and in the future. Paul, being unfamiliar with replacement theology, tells of a day when all Israel will be saved (Rom 11:26). But not now. At the present time there is only a remnant of believing Jews. For the most part, the nation rejected her Messiah (John 1:11).

At this pivotal verse, Paul is raising a seeming injustice. Gentiles did not pursue righteousness. Yet they found it. On the other hand, Israel, which pursued righteousness via the law, did not attain it (Rom 9:31). Is that fair?

Even the Righteousness of Faith

Yes. It is fair because one can only attain righteousness by faith in Christ. That is why Paul calls it "the righteousness of faith," or, *the righteousness which is sourced in faith*. There is no other way to be justified—declared righteous—by God, except by faith in Christ.

Of course, Paul is speaking in generalities here. Some Gentiles have indeed pursued and found righteousness (e.g., Cornelius in Acts 10; Lydia in Acts 16). However, as a whole, the Gentiles were not seeking righteousness at all, whether the righteousness of faith or the righteousness of law keeping.

Hodges says, "The righteousness that has been obtained by Gentiles is quite different in character from the kind pursued by Israel."[1] He continues,

> That nation actually *is* pursuing a form of righteousness, Paul says. But it is not a faith-righteousness that they pursue, but rather the law of righteousness. That is to say, they are seeking righteousness before God by means of Torah, *the law* that prescribes righteous conduct. But this pursuit, as Paul has already shown in Romans (see 3:19-20) has failed...Though Israel pursued legal righteousness with zeal (see 10:2), such righteousness is in fact *out of their reach*. They have not reached the goal.[2]

Nygren writes,

> If God has determined that righteousness shall belong to those who believe, and only to them, then in the nature of the case Israel cannot be participant in that righteousness, since she seeks to win it by way of the law.[3]

He adds, "So Israel's rejection is her own fault."[4]

F. F. Bruce comments,

> The gospel, with its proclamation of the 'righteousness' of God bestowed on believers, came to the Jew first, and also to the Gentile, but (on the whole) it was accepted

---

[1] Zane C. Hodges, *Romans* (Corinth, TX: Grace Evangelical Society, 2013), 286.
[2] Ibid., 286-87.
[3] Anders Nygren, *Commentary on Romans* (Minneapolis, MN: Augsburg Fortress, 1978), 377.
[4] Ibid.

by the Gentile first. The Gentiles responded gratefully to the message which assured them of their acceptance by God on the ground of faith, and it was 'reckoned to them as righteousness.' The Jews (for the most part) continued to pursue the path of legal righteousness, seeking acceptance with God on the basis of their law-keeping, and yet never attained their goal. The reason was simple: they were following the wrong path. Acceptance by God was assured to faith and not to the works enjoined by the law.[5]

No amount of good intentions can turn law keeping into justification by God. For no one keeps the law perfectly (Rom 3:23). The only way to be justified before God is to obtain *the righteousness of faith*.

---

[5] F. F. Bruce, *Romans*, 2nd ed. (Downers Grove, IL: InterVarsity, 1985), 186.

FORTY-SEVEN

Do Not Be Ashamed of Being Justified by Faith in Christ (Romans 9:32-33)

Why? Because they did not seek it by faith, but as it were, by the works of the law. For they stumbled at that stumbling stone. As it is written: "Behold, I lay in Zion a stumbling stone and rock of offense, and whoever believes on Him will not be put to shame."

Jesus Is a Stumbling Stone and Rock of Offense

The one-word question "Why?" looks back to the preceding verses. Why didn't Israel obtain righteousness (9:30-31)? "Because they did not seek it by faith, but as it were, by the works of the law." Faith in Christ is the only way for anyone to be justified before God.

Instead of believing in Messiah, they "stumbled at that stumbling stone" (from Isa 28:16 and possibly Isa 8:14). Hodges suggests that *stumbling* is too weak of a translation and that a better translation would be "a stone *of collision*."[1] He writes, "Obviously Israel had collided violently with her promised Messiah, Jesus Christ, with the result that He died a violent death at her hands."[2]

Cranfield writes,

> Its [Israel's] determination to establish its own righteousness by its works naturally made it blind to the righteousness which God was making available in Christ as

---

[1] Zane C. Hodges, *Romans: Deliverance from Wrath* (Corinth, TX: Grace Evangelical Society, 2013), 287.
[2] Ibid.

a free gift, while its failure to recognize Christ as the true innermost substance of the law could only drive it deeper into legalistic misunderstandings and perversions of the law.[3]

Sadly, many Jews and Gentiles continue to this day to collide with the Stone of collision. Rather than believing in Jesus in order to be justified, countless people seek to be justified by their works. But justification is by faith alone, apart from works.

Whoever Believes in Him Should Not Be Ashamed of Him

Most translations understand the ending of v 33 as a statement of fact: "whoever believes on Him *will not be put to shame*." However, some translations have a more neutral translation, which can be taken as a statement or a command: "whoever believes on Him *shall not be ashamed*" (YLT, Darby, GNV, RGT). When Paul cites these words again in Rom 10:11, he uses it with the force of a command (compare Rom 10:9-10). See also Rom 1:16; 2 Tim 1:8. Hodges suggests that Paul's point in both the end of v 33 and in 10:11 is that "the believer in Jesus should never *be ashamed* of Him and of his identification with Him."[4]

If a statement is what Paul intended, then the point would be that those who believe on Him for their justification will not be ashamed of themselves for that faith. F. F. Bruce comments, "Those who trust in Christ as the Saviour whom God has provided need never fear that their trust will prove ill-founded. God vindicates his people's faith…"[5]

Since so many people reject justification by faith alone, even in Evangelicalism today, there is opposition when we proclaim the faith-alone message. We are often accused of promoting *easy*

---

[3] C. E. B. Cranfield, *The Epistle to the Romans,* vol. 2 (New York, NY: T&T Clark, 1975), 512.
[4] Hodges, *Romans,* 288-89.
[5] F. F. Bruce, *Romans,* 2nd ed. (Downers Grove, IL: InterVarsity, 1985), 188.

believism, antinomianism, and *cheap grace.* But to be ashamed of the faith-alone message is ultimately to be ashamed of the Lord Jesus Christ. He is the one who gave us this message. We are to keep the faith (2 Tim 4:7).

FORTY-EIGHT

Christ Is the End of the Law for Righteousness for the Believer (Romans 10:4)

For they being ignorant of God's righteousness, and seeking to establish their own righteousness, have not submitted to the righteousness of God. For Christ is the end of the law for righteousness to everyone who believes.

Christ Is the End of the Law for Righteousness

Romans 10:4 is set against the backdrop of the zealous strivings of the Jewish people (Rom 10:2) "to establish their own righteousness" by observance of God's commandments (10:3). What is needed is not the righteousness of man, but "the righteousness of God." What man calls *righteousness*, God calls *falling short of the glory of God* (Rom 3:23).

In what sense is Christ "the end of the law for righteousness"? The word translated as *end* is the Greek word *telos*. It has two major senses: *termination* and *goal*. Commentators are evenly divided over which sense is in view here. Is Christ the goal to which the law pointed? Is He the termination of the law entirely? Some think that Paul means both that Christ is the one who terminated the law and the one who is its goal, that is, its fulfillment.

The sense of goal/fulfillment certainly fits the context. F. F. Bruce writes, "Since Christ is the goal of the law, since in him the law has found its perfect fulfilment, a righteous status before God is available to everyone who believes in him."[1]

The words *for righteousness* show what the goal of the law is. The law could not give one a righteous status before God. "For if there had been a law given which could have given life, truly righteousness would have been by the law" (Gal 3:21). Hodges writes, "In Christ alone is found the realization of the otherwise impossible goal of the law, namely, perfect righteousness."[2]

To Everyone Who Believes

The righteousness which Christ gives is "to everyone who believes." All who believe in Him, whether Jews or Gentiles, have the faith-righteousness which God gives.

No one can obtain right standing with God by works. Such righteousness is given to everyone who believes in Christ.

John Murray says, "Paul is speaking of 'law' as commandment, not of the Mosaic law in any specific sense but of law demanding obedience, and therefore in the most general sense of law-righteousness as opposed to faith-righteousness."[3]

Romans 10:4 champions justification by faith alone, apart from works.

---

[1] F. F. Bruce, *Romans,* 2nd ed. (Downers Grove, IL: InterVarsity, 1985), 190.
[2] Zane C. Hodges, *Romans: Deliverance from Wrath* (Corinth, TX: Grace Evangelical Society, 2013), 294.
[3] John Murray, *The Epistle to the Romans,* vol. 2 (Grand Rapids, MI: Eerdmans, 1968), 51.

FORTY-NINE

With the Heart One Believes unto Righteousness (Romans 10:9-10)

...that if you confess with your mouth the Lord Jesus and believe in your heart that God has raised Him from the dead, you will be saved. For with the heart one believes unto righteousness, and with the mouth confession is made unto salvation. For with the heart one believes unto righteousness, and with the mouth confession is made unto salvation.

You Will Be Saved

Romans 10:9-10 features prominently in many evangelistic tracts and presentations. However, because of confusion over what type of salvation Paul has in mind in these verses, many end up garbling the saving message as a result of appealing to these verses.

Salvation and righteousness are not the same thing here or anywhere in the Bible. The faith-righteousness spoken of here and all through Romans is that of forensic justification before God. The works-salvation in view in these verses and all through Romans refers to *deliverance from God's wrath in this life*, not to salvation from eternal condemnation.[1] Compare Rom 1:16-17 with Rom 1:18-32. See also Rom 5:9-10 (where salvation potentially follows justification) and Rom 10:13.

---

[1] See Zane C. Hodges, *Romans: Deliverance from Wrath* (Corinth, TX: Grace Evangelical Society, 2013), 17, 35-41, 143-44, 298-307.

Believing unto Righteousness

The righteousness Paul speaks of in v 10 is the same faith-righteousness he has discussed previously. Justification before God is by faith alone (Rom 3:21–4:25). Often this verse is read as though it said something completely different. Most would paraphrase v 10 in this way: *For with the heart one believes with the result that he is declared righteousness, and all who truly believe demonstrate their faith by confessing the Lordship of Christ with the result that they will obtain final salvation at the Great White Throne Judgment.* But that is not at all what Paul says. Paul does not say that confession proves one's faith. Nor does he ever speak of needing some *final salvation* in order to avoid eternal condemnation. The believer is secure now and forever. The moment he believed in Christ, his salvation, in the sense of regeneration, was final.

The words *one believes unto righteousness* echo the theme of justification by faith alone, apart from works, seen all through Romans.

Believing with the Heart in Romans 10:10

Some think that Paul is saying that justifying faith is not faith at all. Instead, it is a special *heart response* to the Lordship of Christ. A person submits to Christ and determines to follow Him. That is what justifying faith really is.

But Paul has something internal, believing with the heart, and external, confessing with the mouth, in view in these verses. In order to be justified, that is, in order to have imputed righteousness, one merely needs to believe in Christ. Belief is internal. The word *heart* (*kardia*) stands for the inner self where belief occurs. The word *mouth* stands for external behavior.

Confession unto Salvation

To confess Christ in these verses and in Rom 10:13 refers to corporate worship. It especially has in mind Jewish believers during the Tribulation, as v 13, a quote of Joel 2:32, shows. The application in the present time is to believers who gather with other believers in church in corporate worship. Such people are being saved from God's wrath by their public confession of Christ (and the subsequent life, of course, which is consistent with one who is walking in fellowship with God).

Verses 9 and 10 have two conditions, believing and confessing. While some go to great lengths to try and merge these into one condition, they cannot succeed, for confession of Christ is not the same as believing in Him for justification. Verse 10 explains v 9. In v 10 Paul explains that there is one condition for justification, faith in Christ, and two conditions for *salvation/deliverance*, faith in Christ and confessing Christ. If a person merely confesses Christ, but does not believe in Him for righteousness, he is a false professor and will not be saved from God's wrath now (nor is he justified). If a person merely believes in Christ for his justification, but does not confess Him, then he is justified, but he will not be saved from God's wrath in this life. To escape God's wrath here and now, one must believe in Christ *and* confess Him regularly.

It should be noted that whereas v 9 speaks of believing *that God has raised Him from the dead*, v 10 merely speaks of *believing* unto righteousness. Hodges notes, "When one calls on **Jesus** with his mouth in order to be delivered, he therefore must have faith in his heart **that God has raised Him from the dead.** When these two conditions obtain, the person who calls on Him **will be delivered** (see v 13 below)."[2] In v 10 Paul, as he has done throughout Romans, makes it clear that what the justified person believes Jesus for is "righteousness," that is, justification.

Romans 10:10 teaches justification by faith alone: "For with the heart one believes unto righteousness…"

---

[2] Hodges, *Romans,* 299. For a fuller discussion of Rom 10:9-10, see pp. 298-301.

FIFTY

To Save Those Who Believe (1 Corinthians 1:21)

For since, in the wisdom of God, the world through wisdom did not know God, it pleased God through the foolishness of the message preached to save those who believe.

God's Wisdom Is What Men Consider Foolishness

When it comes to wisdom, there is a discrepancy between what God considers wise and what the world considers wise. The world thinks that "the message of the cross is foolishness" (1 Cor 1:18). But God knows better. The message of the cross is wisdom, "the wisdom of God."

By dying on the cross, the Lord Jesus made everyone savable (John 1:29; 1 John 2:2). But until people see the truth about Jesus' promise of everlasting life to all who believe in Him, they remain spiritually dead, lacking everlasting life.

Through the Message Preached to Save Those Who Believe

The message which Paul preached was "the message of the cross." It is also the message of "Christ crucified" (1 Cor 1:23; 2:2). We know from the Book of Acts and Paul's epistles that the message of the cross and Christ crucified was a simple yet profound message. Contrary to human wisdom, God justifies (declares righteous) and gives everlasting life to (regenerates) all who believe in the crucified and risen Savior for their eternal destiny

(Acts 13:46; 16:30-31; Rom 3:21-31; 4:4-5; 1 Cor 1:21; Gal 2:16; Eph 2:5, 8-9; 1 Tim 1:16).

Paul is not suggesting here that all who believe that Jesus died on the cross for our sins are born again. The message of the cross is a faith-alone, apart from works, message.

Of course, someone who believes that Jesus died on the cross for our sins *should then believe in Jesus for his eternal destiny* (1 Tim 1:16). The cross is the greatest apologetic to lead people to believe the promise of everlasting life. Sadly, however, it is possible to believe in Jesus' substitutionary death and in works salvation at the same time. Christianity today is filled with millions who believe in Jesus' death, but who do not believe the faith-alone message, the promise of everlasting life for those who simply believe in Him.

Many commentators illustrate this very point in their discussion of the words "to save those who believe." Rather than saying that God saves all who believe in Christ, they say that the present tense here shows that one needs "the habit of faith,"[1] "a continuing faith,"[2] and a "total commitment to the one who is trusted."[3] Robertson and Plummer explicitly say that if Paul had said *tous pisteusantas* (aorist participle), he "might mean that to have believed once was enough."[4] But since he used a present articular participle, they think Paul was saying that continuous lifelong faith is required. (If so, then one is not saved until he breathes his last while still believing.)

Johnson has the right idea when he says that the underlying Greek (*tous pisteuontas*) means "the believers."[5] The present

---

[1] Archibald Robertson and Alfred Plummer, *A Critical and Exegetical Commentary on the First Epistle of St Paul to the Corinthians*, 2nd ed. (Edinburgh: T&T Clark, 1961), 21.
[2] Leon Morris, *The First Epistle of Paul to the Corinthians*, 2nd ed. (Grand Rapids, MI: Eerdmans, 2000), 45.
[3] Roy E. Ciampa and Brian S. Rosner, *The First Letter to the Corinthians* (Grand Rapids, MI: Eerdmans, 2010), 98.
[4] Robertson and Plummer, *First Corinthians*, 21.
[5] Alan F. Johnson, *1 Corinthians* (Downers Grove, IL: InterVarsity, 2004), 59.

articular participle is a substantive noun. It says nothing about whether the verbal action continues.[6]

There is but one condition for salvation in 1 Cor 1:21—believing on Jesus Christ, the One who died on the cross for us so that we might be saved by faith in Him (John 1:29; 1 John 2:2).

---

[6] Compare John 11:26 where "he who lives" and "he who believes" are both present articular participles joined by the word *and*: "He who lives and believes in Me shall never die." If *he who believes* refers to faith that never stops, then *he who lives* refers to physical life that does not end in physical death. In that case, the moment a person died, we would be sure he did not have everlasting life since he was no longer meeting the two conditions of ongoing living and believing.

FIFTY-ONE

By Faith We Know We Will Have Glorious Eternal Bodies (2 Corinthians 5:1, 7)

For we know that if our earthly house, this tent, is destroyed, we have a building from God, a house not made with hands, eternal in the heavens…For we walk by faith, not by sight.

We Know about Our Future Glorified Bodies

Verses 1-8 of 2 Corinthians 5 deal with the promise of bodily resurrection (cf. John 11:25b) and of the resurrected body being eternal and perfect. We groan as the current tents we live in suffer broken bones, cancer, a variety of maladies, and degradation over the decades (2 Cor 5:2, 4). But there is encouragement here. Lowery says that Paul was sustained by "the realization that this [his current physical body] was a temporary and transitory state."[1] Our suffering and groaning cause us to long for the soon return of Christ and the gaining of our glorified bodies. Barnett says that Paul "leaves little doubt that this 'house' is the individual's resurrection body."[2]

(Paul's point is not that we get the glorified bodies when we die. We get them when Jesus returns. Compare 2 Cor 5:9-10 with

---

[1] David K. Lowery, "2 Corinthians," in *The Bible Knowledge Commentary*, New Testament Edition, ed. by John F. Walvoord and Roy B. Zuck (Wheaton, IL: Victor Books, 1985), 566.
[2] Paul Barnett, *The Second Epistle to the Corinthians* (Grand Rapids, MI: Eerdmans, 1997), 258.

1 Thess 4:16-17. Prior to Christ's return, departed believers are with the Lord in some sort of intermediate body.)

These verses are not referring to something that *might happen*. Once a person believes in Christ, then his future is secure.

Faith Is the Sole Reason We Know Our Eternal Destiny Is Secure

The way in which we keep our future bodies in mind is by walking by faith (v 7). We do not currently see our glorified bodies. We see bodies that degrade over time.

I'm now sixty-eight. I've been competing in racewalking for over twenty years. When I was forty-six, I completed the 5,000-meter racewalk event at the USA Track and Field Masters National Track Meet in 30 minutes. Now I can't break 33 minutes. A racewalker friend who is ten years older commented, "My bad times from ten years ago would be phenomenal times now." How true.

The reason I know I am getting a glorified body is not because my current body is getting better and better and the trajectory is toward a perfect one. Quite the opposite. I know I have an eternal glorified body awaiting me because that is what the Lord and His apostles promised. The promise of everlasting life to the believer (John 11:26a) includes the promise of a resurrected glorified body (John 11:25b). Constable is certainly correct when he says that, as believers, "We need never despair, therefore…believing what God has revealed He has in store for us."[3]

The faith-alone message tells us that we are eternally secure and that we await a new tent to live in forever.

---

[3] Thomas Constable, https://netbible.org/bible/2+Corinthians+5.

FIFTY-TWO

By Faith We Know That to Be Absent from the Body Is to Be Present with the Lord (2 Corinthians 5:8)

We are confident, yes, well pleased rather to be absent from the body and to be present with the Lord.

Beam Me Up

I liked Star Trek. I especially loved it when Captain Kirk would say, "Beam me up, Scotty."

We know that if we die before the Rapture, our immaterial self, our soul and spirit, will depart from our temporary body and will go into the presence of the Lord Himself.

I suggested in the last chapter that we will have intermediate bodies if we die before the Rapture. There is Biblical support for my suggestion.

Do you recall the Mount of Transfiguration account? The Lord Jesus was transformed into His glorified presence. But it was not just Peter, James, and John witnessing this transformation (Matt 17:1-13). Moses and Elijah were also present. While Elijah never died, Moses did die and was buried (Deut 34:5-6). Yet at the Mount of Transfiguration, he is recognized by the disciples. Peter says, "Let us make three tabernacles: one for You, one for Moses, and one for Elijah" (Matt 17:4). You don't make a tabernacle for an invisible, disembodied spirit.

The same is true in the account of the rich man and Lazarus in Luke 16:19-31. After death, both men have bodies. The rich man wants Lazarus to dip his finger in water and quench his thirst (Luke 16:24). Abraham is visible as well (Luke 16:23-31).

The point is simple: believers can and should remain certain that to be absent from the body is to be present with the Lord.

We Know Death Brings Us Directly to Christ's Presence by Faith

"For we walk by faith, not by sight" looks simultaneously back to vv 1-6 and forward to v 8. We know by faith in God's promise that when we die, we immediately and consciously go into the presence of the Lord. There is no down time. Garland says that Paul clearly "shows that as soon as we are away from the physical body we are present with the Lord in a new dimension…"[1]

Kruse says, "As the parenthesis of v 7 threw light backward upon the meaning of v 6, so too it throws light forward upon the statement in v 8. To be away from the body means to be at home with the Lord…"[2]

Hodge comments on Paul's attitude in 2 Cor 5:8, "Death is not an object of dread, but of desire."[3]

While we may not typically view a text like this as a faith-alone text, it surely is. There is no condition of works or perseverance for the believer to go directly at death into the Lord's presence. That is guaranteed the very moment we believe in Christ for everlasting life.

---

[1] David E. Garland, *2 Corinthians* (Nashville, TN: Broadman & Holman, 1999), 265.
[2] Colin G. Kruse, *2 Corinthians* (Downers Grove, IL: InterVarsity, 2015), 159.
[3] Charles Hodge, *An Exposition of the Second Epistle to the Corinthians*, (New York, NY: Robert Carter & Brothers, 1860), 123.

FIFTY-THREE

Triply Justified by Faith, Not Works (Galatians 2:16)

...knowing that a man is not justified by the works of the law but by faith in Jesus Christ, even we have believed in Christ Jesus, that we might be justified by faith in Christ and not by the works of the law; for by the works of the law no flesh shall be justified.

Not Justified by Works of the Law

Boice identifies the emphasis of this verse: "The threefold repetition of the doctrine of justification by faith in this one verse is important, because it shows the importance the apostle gives to the doctrine."[1]

Some commentators suggest that Paul was not renouncing justification by works, but instead only justification by works *of the Law of Moses*. While it is true that Paul denied justification by works of the Law of Moses, he meant more than that, as Rom 4:1-8 shows. One cannot be justified before God by works of any kind. George says that what is being contrasted in Galatians is "God's free initiative in grace versus human efforts toward self-salvation."[2]

The context here is Paul's public rebuke of Peter and Barnabas for withdrawing from Gentiles, evidently at the Lord's Supper. Peter and Barnabas were kowtowing to Judaizers regarding the

---

[1] James Montgomery Boice, "Galatians," in *Romans–Galatians: The Expositor's Bible Commentary* (Grand Rapids, MI: Zondervan, 1976), 449.
[2] Timothy George, *Galatians* (Nashville, TN: Broadman & Holman, 1994), 195.

OT dietary laws, which were no longer in force (see Peter's three visions in Acts 9).

When Peter and Barnabas withdrew from the Gentiles, they "were not being straightforward about the truth of the gospel." While they did not verbally say that one had to do more than believe in Jesus to be justified before God, their actions implied that. Campbell says that they "were denying by their actions the truth that on the basis of Jesus Christ's death and resurrection Jews and Gentiles who believe are accepted equally by God."[3]

Verse 16 is a statement Paul made in front of the believers in Antioch, and that statement has direct relevance to the believers in Galatia, and all believers everywhere as well.

Justified by Faith in Christ

Three times Paul refers to believing in Jesus in order to be justified before God. "By faith in [Jesus] Christ" occurs twice for emphasis. He also uses the verb *believe* (*pisteuō*) in conjunction with one of the references to faith: "Even we have believed in Jesus Christ" for the purpose "that we might be justified by faith in Christ." The word *we* refers to Jewish believers, including Peter and Barnabas. When they withdrew from table fellowship with Gentiles, they were essentially contradicting their own justification by faith "and not by the works of the law."

By withdrawing from the Gentile believers, Peter and Barnabas were unintentionally calling into question justification by faith alone (Gal 2:14). Justification is by faith in Christ, apart from works. It really is that simple.

---

[3] Donald K. Campbell, "Galatians" in *The Bible Knowledge Commentary*, New Testament Edition, ed. by John F. Walvoord and Roy B. Zuck (Wheaton, IL: Victor Books, 1985), 595.

FIFTY-FOUR

Receiving the Spirit by Faith, Not Works (Galatians 3:2)

This only I want to learn from you: Did you receive the Spirit by the works of the law, or by the hearing of faith?

Receiving the Spirit

Paul is amazed that Judaizers had bewitched the believers in Galatia (Gal 3:1). That leads to the question raised in v 2. How did the Galatians receive the Spirit?

When a person believes in Christ, many things happen to him. He is justified by God the Father right then. The Holy Spirit regenerates him, baptizes him into the Body of Christ, and seals him forever. The Spirit also takes up permanent residence in the believer. This is called *indwelling*. Here Paul refers to the initiation of the Spirit's indwelling as the time when the readers *received the Spirit*. To receive the Spirit is another way of speaking of regeneration or justification, since they all occur simultaneously.

Not by the Works of the Law

Paul's question is rhetorical. The answer is obvious. The readers were Gentile unbelievers when Paul evangelized them. He did not preach the Law of Moses to them. They did not receive the Spirit by works of the law. Yet when Judaizers came into their churches, they were being duped into thinking that in order to retain the Spirit and their justification, they had to keep the law. That makes no sense.

By the Hearing of Faith

The expression "by the hearing of faith" (*ex akoēs pisteōs*) sounds a bit wooden. It has been variously explained by commentators as "[by] listening to the doctrines of the faith,"[1] "by hearing God's word with faith,"[2] "by faith in the Word of God,"[3] "by faith in the gospel message,"[4] "[by] hearing and believing,"[5] and "on the basis of believing what you heard."[6]

Regardless of how we render that expression, Paul's point is that the readers received the Spirit and were justified *by faith in Christ, not by works of the law.*

---

[1] J. B. Lightfoot, *The Epistle of St. Paul to the Galatians* (Grand Rapids, MI: Zondervan, 1976), 135.
[2] Homer A. Kent, Jr., *The Freedom of God's Sons: Studies in Galatians* (Winona Lake, IN: BMHC, 1981), 82.
[3] Warren W. Wiersbe, *Be Free: An Expository Study of Galatians* (Colorado Springs, CO: David C. Cook, 1975), 65.
[4] Ronald Y. K. Fung, *The Epistle to the Galatians* (Grand Rapids, MI: Eerdmans, 1988), 130.
[5] R. Alan Cole, *Galatians*, 2nd ed. (Grand Rapids, MI: Eerdmans, 1989), 132; Fung, *Galatians,* 131.
[6] Richard N. Longenecker, *Galatians* (Dallas, TX: Word Books, 1990), 103; Scot McKnight, *Galatians* (Grand Rapids, MI: Zondervan, 1995), 140.

FIFTY-FIVE

Supply of the Spirit and Working of Miracles by Faith, Not by Works (Galatians 3:5)

Therefore, He who supplies the Spirit to you and works miracles among you, does He do it by the works of the law, or by the hearing of faith?

The Supply of the Spirit & the Working of Miracles

Paul uses various expressions to refer to regeneration. "He who supplies the Spirit to you" refers to the initial reception of the Holy Spirit by the readers when they first believed in Christ for everlasting life. The reference to "He who…works miracles among you" refers to the miraculous works which Paul did in their midst by the power of the Holy Spirit. It might also include any additional miracles that God did among them after Paul left. Though he does not mention God's name explicitly, Paul puts the attention where it belongs, on God, who is the Source of the Spirit and of the miracles that they witnessed. Constable correctly points out that "God did not perform them [the miracles] because the Galatians did something special to earn them."[1]

Not by the Works of the Law

Paul denies that the Spirit's indwelling ministry or the miracles done among the Galatians were due to "the works of the law." The believers in Galatia did not receive the Spirit by means

---

[1] Thomas Constable, https://netbible.org/bible/Galatians+3.

of the works of the law. Nor did God do miracles among them because of works of the law. To this point Campbell adds the important fact that when Paul arrived in Galatia, "The Galatians did not [even] know the Law, and Paul's message was that of justification by faith."[2]

Paul is once again denying justification/regeneration by works.

By the Hearing of Faith

The same odd expression found in v 2 is repeated here in v 5 (*ex akoēs pisteōs*, "by the hearing of faith"). The basis of the indwelling Spirit and the miraculous works that were done in Galatia is faith in the saving message that they heard. See chap. 54 for details.

There were people, whom we call *Judaizers*, who were distorting the gospel of Christ (Gal 1:8-9). They were saying that faith in Christ was not enough to make it into Christ's kingdom. They were essentially teaching justification by law-keeping (see Gal 5:4; cf. Acts 15:1). But justification is by faith in Christ, apart from works. While justified people are expected by God to produce lives full of good works, those good works are not a condition either of being justified or remaining justified. Temporary or even ongoing failure is possible for believers (as the Book of Galatians shows). Justification is by faith alone. For a person who believes in Christ to be misled—to take his eyes off Christ—and then to buy into a works-salvation mindset, is like being bewitched (Gal 3:1-2). George says that in the case of the Galatians, Paul was telling them that those who were teaching them justification by works were "like evil magicians...trying to seduce [them] from the way of Christ to a counterfeit gospel."[3]

---

[2] Donald K. Campbell, "Galatians" in *The Bible Knowledge Commentary*, New Testament Edition, ed. by John F. Walvoord and Roy B. Zuck (Wheaton, IL: Victor Books, 1985), 597.

[3] Timothy George, *Galatians* (Nashville, TN: Broadman & Holman, 1994), 214.

FIFTY-SIX

Abraham's Justification by Faith in Messiah (Galatians 3:6)

—just as Abraham "believed God, and it was accounted to him for righteousness."

Abraham Once Again

Abraham was the revered patriarch of Judaism. But he also was and remains the revered patriarch of Christianity. Paul loves to cite him as proof of justification by faith alone. He also discusses Gen 15:6 and Abraham's justification by faith alone in Rom 4:1-3, 9, 12, 13, 16; Gal 3:7, 8, 9, 14.

Abraham Believed God Concerning the Messiah

While some think that Paul is simply saying that Abraham believed in the existence of God and was justified on that basis, Gen 15:1-6 shows clearly that Abraham believed in the coming Messiah for his eternal destiny. Compare also Christ's words in John 8:56 and the words of the author of Hebrews in Heb 11:10. See chap. 37, which concerns Rom 4:3, for a fuller discussion of Gen 15:6.

Abraham's Faith in Messiah Was Accounted as Righteousness

In Greek, the word *righteousness* is a noun in the same word family as the verb *justified*. We might translate this as "his faith was accounted for justification." God credited Abraham with righteousness because of his faith in the coming Messiah.

Wiersbe writes, "The word *accounted* in Galatians 3:6 and *counted* in Genesis 15:6 mean the same as *imputed* in Romans 4:11, 22-24...When the sinner trusts Christ, God's righteousness is put into his account..."[1] Cole says that Abraham "could never win [this justification] by his own efforts."[2]

After showing that the Jews in Jesus' day cited Gen 15:6 to prove that Abraham was justified *by his deeds*, Longenecker writes:

> But Paul cites Gen 15:6 without any reference to Abraham's meritorious deeds of Gen 14 as a basis for his reception by God or to Abraham's acceptance of circumcision in Gen 17 as a condition. His emphasis, as even his contextual omissions reveal, is on faith alone, apart from righteous deeds or circumcision.[3]

Abraham was called "a friend of God" in Scripture (2 Chron 20:7; Isa 41:8; Jas 2:23). His *friendship with God* was based upon the good works which he did after that, especially when he freely offered up his only son, Isaac (Gen 22:1-19).

Paul does not say, "Abraham served God, and it was accounted to him for righteousness." The sole issue in justification before God is faith in Christ.

In the verses that follow, Gal 3:7-14, Paul emphatically rejects justification by works and repeatedly and enthusiastically pronounces justification by faith in Christ. The words *faith* (*pistis*) and *believe* (*pisteuō*) occur a whopping six times in Gal 3:5-9 and another three times in Gal 3:10-14.

---

[1] Warren W. Wiersbe, *Be Free: An Expository Study of Galatians* (Colorado Springs, CO: David C. Cook, 1975), 68.
[2] R. Alan Cole, *Galatians,* 2nd ed. (Grand Rapids, MI: Eerdmans, 1989), 134.
[3] Richard N. Longenecker, *Galatians* (Dallas, TX: Word Books, 1990), 114.

FIFTY-SEVEN

Only Believers Are Sons of Abraham (Galatians 3:7)

Therefore, know that only those who are of faith are sons of Abraham.

Only Those Who Are of Faith

The Lord Jesus said to His mostly rebellious Jewish audience in John 8:33-59. They claimed to be Abraham's descendants. Yet they said that Jesus was born of fornication (John 8:41), and they said He was a Samaritan and had a demon (John 8:48, 52).

Paul was, of course, a Jew, "a Hebrew of the Hebrews" (Phil 3:5) and "the seed of Abraham" (2 Cor 11:22). But that was merely his *physical* heritage. He knew that his spiritual heritage depended solely on faith in the Lord Jesus Christ.

Are Sons of Abraham

I intentionally skipped discussing the word *only* near the start of this verse. It is not actually found in the Greek text. That is clearly the sense, however. The Greek could more woodenly be translated: "Know, therefore, that those who are of faith, these are the sons of Abraham." Paul is speaking of *spiritual sonship*. The Jewish people are the physical descendants of Abraham, Isaac, and Jacob. Paul learned that the *spiritual* seed of Abraham are not Jews, but anyone who believes in Jesus, whether Jewish or Gentile. Those who do not believe in Jesus, even if they are Jews by birth, are not the sons of Abraham spiritually.

Today, some Gentiles pronounce themselves the spiritual seed of Abraham on the basis not of faith in Christ, but because of their supposed faithfulness to Christ. Though they are not Jewish, they are repeating a flawed understanding of the Scriptures that the Lord Jesus Himself contended with and rejected repeatedly. Jesus said that only those who believe in Him are the spiritual descendants of Abraham (John 8:45-47, 56, 58).

Wiersbe writes,

> The Jewish people were very proud of their relationship with Abraham. The trouble was, they thought that this relationship guaranteed them eternal salvation. John the Baptist warned that their *physical* descent did not guarantee *spiritual* life (Matt. 3:9). Jesus made a clear distinction between 'Abraham's seed' physically and 'Abraham's children' spiritually (John 9:33-47).[1]

Ridderbos comments, "Faith is therefore the criterion for being sons of Abraham."[2] Longenecker adds, "Paul's use of the phrase *hoi ek pisteōs* ('those who rely on faith') in all likelihood arises from and counters the Judaizers' call for Gentile Christians to be 'those who rely on the law' (*hoi ek nomou*) for perfection in their lives."[3]

The righteous, those justified by God, are those who, like Abraham, believe in Christ for eternal standing in the family of God. Faith alone is the key that unlocks justification before God.

---

[1] Warren W. Wiersbe, *Be Free: An Expository Study of Galatians* (Colorado Springs, CO: David C. Cook, 1975), 69.
[2] Herman N. Ridderbos, *The Epistle of Paul to the Churches of Galatia* (Grand Rapids, MI: Eerdmans, 1953), 120.
[3] Richard N. Longenecker, *Galatians* (Dallas, TX: Word Books, 1990), 114.

FIFTY-EIGHT

The Old Testament Foresaw Justification by Faith for Gentiles (Galatians 3:8)

And the Scripture, foreseeing that God would justify the Gentiles by faith, preached the gospel to Abraham beforehand, saying, "In you all the nations shall be blessed."

Scripture Foresaw That God Would Justify the Gentiles by Faith

Paul connects the justification of Abraham by faith with the justification of Gentiles in his day by faith. The same way in which Abraham was justified—by faith in Christ—is the way in which Gentiles are justified today.

The faith-alone message did not originate with Paul. Moses proclaimed that same message in Genesis. The expression *the Scripture* refers to what we call the OT, which taught justification by faith alone and understood that all are justified in this way. The OT even foresaw a time when many more Gentiles than Jews would believe in Messiah. Indeed, Paul calls this *the gospel.*

Campbell comments, "the justification of uncircumcised Gentiles was anticipated in the universal aspect of the Abrahamic Covenant when God **announced the gospel** (lit., 'the good news') **…to Abraham.**"[1]

---
[1] Donald K. Campbell, "Galatians" in *The Bible Knowledge Commentary*, New Testament Edition, ed. by John F. Walvoord and Roy B. Zuck (Wheaton, IL: Victor Books, 1985), 597.

Martyn adds:

> *The Scripture.* For the first time in the letter Paul uses this term, doing so in an arresting manner, indicating that scripture is not a passive text to be quoted and interpreted by human beings as they will. On the contrary, it is alive, having, as it were, eyes and intelligence and a mouth.[2]

Preached the Gospel to Abraham Beforehand

Paul indicates that "The Scripture...preached the gospel to Abraham beforehand." He is using *the Scripture* to refer to the Lord who spoke with Abraham and told him *the gospel.*

What is this gospel message that was preached to Abraham? We might think that it is Gen 15:6. But Paul goes back years earlier, to the time after Abraham (then Abram) had left Ur of the Chaldeans with his father, wife, nephew, and all of their servants and possessions. In fact, the Lord waited until Abraham's father died in Haran before He gave the wonderful gospel promise to him. Campbell notes, "It should not be overlooked that Paul referred to Scripture speaking as though God were speaking, so it can rightly be affirmed that what the Bible says, God says."[3] So, what gospel did Abraham know?

"In You All the Nations Shall Be Blessed"

Paul is here linking Gen 15:6 with Gen 12:3. Genesis 12:3 reads, "I will bless those who bless you, and I will curse him who curses you; and in you all the families of the earth shall be blessed." Paul paraphrases the end of v 3 in this way: "in you all the nations shall be blessed."

In what sense is the blessing of the nations—the Gentiles—*gospel*? It is *gospel*, or *good news*, in the sense that all who believe

---
[2] J. Louis Martyn, *Galatians* (New York, NY: Doubleday, 1997), 300.
[3] Campbell, "Galatians," 597.

in the Messiah, including Gentiles, are justified by God. That is the connection between Gen 15:6 and Gen 12:3.

Some scholars think that Abraham believed in the Messiah in Gen 12:3 and that Gen 15:6 is a summary statement that looks back to his earlier faith. In light of the way Paul uses Gen 15:6 and Gen 12:3, it is more accurate to say that Gen 12:3 was alluding to justification by faith alone, but that Abraham did not understand and believe that until the Lord met with him again (Gen 15:1-6).

Martyn comments:

> So equipped already in Abraham's time, scripture foresaw that God would one day rectify the Gentiles by faith. And gifted with such foresight, it did nothing less than preach the gospel itself ahead of time to the patriarch, telling him that in him, the man of faith, all the Gentiles would one day be blessed.[4]

It is blessed good news that Gentiles are justified by faith in Messiah, in the same way Abraham and all Jewish spiritual sons of Abraham are justified (Gal 3:7). God's calling of Abraham was good news not only for Jews who shared his faith in Messiah, but also for Gentiles who believed the faith-alone message.

Kent says, "This was no innovation originated by Paul. It was announced long ago to Abraham, hundreds of years before Moses ever wrote it down in Scripture."[5]

Galatians 3:8 is another powerful faith-alone verse.

---

[4] Martyn, *Galatians,* 300.
[5] Homer A. Kent, Jr., *The Freedom of God's Sons: Studies in Galatians* (Winona Lake, IN: BMHC, 1981), 86. See also, Scot McKnight, *Galatians* (Grand Rapids, MI: Zondervan, 1995), 152, who says, "His [Paul's] logic is this…[Gentiles] must be justified as Abraham was: that is, by faith, not [by] works of the law."

FIFTY-NINE

Those Who Are of Faith (Galatians 3:9)

So then those who are of faith are blessed with believing Abraham.

Those Who Are of Faith

Paul here concludes his discussion of Abraham's justification and Gen 15:6. The word *so* looks back to 3:1-8. The expression *those who are of faith* is powerful. Paul is thinking here of those who believe in the Messiah for their eternal destiny. The words *of faith* contrast with the expression *of the law* (Gal 3:5, 10, 13). Cole cleverly paraphrases *of faith* as "[of] the 'faith people.'"[1]

This is a sort of spiritual lineage. If you were Irish, you might say, "I'm of Neill," "I'm of Drugain," or "I'm of Domhnaill." Those are clans, physical lineage. Christians are part of the clan of faith. That is why we call ourselves *believers*. We are faith people.

Kent comments, "They receive by faith the blessing of a perfect standing with God, just as Abraham did. It is these who are 'of faith.'"[2]

Are Blessed

The blessedness referred to in v 9 looks back at the blessing of justification by faith alone in the previous verse (3:8). By faith

---

[1] R. Alan Cole, *Galatians*, 2nd ed. (Grand Rapids, MI: Eerdmans, 1989), 137.
[2] Homer A. Kent, Jr., *The Freedom of God's Sons: Studies in Galatians* (Winona Lake, IN: BMHC, 1981), 87.

justification is a blessing given to all who are "of faith" and who are spiritually related to Abraham. Fung says, "God has promised that the Gentiles will be blessed through Abraham and since his blessing was in the first instance that of justification by faith, then those who exercise faith in God are blessed—that is, justified—'along with Abraham, the man of faith' (NIV)."[3]

With Believing Abraham

The expression *believing Abraham* is a fitting capstone to this portion of Galatians. Abraham is and was and always will be *the believing one,* or *the believer.*

A few English translations (KJV, NEB, GNV, MEV, WYC) unfortunately translate *pistō* here as *faithful.* That is misleading. The point here is not that Abraham was *the faithful one.* Instead, he was *the believing one.* Longenecker writes, "The translation 'believing' more exactly expresses its meaning (certainly not 'trustworthy' as in Sir 44:20 or 'faithful' as in KJV and NEB)."[4]

In a sense it is unfortunate that some believers prefer to call themselves *Christians.* While *Christian* is a great term, it is not understood in our culture to refer to those *who believe in Christ.* It is understood to refer to those *who follow Christ.* It is certainly true that all believers should follow Christ. But our core identity is found in the fact that we are believers, not that we are followers. Following without believing is unproductive and misleading.

In Gal 3:9, Paul uses two cognate forms of the noun *faith* (*pisteōs* and *pistō*). Justified people are "of faith" people and they are spiritual kin to "believing Abraham." Paul is emphasizing the faith-alone message.

---

[3] Ronald Y. K. Fung, *The Epistle to the Galatians* (Grand Rapids, MI: Eerdmans, 1988), 140.
[4] Richard N. Longenecker, *Galatians* (Dallas, TX: Word Books, 1990), 116.

SIXTY

Receiving the Promise of the Spirit Through Faith (Galatians 3:14)

[Christ has redeemed us from the curse of the law] ... that the blessing of Abraham might come upon the Gentiles in Christ Jesus, that we might receive the promise of the Spirit through faith.

The Blessing of Abraham

Paul established Abraham's blessing which extends to the Gentiles (from Gen 12:3), is justification by faith alone (Gal 3:8-9). Then in vv 10-13, Paul brought in the other side of the blessing-cursing motif. Those who are "of the works of the law are under the curse" spoken of in Deut 27:26 (which Paul quotes). "Christ has redeemed us from the curse of the law, having become a curse for us," as Deut 21:23 says (which Paul also quotes).

Those seeking to be justified by works are under a curse. But those justified by faith in Christ are experiencing the blessing God intended for them. Verse 14 begins with *hina* (*that, so that*), expressing one of the purposes of Christ's becoming a curse for us.

He became a curse for us (universal atonement) so that Gentiles might receive the blessing of Abraham.

That blessing is "in Christ Jesus." In Paul's writings, the words "in Christ" (*en Christō*) or "in Christ Jesus" refer to those who are justified and born again, that is, to those who believe in Him. The blessing of justification does not come upon *all Gentiles*. It only comes upon those who believe in the Lord Jesus Christ and hence are "in Christ Jesus."

The Promise of the Spirit

Chafer famously said that there were thirty-three major works of God that occur when a person believes in Christ for everlasting life. One of those works of God is the permanent indwelling of the Holy Spirit in the believer.[1] In Scripture this is sometimes called "the promise of the Spirit" (Acts 2:33; Gal 3:14; Eph 1:13; see also Acts 10:47).[2] Only those who believe in Christ and hence are "in Christ" receive the promise of the Spirit. This ministry of the Spirit is a second reason why Christ became a curse for us.[3]

Through Faith

The promise of the Spirit, like justification and regeneration, is for those who believe in Christ, not for those who seek justification by works. The words "through faith" indicate that the means through which the Spirit is received, and justification occurs, is faith. Ridderbos writes, "Faith is the means by which, and the way in which, God grants the gifts of the Spirit to the

---

[1] Before Cornelius and his Gentile household came to faith under the preaching of Peter (Acts 10:43-48), the reception of the Spirit in terms of permanent indwelling did not occur when a person believed, but after he repented and was baptized (Acts 2:38, in reference to Jews) or after the Apostles laid hands on the person (Acts 8:15-17, in reference to Samaritans). Since the Acts 10 experience of the Gentiles, with one notable exception (i.e., the disciples of John the Baptist in Ephesus who received the Spirit after Paul baptized them and then laid hands on them, Acts 19:1-7), the Spirit has been received whenever a person believes in Christ (1 Cor 12:13).

[2] Kent, however, suggests that the promise of the Spirit refers to "regeneration to all who believe." See Homer A. Kent, Jr., *The Freedom of God's Sons: Studies in Galatians* (Grand Rapids, MI: Baker, 1976), 90. In light of other uses of this expression in the NT, this refers to the indwelling of the Spirit. While those two ministries of the Spirit are similar, they are not the same.

[3] The promise of the Spirit is part of a second *hina* clause, expressing a second purpose or intended result of Christ's death. See Ronald Y. K. Fung, *The Epistle to the Galatians* (Grand Rapids, MI: Eerdmans, 1988), 151.

redeemed by Christ."[4] Hoehner, referring to the same expression in Eph 2:8, says, "the words *dia pisteōs*, 'through faith,' denote the subjective means by which one is saved."[5] We are not justified through works. Faith alone is the human condition for justification to occur.

Longenecker says that v 14 concludes Paul's argument "asserting the centrality of faith" in justification and the reception of the Spirit.[6]

---

[4] Herman N. Ridderbos, *The Epistle of Paul to the Churches of Galatia* (Grand Rapids, MI: Eerdmans, 1953), 128.
[5] Harold Hoehner, *Ephesians* (Grand Rapids, MI: Baker, 2002), 340.
[6] Richard N. Longenecker, *Galatians* (Dallas, TX: Word Books, 1990), 124.

SIXTY-ONE

The Promise by Faith to Those Who Believe (Galatians 3:22)

But the Scripture has confined all under sin, that the promise by faith in Jesus Christ might be given to those who believe.

The Scripture Has Confined All under Sin

Though not as well-known as Rom 3:23, Gal 3:22 also asserts the universal sinfulness of man. The Greek word translated as *has confined* refers either to the spiritual bondage that people are in before they believe in Christ (cf. John 8:24, 34; Rom 6:6, 17, 18, 20, 22) or to confinement for one's own good, as in protection. The former better fits v 22 and the use of the same word again in v 23. Longenecker comments, "Paul is then saying that a primary function of the Mosaic law was to bring all humanity under the curse of the law...[it] brought about a knowledge of sin..."[1]

That the Promise by Faith Might Be Given

The word *promise* is not explained here. That word has been used seven times earlier in Galatians 3 (vv 14; 16; 17; 18, twice; 19; 21). It is also used at the end of chap. 3 (v 29). It refers to the blessing of justification, to the related promises of the Holy Spirit (v 14), and of being heirs of God (vv 18, 29; see also Rom 8:17a).

---

[1] Richard N. Longenecker, *Galatians* (Dallas, TX: Word Books, 1990), 144-45.

The words "might be given" allude to the fact that salvation, justification, and the associated blessings are *gifts* of God, not things which we earn by work done.

The words *by faith* intrude into the normal flow of the sentence. The sentence would have been smoother if Paul had said, "that the promise might be given to those who believe." Those intruding words thus give added emphasis to justification by faith alone.

To Those Who Believe

The words *by faith*, discussed in the previous section above, are especially emphatic since they are combined with "those who believe" at the end of the verse. Paul's emphasis all through Galatians 3 (and the whole letter thus far) is that faith in Christ is the sole means of justification. Faith alone is doubly emphatic in this verse.

Kent comments, "Righteousness comes only by God's gift, and sinners receive it by faith."[2] Wiersbe adds, "God does not have two ways of salvation; He has but one—faith in Jesus Christ."[3]

While we are only counting Gal 3:22 as a single verse supporting justification/regeneration by faith alone, it could be counted as two because the verse speaks both of *by faith* and *to those who believe*. Faith alone. Times two.

---

[2] Homer A. Kent, Jr., *The Freedom of God's Sons: Studies in Galatians* (Grand Rapids, MI: Baker, 1976), 102.
[3] Warren W. Wiersbe, *Be Free: An Expository Study of Galatians* (Wheaton, IL: Victor Books, 1975), 81.

SIXTY-TWO

Saved and Sealed (Ephesians 1:13)

In Him you also trusted, after you heard the word of truth, the gospel of your salvation; in whom also, having believed, you were sealed with the Holy Spirit of promise...

In Him You Trusted

The word *trusted* is not in the Greek. It is supplied by the NKJV translations. Other translations read, "when you believed in Him" (HCSB, NET), picking up the idea of believing from later in the sentence. Many simply translate the start of the verse as "In Him you also, after..." (LEB, MEV, NRSV, NASB, WEB, ESV).

While faith is clearly implied in the beginning of the verse, it is probably best to translate the English as closely as possible from the Greek, as many translations do, and simply have the start of the verse pointing to Jesus ("In Him you also") without initially explicitly identifying believing in Him as the response of the readers. Leaving it unstated is a bit more dramatic—something Paul evidently intended.

The Gospel of Your Salvation

The expression *the gospel of your salvation* is understood by many to indicate that Paul is saying that the gospel is the object of saving faith. They often leave Ephesians and go to 1 Cor 15:3-4 to explain what Paul means by *the gospel* here in Ephesians.

However, Paul uses the word *gospel* three other times in Ephesians, and each time it refers to *the good news that in the Church, Jews and Gentiles are united in one body* (cf. 3:6; 6:15, 19). In

Eph 6:19, Paul speaks of *the mystery of the gospel*. The death of Messiah for our sins was not a mystery. It was clearly revealed in Gen 3:15; Isa 52:13–53:12; Matt 16:21; Luke 2:34-35). It was also revealed in the type of Abraham's offering his only son, Isaac (Gen 22:1-14). But the Church, Jews and Gentiles united in one body, was not clearly revealed in the OT.[1]

The word *salvation* only occurs one other time in the letter, "the helmet of salvation" (Eph 6:17). That is not clear as to what type of salvation is meant. However, the verb form *save* is found in Eph 2:5, 8. There it clearly indicates that in Ephesians, salvation refers to being made alive, that is, given everlasting life.

The genitive *of your salvation* most likely is a possessive genitive, referring to salvation's good news.[2] The point would be that during this age, the new birth possesses the good news of the Church. Our common birth makes us spiritual brothers and sisters.

Having Believed, You Were Sealed with the Holy Spirit

The salvation (=regeneration, Eph 2:5, 8) and the sealing both occurred when the Ephesians believed in Christ for their eternal salvation. Both regeneration and sealing are ministries of the Holy Spirit that occur when someone first believes in Christ.[3]

---

[1] I believe that the Church is prophesied in the OT in places like Psalm 45, but that without the further revelation of the NT, it could not be understood. However, the death of Messiah could and should have been understood from the OT and from the teaching of the Lord Himself. He directly told the disciples that He was going to be killed and that He would rise on the third day (e.g., Matt 16:21).

[2] Hoehner suggests that this is a genitive "of content, namely, 'the gospel which has for its content salvation'" (Harold W. Hoehner, *Ephesians: An Exegetical Commentary* [Grand Rapids, MI: Baker, 2002], 237). He adds, "The truth of the message is the good news of deliverance of people from their bondage to sin" (p. 237). He is not clear as to what he means by deliverance from sin's bondage.

[3] Two other ministries of the Spirit that occur then are permanent indwelling and baptism into the Body of Christ. Those four ministries can be remembered with the acronym RIBS (regeneration, indwelling, baptizing, and sealing).

Hoehner writes, "The aorist participles in relation to the main verb…could be regarded as temporal…'after having heard and believed, you were sealed'…The picture is that when they heard, they believed and hence were sealed."[4]

There is no mention here of anything other than belief in Christ (belief in what you heard about Him and His promise of everlasting life) as the condition. This is another faith-alone verse. Anyone who simply believes in Jesus is saved and sealed forever.

---

[4] Hoehner, *Ephesians*, 237.

SIXTY-THREE

Salvation by Grace Through Faith, Apart from Works (Ephesians 2:8-9)

For by grace you have been saved through faith, and that not of yourselves; it is the gift of God, not of works, lest anyone should boast.

Saved by Grace Through Faith

Ephesians 2:8 is speaking of the past salvation of the readers. Paul uses a perfect tense ("you have been saved"). In Greek the perfect tense refers to something which occurred in the past and which has an abiding result. In Eph 2:8 the perfect tense means that the Christians in Ephesus were saved in the past; they are still saved now; and they will remain saved forever. Paul is saying that the readers have everlasting life that can never be lost.

How do we know that the salvation in Eph 2:8 refers to everlasting life? The first part of v 8 is a repetition of the end of Eph 2:5: "by grace you have been saved." In Eph 2:5 that salvation is described as "He made us alive together with Christ." *Being made alive with Christ* refers to the new birth, being born again.

The means by which this *by grace salvation* was received was "through faith." While Paul does not specifically mention faith *in Christ,* that is clear from v 5.

The fact that eternal salvation is through faith is emphasized in the words that follow.

That Not of Yourselves

Some theologians suggest the words *that not of yourselves* refer to faith. However, the word *faith* (*pistis*) is feminine in Greek. But the word *that* (*touto*) is neuter. Neuter pronouns in Greek do not normally refer to feminine antecedents. Instead, neuter pronouns refer to the entire idea just stated ("by grace you have been saved"). Hoehner writes, "Rather than any particular word, it is best to conclude that *touto* refers back to the preceding section... the concept of salvation by grace through faith."[1]

Paul is saying that the salvation of the Ephesian believers is not of themselves. That is made clear in what he goes on to say.

It Is the Gift of God

The word *it* is not in the Greek. Literally, it reads, *the gift of God*.[2] Salvation is not of our own doing; it is the gift of God. That same teaching is found in the Lord Jesus' words in John 4:10 to the woman at the well: "'If you knew the gift of God, and who it is who says to you, "Give Me a drink," you would have asked Him, and He would have given you living water.'" He went on to explain that the gift of God is everlasting life (John 4:14). Salvation (everlasting life) is also called a gift in Rom 5:15-18; 6:23; Heb 6:4; Jas 1:17-18; and Rev 22:17.

Not of Works, Lest Anyone Should Boast

Still discussing salvation/everlasting life, Paul says that it is "not of works, lest anyone should boast." In Galatians, Paul repeatedly said that justification is not of works. Here in Ephesians he says that regeneration is not of works. The fact that it is not of works means that there is no ground for boasting.

---

[1] Harold W. Hoehner, *Ephesians: An Exegetical Commentary* (Grand Rapids, MI: Baker, 2002), 343.
[2] Paul put *God* first in Greek to emphasize that this is *His gift*: *Theou to dōron* (lit., "of God the gift").

If you got into Christ's kingdom because your works were better than the works of most people, then you'd have a basis for boasting. But since salvation is not of works—even works we do *after we are born again*—then boasting is eliminated.[3] Hoehner says, "From God's vantage point it is grace, not a human being's works, that is the basis of salvation. From a human's vantage point, it is faith and not works that is the means to salvation."[4]

Salvation is by grace, through faith, and apart from works. It is by faith alone.

---

[3] Some commentators suggest that Eph 2:10 means that those who are saved will necessarily persevere in a life of good works. However, they fail to give careful attention to the shift in pronouns. In Eph 2:8-9 the second-person plural pronoun is used. Paul is talking about the readers—*you*. But in v 10, the first-person plural pronoun is used: *we*. The reason for the shift is obvious when we consider Eph 2:11-22. Verses 11-22 show that the first-person plural refers to the Church, the Body of Christ, Jews and Gentiles united in one body. The Church is "God's masterpiece, created in Christ Jesus for good works, which God prepared beforehand that we should walk in them." Paul is not referring to individual believers in v 10. He is not making some promise that all believers will overflow in good works. Anyone reading the Corinthian epistles, for example, knows that not all believers in the early church were stellar examples of holiness. I can *apply* Eph 2:10 by realizing that as a part of the Body of Christ *I should be producing the good works that God has prepared for the Body of Christ to do* (see Ephesians 4-6 for the types of works Paul has in mind). But it is a terrible misapplication of Eph 2:10 to base one's assurance of everlasting life on the quality of his lifestyle. Of course, anyone who tries to find assurance in his flawed works will find himself unsure of his eternal destiny. Only by continuing to believe the promise of life can we maintain assurance of salvation.

[4] Hoehner, *Ephesians,* 345.

SIXTY-FOUR

Righteousness Through Faith in Christ (Philippians 3:9)

...and be found in Him, not having my own righteousness, which is from the law, but that which is through faith in Christ, the righteousness which is from God by faith...

Not Having My Own Righteousness from the Law

The word *righteousness* (*dikaiosunē*) is the noun form of the verb *justify* (*dikaioō*). While it is sometimes used of *the experiential righteousness* that believers can enjoy in this life (e.g., Eph 5:9; Phil 1:11; 1 Tim 6:11; 2 Tim 2:22; 3:16; Heb 11:33; 12:11; 1 Pet 2:24; 2 Pet 2:21; 1 John 2:29; 3:7), *dikaiosunē* here refers to *positional righteousness*, right standing with God (i.e., justification). Fee calls personal righteousness "behavioral righteousness" and says, "to get there one must first receive *the righteousness that comes from God*."[1] Experiential righteousness is less than perfection (e.g., Phil 3:12-14; 1 John 1:8, 10). But positional righteousness is perfection (Heb 10:10, 14).

Martin comments, "Justification here carries the eschatological meaning of vindication at the divine court by the possessing of an acceptable **righteousness**, i.e., right relationship with God, granted by God himself."[2]

---
[1] Gordon D. Fee, *Philippians* (Downers Grove, IL: IVP Academic, 1999), 146.
[2] Ralph P. Martin, *Philippians* (Grand Rapids, MI: Eerdmans, 1976), 131-32.

Having Righteousness Which Is Through Faith in Christ

Both mentions of faith in this verse are given as the means by which a person is justified before God. Paul indicates that he knows that he has righteousness "which is through faith in Christ." It is not "[his] own righteousness." It is the righteousness of Christ that is imputed to a person when he believes in Christ for his eternal destiny.

Paul was justified, and he was sure that he was because the only condition of justification before God is having faith in the Lord Jesus Christ.

The Righteousness Which Is from God by Faith

The second mention of faith in this verse is emphatic. The righteousness that Paul has through faith in Christ is "righteousness which is from God by faith." The precise Greek expression, *epi tē pistei*, is only found here in the NT, though Paul expresses this same *by-faith* idea in different words often in his letters (e.g, [*tē*] *pistei* with no preposition, Rom 3:28; 5:2; 11:20; 2 Cor 1:24; *ek pisteōs*, Rom 3:30; 5:1; 9:32; Gal 2:16; 3:8, 11, 22, 24; 5:5; *dia pisteōs*, 2 Cor 5:7; Gal 2:16; *en pistei*, Gal 2:20). Vincent comments, "It belongs to the nature of God's righteousness as imparted to man that it rests upon faith (Rom. 4:5)."[3]

When a person believes in Christ, God the Father imputes Christ's righteousness to his account and declares him forever righteous. The sole condition is faith in Christ. Nothing else.

---

[3] Marvin R. Vincent, *The Epistles to the Philippians and to Philemon* (Edinburgh: T&T Clark, 1897), 103.

SIXTY-FIVE

Believing on Him for Everlasting Life (1 Timothy 1:16)

However, for this reason I obtained mercy, that in me first Jesus Christ might show all longsuffering, as a pattern to those who are going to believe on Him for everlasting life.

Paul Obtained Mercy

Paul recounted his experience when he told Timothy, "I was formerly a blasphemer, a persecutor, and an insolent man; but I obtained mercy because I did it ignorantly in unbelief" (1 Tim 1:13). He went on to say, "Christ Jesus came into the world to save sinners, of whom I am chief" (1 Tim 1:15).

The words *for this reason I obtained mercy* in v 16 do not look back to the previous verses. Instead, they look to the words that follow. While God poured out mercy upon Paul for Paul's own sake, He had a bigger picture in mind as well. Paul goes on to speak of that bigger purpose.

Jesus Christ First Showed All Longsuffering toward Paul

The longsuffering and mercy that God showed to Paul was not the end of the story. It was the beginning of Paul's ministry as the Apostle to the Gentiles. The word *first* shows that God knew that Paul would become a champion for the saving message, especially to Gentiles.

The mercy and patience that God demonstrated toward Paul became a paradigm for all who would follow in his footsteps.

Paul Was a Pattern, an Example for Us

The word *pattern* (*hupotupōsis*) refers to an example for others. The leading dictionary of NT Greek says, "as a model prototype 1 Tim 1:16 (as prime recipient of extraordinary mercy in view of his infamous past, Paul serves as a model for the certainty of availability of mercy to others)."[1]

If God would save a person who hated Jesus Christ and who persecuted and even participated in the killing of Christians, then God is willing and able to save anyone.

Believing on Him for Everlasting Life

Paul speaks of himself as an example of those *who are going to believe on Him (Christ) for everlasting life*. Paul came in on the ground floor of the Church. He was one of the first to come to faith. Those who have been born again in the past two thousand years all did so in the same way, by believing in Jesus Christ for everlasting life.

The expression *for everlasting life* expresses the content of saving faith. Guthrie comments, "Christ is the firm basis of faith. Such unshakeable assurance serves not only in this life but in eternity."[2] Hiebert adds, "The expression 'on him'…pictures the faith as resting on Christ as the sure and abiding foundation. The goal of that faith is 'unto eternal life.' It is imparted to us now but finds its consummation in eternity."[3]

People today believe in Jesus for a variety of reasons: for a good marriage, for health, for wealth, for an abundant life, and

---

[1] Bauer, Danker, Arndt, and Gingrich, *A Greek-English Lexicon of the New Testament and Other Early Christian Literature*, 3rd ed. (Chicago, IL: University of Chicago Press, 2000), 1042.
[2] Donald Guthrie, *The Pastoral Epistles*, rev. ed. (Grand Rapids, MI: Eerdmans, 1957, 1990), 76.
[3] D. Edmond Hiebert, *First Timothy* (Chicago, IL: Moody Press, 1957), 44.

so forth. But the Lord does not promise those things to the one who believes in Him.[4] What He promises to the one who believes in Him is everlasting life.

If a person believes in Jesus *for everlasting life*, then he has it. But until and unless a person believes in Jesus for that life, he remains unregenerate no matter how religious, no matter how committed, no matter how prayerful, no matter how loving and kind. There is only one way to be eternally saved and that is to believe in Jesus for everlasting life.

---

[4] In order to have a good marriage, both spouses must not only believe in the Lord Jesus for everlasting life, but they must also follow Him day by day. Good health is not guaranteed to anyone. Nor is financial prosperity. An abundant life is indeed promised to the believer *who follows Christ* (John 10:10; Rom 8:6). That which is guaranteed the person who believes in Christ is regeneration and the associated blessings of justification, the indwelling ministry of the Holy Spirit, and being baptized by the Spirit into the Body of Christ.

SIXTY-SIX

I Know Whom I Have Believed (2 Timothy 1:12)

For this reason I also suffer these things; nevertheless I am not ashamed, for I know whom I have believed and am persuaded that He is able to keep what I have committed to Him until that Day.

Suffering, But Not Ashamed

Two verses earlier, in v 10, Paul referred to "our Savior Jesus Christ, who has abolished death and brought life and immortality to light through the gospel." The life to which Paul refers is the everlasting life which Jesus gives to all who believe in Him.

In v 8, Paul urged Timothy: "do not be ashamed of the testimony of our Lord, nor of me His prisoner, but share with me in the sufferings for the gospel according to the power of God." He then added, [he] who has saved us and called us with a holy calling, not according to our works, but according to His own purpose and grace…" Here in v 12, Paul again mentions suffering for Christ and His gospel (*these things*), yet not being ashamed. Paul was again in prison in Rome as he wrote this letter. He knew he was about to be killed for his faith (2 Tim 4:6, "the time of my departure is at hand"). Yet he was not ashamed. Indeed, that is an understatement. Paul was overjoyed and proud to suffer for His Savior. He knew that such suffering would result in eternal rewards, as he is about to indicate.

I Know Whom I Have Believed

The words *I know whom I have believed* refer to Paul's belief in Christ to save him (v 9), that is, to give him everlasting life (v 10). Some Calvinists have suggested, especially considering Paul's remarks in 1 Cor 9:27, that Paul was not sure that he believed in Christ and hence was not sure of his eternal destiny. But here Paul indicates he knows that he believes in Christ. The issue in 1 Cor 9:27 is ruling with Christ in the life to come (compare 1 Cor 9:24-26 and 2 Tim 4:6-8).

This verse, understood in the context (esp. vv 8-9), is another faith-alone verse. Paul was sure of his eternal destiny because of the promise of Him in whom he believed.

Hiebert writes, "God is pictured as the Trustee with whom he has deposited for safekeeping his temporal and eternal welfare… His labors in the proclamation and defense of that message [the gospel] lead him to think of the day of future reward."[1] That statement about future reward is found in the words which follow, in the second half of v 12.

I'm Persuaded He Will Reward Me on That Day

The end of v 12 is about eternal rewards, not eternal destiny: "[I] am persuaded that He is able to keep what I have committed to Him until that Day." The words *that Day* refer to the Judgment Seat of Christ, the Bema (cf. 2 Cor 5:9-10). Hiebert writes, "'Against that day' looks forward to that future day when Paul will stand before the judgment seat of Christ to receive his reward for his Gospel labors."[2]

Rather than repeating *belief* (e.g., *I know whom I have believed, and I believe that He is able…*), Paul uses a synonym for belief. To be persuaded is to be convinced or to believe. Paul is persuaded that Christ can and will keep the works which he committed to Him until the Bema. At the Bema, Christ will reward

---

[1] D. Edmond Hiebert, *Second Timothy* (Chicago, IL: Moody Press, 1958), 43.
[2] Ibid., 44.

Paul for the suffering he endured for His name. Guthrie says, "Paul sees it as of paramount importance to be able to give a good account of his stewardship."[3]

Of course, there could be no certainty of eternal rewards unless Paul knew that the Person in whom He believed guaranteed his eternal destiny. If Paul's salvation was in doubt, then so would be any eternal rewards.

Everlasting life is by faith alone, apart from works. In addition, God guarantees that any suffering believers experience for Christ (along with any other good works we do) will be rewarded at the Bema.

---

[3] Donald Guthrie, *The Pastoral Epistles*, rev. ed. (Grand Rapids, MI: Eerdmans, 1957, 1990), 145.

SIXTY-SEVEN

Salvation Through Faith in Christ Jesus (2 Timothy 3:15)

...from childhood you have known the Holy Scriptures, which are able to make you wise for salvation through faith which is in Christ Jesus.

The Scriptures Can Make You Wise for Salvation

Paul is here reminding Timothy of his spiritual heritage. From his childhood he was taught "the Holy Scriptures," a reference to the OT since when Timothy was a child the NT Scriptures did not yet exist.

Many people think that the OT does not tell people in this age what they must do to be saved. But Paul says that the OT indeed can make one "wise for salvation."[1] Hiebert favorably quotes Bernard as saying, "'Salvation, the salvation of man, is the final purpose of the whole Bible.'"[2] MacDonald writes, "This means,

---

[1] However, *The NIV Bible Commentary*, vol. 2: New Testament, ed. by Kenneth L. Barker and John Kohlenberger III (Grand Rapids, MI: Zondervan, 1994) takes a different view. It suggests that "the OT Scriptures, which were able to make him 'wise' *in preparation* 'for salvation through faith in Christ Jesus'...disciplined him in obedience to God and also pointed forward to the coming Messiah, through whom salvation by faith would become available" (p. 915, emphasis added). It seems to be saying that obedience and reading the OT were a way in which one could prepare himself to be ready for salvation, which was not available before, but which became available after Jesus' death, burial, resurrection, and ascension.

[2] D. Edmond Hiebert, *Second Timothy* (Chicago, IL: Moody Press, 1958), 98.

first of all, that men learn the way of **salvation** through the Bible. It might also carry the thought that assurance of salvation comes through the word of God."³

That Paul is speaking of regeneration is evident in what he goes on to say.

Through Faith in Christ Jesus

Salvation is "through faith in Christ Jesus." Here is another faith-alone text. Hiebert says,

> Saving faith centers in and rests upon Christ as revealed in the Scriptures. Faith is the means through which the salvation in the Word is grasped. Faith in Christ is the link which unites the Old and New Testaments.⁴

Guthrie comments,

> That salvation [which] is appropriated only *through faith in Christ Jesus* is also thoroughly Pauline. The mere reading of Scripture is ineffective in securing salvation unless faith is in operation, centred entirely in Christ. This was evident in the case of the unbelieving Jews.⁵

And MacDonald writes,

> **Salvation is through faith which is in Christ Jesus.** We should mark this well. It is not through good works, baptism, church membership…or any other way that involves human effort or merit. **Salvation is through faith in the Son of God.**⁶

---

³ William MacDonald, *Believer's Bible Commentary*, New Testament (Nashville, TN: Thomas Nelson, 1990), 939.
⁴ Hiebert, *Second Timothy*, 99.
⁵ Donald Guthrie, *The Pastoral Epistles,* rev. ed. (Grand Rapids, MI: Eerdmans, 1957, 1990), 175.
⁶ MacDonald, *Believer's Bible Commentary*, 939.

SIXTY-EIGHT

Salvation by Grace Through Faith in Christ (Titus 3:5-8)

...not by works of righteousness which we have done, but according to His mercy He saved us, through the washing of regeneration and renewing of the Holy Spirit, whom He poured out on us abundantly through Jesus Christ our Savior, that having been justified by His grace we should become heirs according to the hope of eternal life. This is a faithful saying, and these things I want you to affirm constantly, that those who have believed in God should be careful to maintain good works. These things are good and profitable to men.

Not by Works of Righteousness Which We Have Done

Paul does not state his point succinctly in one verse. It takes him four verses to tie together the divine and human side of salvation.

Paul starts in v 4 with a statement that this salvation/justification is not by works of righteousness which we have done. In many other places in his letters (e.g., Gal 2:16; Eph 2:8-9), Paul follows up a statement like this with a direct statement that our salvation is by or through faith in Christ. Here it is implicit, until Paul refers to belief in v 8. Litfin writes, "God in His grace saves those who believe, not because of any righteousness in them…but because of His mercy."[1]

---

[1] A. Duane Litfin, "Titus," in *The Bible Knowledge Commentary*, New Testament Edition, ed. by John F. Walvoord and Roy B. Zuck (Wheaton, IL: Victor Books, 1983), 766.

Why doesn't Paul explicitly mention faith in Christ in v 5? Litfin says, "No mention is made here of the role of faith in the process because Paul's entire focus was on what God has done, not on human response."[2]

He Saved (Regenerated) Us by His Grace

Paul speaks of salvation (= washing of regeneration[3]) and justification in vv 5 and 7. In v 7 Paul indicates that this salvation/justification is by God's grace.

The *hope of eternal life* in v 7 refers to the certain yet future time when we will experience the fullness of eternal life. We are eagerly awaiting our glorified bodies and the coming of the kingdom. Hiebert writes, "The experiential realization of the inheritance awaits the day of our Lord's return. Our being heirs is in full accord with our 'hope of eternal life.' Eternal life is ours now, but its consummation likewise awaits the time when Christ shall come for His church."[4]

Likewise, Guthrie comments,

> The heirs are not yet possessors in the fullest sense, as the words *having the hope of eternal life* show…the justified believer may look forward towards the full appropriation of his inheritance. The words do not exclude any present possession of *life*, but rather anticipate its complete realization…[5]

---

[2] Ibid.
[3] When a person is regenerated, he is cleansed (cf. John 13:10; 15:3). The expression, *the washing of regeneration,* refers to the positional cleansing which occurs when one is born again.
[4] D. Edmond Hiebert, *Titus and Philemon* (Chicago, IL: Moody Press, 1957), 73.
[5] Donald Guthrie, *The Pastoral Epistles*, rev. ed. (Grand Rapids, MI: Eerdmans, 1957, 1990), 219.

Those Who Have Believed in God

Typically, Paul speaks of those who have believed *in Christ*. The reference here to believing "in God" either is a reference to the deity of Christ, or it is a reference to the fact that when we believe in Christ, we are also believing in God the Father who sent Him (e.g., John 5:24). I think the former is more likely here.

Tying v 8 together with vv 4-7, Paul is explicitly saying that we are not saved by works of righteousness which we have done, but we are saved by believing in the Lord Jesus Christ for everlasting life. In v 8, Paul brings forth the moral imperative that "those who have believed in God should be careful to maintain good works." While good works are not the basis of our salvation, nor are they guaranteed, they are the reasonable and expected result of one who has been given everlasting life as a gift. The faith-alone salvation which we have should produce an ongoing and powerful sense of gratitude and love for Christ in us.

SIXTY-NINE

Whoever Believes That Jesus Is the Christ Is Born of God (1 John 5:1)

Whoever believes that Jesus is the Christ is born of God, and everyone who loves Him who begot also loves him who is begotten of Him.

Whoever Believes That Jesus Is the Christ

Do you recall ever seeing 1 John 5:1 in a tract? Probably not. Most tracts think that the condition of everlasting life is a special type of faith that includes turning from sins, surrender, and commitment, and which necessarily results in lifelong obedience. The idea that a person is born again if he simply believes some fact like "Jesus is the Christ" is either not considered at all, or is rejected as being *easy believism, cheap grace, historical faith*, or *simply believing some historical facts about Jesus.*

In John's writings, to believe "that Jesus is the Christ [Messiah]" has specific content. It is always to believe that Jesus, as the promised Messiah, guarantees everlasting life that cannot be lost to all who believe in Him. See John 4:1-42 (chap. 8–10), John 11:25-27 (chaps. 17–19), and John 20:30-31 (chap. 22). That is precisely what John is saying again in this verse,[1] as the following words make clear.

---

[1] Derickson, however, suggests that "It is a correct recognition of the deity of Jesus." See Gary W. Derickson, *1,2,&3 John* (Bellingham, WA: Lexham Press, 2014), 489. See also p. 490.

Is Born of God

The verb and its modifier tell us the identity of the person who believes "that Jesus is the Christ." Such a person "is born of God." That is who he is.[2]

Though the NKJV and some other translations (e.g., NIV, KJV, NASB, MEV, RSV) use a present tense here (*is born*), the Greek and some other translations (HCSB, NET, LEB, CEB) have a perfect tense (*has been born*). Smalley comments, "The perfect tense of *gegennētai*...indicates, as often in 1 John, a past act with continuing effects in the present."[3] A present tense translation is acceptable if the translator believes that the emphasis is on the current state. In any case, John is saying that such a person has been, is, and always will be born of God. Being a child of God is his permanent status.[4]

Everyone who believes that Jesus is the Christ is born of God. It is that simple. Of course, the expression "born of God" hearkens back to Jesus' words to Nicodemus in John 3 (esp. John 3:3, 5). See also John 1:13. Anyone who is born of God has everlasting life, for the new birth occurs when a person is given everlasting life.

But why is John telling us this in the middle of a section dealing with our call to love our Christian brothers and sisters (1 John 4:20–5:3a)? The answer is found in the closing words of this verse.

---

[2] Derickson sees this as *part* of what defines a Christian. However, he sees behavior as even more significant, indicating that "conduct does indeed define a Christian" (*1, 2, & 3 John*, 494). By contrast, see the comments by Hodges in note 5 below, and see David R. Anderson, *Maximum Joy: First John—Relationship or Fellowship* (Irving, TX: Grace Evangelical Society, 2005), 225.

[3] Stephen S. Smalley, *1, 2, 3 John* (Waco, TX: Word Books, 1984), 266.

[4] Though Smalley presumably agrees, he makes this statement, "The regenerate Christian (past) must constantly live out (present) his faith in Jesus as Messiah, and also give his sustained allegiance to the love command" (*1, 2, 3 John*, 266-67). He may be suggesting that God guarantees that the born-again person will persevere in faith and good works. Or he may simply be saying that in order to be a faithful disciple, a Christian must do that.

We Love God by Loving His Children

Do you remember the account of a Jewish lawyer, an expert in the Law of Moses, who asked Jesus, "And who is my neighbor?" (Luke 10:29)? Jesus had just said that a summation of the Law was that you shall love the Lord with all your heart, soul, strength, and mind, and "your neighbor as yourself" (Luke 10:27). The lawyer was looking for a way to limit those whom he needed to love. Christians are capable of the same sort of thinking. We might wonder, "And who is my brother?"

Hodges writes,

> This strips a well-known excuse from the hands of those who might wish to use it: "I don't need to love *him*. The way *he* lives he could not possibly be a Christian!" The church has more than a few "fruit inspectors" like this, who are more than ready to tell us who is saved and who is not. But many such "inspectors" have never been born again *themselves,* because they have never understood the grace of God who "imputes righteousness apart from works" (Romans 4:6).
>
> When it comes to loving a Christian brother, whether or not he is living worthily of his Christian faith is totally irrelevant…I love the child of God…because I love the Father of that child![5]

---

[5] Zane C. Hodges, *The Epistles of John* (Denton, TX: Grace Evangelical Society, 1999), 212-13.

SEVENTY

He Who Has the Son Has Life (1 John 5:9-12)

If we receive the witness of men, the witness of God is greater; for this is the witness of God which He has testified of His Son. He who believes in the Son of God has the witness in himself; he who does not believe God has made Him a liar, because he has not believed the testimony that God has given of His Son. And this is the testimony: that God has given us eternal life, and this life is in His Son. He who has the Son has life; he who does not have the Son of God does not have life.

God Testified That He Gives Eternal Life

Have you ever testified in a court of law? If so, you know it is a solemn responsibility.

We often use the language of testifying when we talk about telling others how we came to faith in Christ. We call that *giving your testimony*.

Unfortunately, not all Christian testimonies accurately present the faith-alone message. Often the idea is given that the person was saved (frequently left unclear as to whether this is permanent) because he turned from his sins and committed his life to Christ. Belief in the testimony of God is typically not mentioned.

"And this is the testimony: that God has given us eternal life, and this life is in His Son" (v 11). Of course, Jesus *is* "the life" (John 11:25; 14:6; 1 John 1:2; 5:21). To have everlasting life is to have Jesus Christ. He is the life. Believers have the life.

John makes it clear that the people who have the life and the Son are those who believe in Him.

To the One Who Believes in His Son

Verses 9-10 are all about faith in Christ. John begins by using a figure of speech: "If we receive the witness of men, the witness of God is greater..." He then speaks plainly: "He who believes in the Son of God has the witness in himself..."

God the Father rarely is quoted in the NT. At Jesus' baptism and transfiguration, the Father indicates that Jesus is His beloved Son and calls upon all to hear Him. When John speaks of the testimony of God, he is referring to the words of Jesus. Jesus said what the Father sent Him to say (cf. John 5:24). Hodges comments, "But John claims that **God has testified of His Son** and the words that follow in verses 11-12 show that this testimony is derived directly from words spoken by Jesus Himself in the hearing of the apostles...His own words are equivalent to the very words of **God**."[1]

What does it mean to *have the witness in you*? It means that you are a carrier of the testimony. It resides in you. You can infect others with the witness if you share the witness that is within you. That witness is the fact that all who believe in the Son have everlasting life. John goes on to stress that point in v 12.

He Who Has the Son Has Life

Since Jesus is the life, to have Him is to have life. It is impossible to have Jesus, who is everlasting life (1 John 5:20), and yet not have everlasting life. Wiersbe is certainly correct when he says, "Eternal life is a gift; it is not something that we earn (John 10:27-29; Eph. 2:8-9). But this gift is a Person—Jesus Christ."[2]

---

[1] Zane C. Hodges, *The Epistles of John* (Denton, TX: Grace Evangelical Society, 1999), 222-23.
[2] Warren W. Wiersbe, *The Bible Exposition Commentary*, vol. 2 (Wheaton, IL: Victor Books, 1996), 528.

Conversely, the one who does not have the Son does not have life. Unbelievers, no matter how nice they may be, need everlasting life. We who have the witness in us should be available. If the opportunity arises, we should share the testimony with them, that God gives everlasting life to all who believe in the Lord Jesus Christ. Of course, moral unbelievers will object. They may say, as I've often heard, that bad people can't go to heaven. When we point out that we are all sinners (Rom 3:23), they counter with, "Yes, but you can't be *too sinful*." By unleashing the witness, we plant a seed, which then has a chance to germinate. As the person thinks about what you said, he might begin to pray, read the Gospel of John, and ask you or others questions.

Anderson writes,

> What must I do to have the Son? The only requirement mentioned in 1 John (or anywhere in the Bible, for that matter) is to believe. There is absolutely no mention of one's performance, one's fruit, or one's obedience as a requirement for having the Son or for having assurance.[3]

---

[3] David R. Anderson, *Maximum Joy: First John—Relationship or Fellowship?* (Irving, TX: Grace Evangelical Society, 2005), 238-39.

SEVENTY-ONE

That You May Know That You Have Eternal Life (1 John 5:13)

These things I have written to you who believe in the name of the Son of God, that you may know that you have eternal life, and that you may continue to believe in the name of the Son of God.

To You Who Believe in the Name of the Son of God

John is writing to mature believers (1 John 2:12-14) who are under attack by false teachers (1 John 2:18, 22; 4:3). John had said that the antichrists were trying to deceive the readers concerning the Lord's promise of eternal life (1 John 2:24-26).

Assurance of everlasting life is vital to fellowship with God. That is why in a book about fellowship (1 John 1:3-4), John has a section on assurance (1 John 5:6-13). Verse 13 is the culmination of John's discussion on assurance.

The readers had not been deceived by the false teachers—yet. But they might become deceived. That is what John goes on to say in the rest of v 13.

That You May Know That You Have Eternal Life

Since the readers currently believe in the name of the Son of God (1 John 5:13a), they know that they have everlasting life. That is, they believe the promise of life (1 John 2:24-26) and currently have the witness in themselves (1 John 5:10).

The NKJV, MEV, and WEB translations supply the words *continue to* before the word *believe* in the third part of v 13, discussed below. But to be consistent, they should have supplied those words in the second part of v 13 as well: "that you may *continue to* know that you have eternal life." The readers knew that currently. But the danger is they would be deceived by the false teachers (1 John 2:24-26).

The reason for supplying these words is the context, not the verb tense. The verb (*eidēte*) is a perfect active subjunctive.[1] A perfect tense refers to a past event that has an abiding result. But the subjunctive mood introduces conditionality. John is giving this information on assurance so that (*hina*) they might continue to know that they have everlasting life.[2]

That You May *Continue to* Believe in the Name of the Son of God

Most Greek manuscripts of 1 John 5:13 contain the words "that you may *continue to* believe in the name of the Son of God." Translations which rely on the so-called Critical Text do not print these words (e.g., NIV, NASB, NET, HCSB). But they are found in most manuscripts, and it is not likely that any copyist would ever have added these words.

Note the symmetry with the first part of v 13. The readers currently *believe in the name of the Son of God* (1 John 5:13a).

---

[1] There are five other uses of *eidēte* in the NT: Matt 9:6; Mark 2:10; Luke 5:24; Eph 6:21; and 1 John 2:29. All but the last of those occur in purpose (*hina*) clauses. Ephesians 6:21 probably means, *that you may continue to know my affairs and how I am doing*. The three references in the Synoptics are flexible enough to cover those who did not already know that Jesus had the power to forgive sins as well as those who need to continue to believe that (e.g., His disciples).

[2] Hodges understands 1 John 5:13 differently. He understands "to you who believe in the name of the Son of God" to refer to people who have believed in the past, but who may be experiencing doubt at the time of the letter. He understands "that you may know that you have eternal life" to refer to regaining lost assurance. See Zane C. Hodges, *The Epistles of John* (Denton, TX: Grace Evangelical Society, 1999), 228-29. While the present active participle *tois pisteuousin* does not by itself indicate that the readers were currently believing, the context of 1 John 5:9-12 shows that they were (see also 1 John 2:12-14, 24-26).

John wishes that they will continue to do so (1 John 5:13c). The words *continue to* have been supplied by the translators. Otherwise, the verse would not make sense.[3] The antichrists were trying to strip the readers of assurance of everlasting life (cf. 1 John 2:24-26). John had urged them earlier in the letter to "let that abide [remain, continue] in you which you heard from the beginning…the promise that He has promised us—eternal life" (1 John 2:24-25). Now he repeats that idea here.

Derickson accepts the third part of v 13 as original, and he holds that John is urging the readers *to continue to believe* in the name of the Son of God. He writes:

> Believers must keep believing if they are to keep enjoying eternal life—a quality of life—that Jesus came to give…John is assuring his readers that he knows they do believe in Jesus. His desire is that they continue to do so, not in order to gain or maintain their salvation but to continue enjoying the eternal life that comes from a healthy relationship with Jesus, who is that life.[4]

Faith alone is the sole means of regeneration and of assurance of regeneration.

---

[3] Hodges, however, suggests that, "This continuing faith was to have a different object than the 'testimony of God' about His gift of life. And that object [the promise of answered prayer] is now stated [in 5:14]," *The Epistles of John*, 229. While possible, the contextual tie *backwards* with the first part of v 13 suggests that the object of faith is the testimony of God.

[4] Gary W. Derickson, *1,2,&3 John* (Bellingham, WA: Lexham Press, 2014), 531.

SEVENTY-TWO

The Free Water of Life to Him Who Thirsts (Revelation 21:6)

And He said to me, "It is done! I am the Alpha and the Omega, the Beginning and the End. I will give of the fountain of the water of life freely to him who thirsts."

I Will Give

In the penultimate chapter in the NT, the Lord reiterates the promise of life He made to the woman at the well (John 4:10-14) and to the five thousand whom He had miraculously fed (John 6:35, "he who believes in Me will never thirst"). Just as He told the woman and the five thousand that He gives this living water, so He repeats that good news here.

The Fountain of the Water of Life

Why does the Lord speak of *the fountain of the water of life* and not simply *the water of life*? He did the same thing in John 4:14: "'Whoever drinks of the water that I shall give him will never thirst. But the water that I shall give him will become in him a fountain of water springing up into everlasting life.'"

The water of life is not everlasting life. Instead, it is the message that results in everlasting life when one believes, that is, drinks it. That is the message that Jesus is the Christ (1 John 5:1; see chap. 69), and He guarantees everlasting life that cannot be lost to all who believe in Him for it (John 11:26; 1 Tim 1:16; see chaps. 18 and 65).

Freely

The word translated *freely* (*dōrean*) is last in the Greek sentence for emphasis. It occurs nine times in the NT and is variously translated as "freely" (Matt 10:8, twice; Rom 3:24; Rev 21:6; 22:17), "without a cause" (John 15:25), "free of charge" (2 Cor 11:7; 2 Thess 3:8), and "in vain" (Gal 2:21). It is an adverb modifying the main verb, "I will give." It is possible to give something with some strings attached.[1] However, if something is given *freely*, then there are no strings attached.

To Him Who Thirsts

Thirsting for the water of life is a figure of speech that refers to longing for everlasting life. To drink living water is to believe in Jesus as He said in John 6:35b, "he who believes in Me shall never thirst."[2] While Rev 21:6 does not explicitly mention faith in Christ, it is included in Section One—Crystal Clear Faith-Alone Verses. That is because this figure of drinking living water is a well-established one for faith in Christ.

The two verses which follow Rev 21:6 speak of the other two types of people in eternity future. Verse 7 speaks of those who not only believe in Christ, but who overcome in this life. Those believers will have superlative experiences in the life to come. They will "inherit all things," and they will have a special relationship with God (the rights of the firstborn son).[3]

---

[1] For example, your employer might give you a car, but with the stipulation that he will take back the car if your sales drop below a certain level. In that case the "free car" is not free. Even if the requirement were small, it would not be free. If your parents gave you a $25,000 car, but you had to pay $2,000 for the tax, title, and license, it would not be free. It would be cheap. It would be a great deal. But you'd have to pay your share.

[2] Of course, it is possible to desire everlasting life and not obtain it if one is not open to what God says (see John 5:39-40). But in Rev 21:6, Jesus is speaking of a type of thirst, or desire, that is fully open to the truth. In Rev 21:6, thirsting results in the quenching of the thirst via hearing the promise of life (the living water) and believing. Both the water of life and the everlasting life to which it leads are free.

[3] The implication is that some believers will not overcome and will not

Verse 8 speaks of those excluded from the kingdom entirely, that is, those sent to the lake of fire (cf. Rev 20:15). They are unbelieving people and people who died in their sins (John 8:24), meaning that they eternally are "abominable, murderers, sexually immoral, sorcerers, idolaters, and liars" who "have their part in the lake which burns with fire and brimstone, which is the second death."[4]

Everlasting life is freely given to all who simply believe in the Lord Jesus Christ for it.

---

inherit all things, but they will nonetheless be in the kingdom. Compare Luke 19:20-26 and 1 Thess 5:9-10. Beckwith, however, sees v 7 as repeating the promise made in v 6 "in another form" (Isbon T. Beckwith, *The Apocalypse of John* [Grand Rapids, MI: Baker, 1919], 752). Ladd seems to see v 7 as an explanation of v 6 (George Eldon Ladd, *A Commentary on the Revelation of John* [Grand Rapids, MI: Eerdmans, 1972], 279). Both John Piper (desiringgod.org) and John MacArthur (gty.org) have articles showing they too believe that only those who both thirst and overcome will be in Christ's kingdom.

[4] They are not excluded from the kingdom because of their sins. Revelation 21:8 does not say or imply that. Compare Rev 20:11-15. They experience the second death because their names are not in the Book of Life. One gets into the Book of Life by believing in Christ for everlasting life during one's lifetime. The point of v 8 is that the kingdom will be a perfect place. There will be no sin in Christ's eternal kingdom on the new earth.

SEVENTY-THREE

Take the Water of Life Freely (Revelation 22:17)

And the Spirit and the bride say, "Come!" And let him who hears say, "Come!" And let him who thirsts come. Whoever desires, let him take the water of life freely.

Come!

Until the end of this age, God is calling upon people to come to Christ through the Spirit, the bride, and God's Word.[1] The Holy Spirit gives this invitation in Scripture (and gave it through His prophets). The bride, a reference to the Church, also extends this invitation as we share the promise of everlasting life with people.

The person who hears should say, "Come!" Hearing most likely refers to believing (cf. John 5:24). The one who comes to Christ by faith should share the call to come to Christ.

Let Him Who Thirsts Come

Thirsting is a figure of speech for longing for everlasting life. It is to be followed by coming: "Let him who thirsts come." Then the Lord adds, "whoever desires (i.e., thirsts), let him take the water of life freely."[2] The Lord is saying that the one who desires everlasting life should come to Christ in faith to receive that life.

---

[1] Some see the first two calls to "Come!" to be related to Christ's statement earlier that He is coming quickly (Rev 22:7, 12; see also Rev 22:20). They suggest that an abrupt shift then occurs when those who hear say, "Come!" However, Ladd shows why this is unlikely. See George Eldon Ladd, *A Commentary on the Revelation of John* (Grand Rapids, MI: Eerdmans, 1972), 295.

[2] Thirsting is equivalent to desiring. Coming to Christ is equivalent to

Let Him Take the Water of Life Freely

As in Rev 21:6, the last word in Rev 22:17 is the word *freely* (*dōrean*). The one who desires everlasting life is invited to take the water of life *freely*. The other uses of the expression *the water of life* (or *living water*) all refer to the message that Jesus is the Christ, the One who guarantees everlasting life to all who believe in Him for it (John 4:10-14; 6:36). That is most likely the sense here as well. The water of life is not everlasting life per se, but it is the message that results in everlasting life when one believes it.

Vacendak writes, "Eternal life is not given to people because they have earned it by doing good deeds. It is a gift, given to those who believe in Christ for it, that is, it is absolutely free (cf. John 4:10, 13-14; Rom 4:4-5; 6:23)."[3]

As in Rev 21:6-8, here too there are three types of people mentioned, except this time the order is different. In Revelation 21 the order was 1) those who receive the free gift, 2) those who overcome, and 3) those who experience the second death, that is, who are cast into the lake of fire. The order in Rev 22:12-17 is 1) those who overcome (vv 12-14), 2) those who are excluded from the kingdom (v 15), and 3) those who receive the free gift (v 17). The message is the same. Those who believe in Christ will be in the kingdom forever. Those believers who "do His commandments" (Rev 22:14) will rule with Christ and receive other rewards. Those who reject Christ will be excluded from Christ's kingdom.

Five verses from the end of the NT is a final faith-alone verse, and a powerful one at that.

---

taking the water of life freely (cf. John 6:35a, "he who comes to Me shall never hunger"). Here is the faith-alone message contained in a figure of speech.

[3] Robert Vacendak, "Revelation," in *The Grace New Testament Commentary*, rev. ed., ed. by Robert N. Wilkin (Denton, TX: Grace Evangelical Society, 2010, 2019), 655.

SECTION 2

Contexually Clear Verses

SEVENTY-FOUR

Rejoice Because Your Names Are Written in Heaven (Luke 10:20)

Nevertheless do not rejoice in this, that the spirits are subject to you, but rather rejoice because your names are written in heaven.

The last twenty-seven verses of our hundred are ones that are not quite as clear *in the actual verse* as the first seventy-three. While they do not *explicitly* state that salvation is by faith alone, that doctrine is *implied* by the context. Hence, I call these "contextually clear faith-alone texts." The first one is a terrific quotation of the Lord Jesus to His believing disciples.

Do Not Rejoice That the Spirits Are Subject to You

The Lord sent out seventy disciples, two by two. They were to go to the towns of Israel and heal the sick and say, "The kingdom of God has come near to you" (Luke 10:9).

Luke tells us, "Then the seventy returned with joy, saying, 'Lord, even the demons are subject to us in Your name'" (Luke 10:17). The Lord Jesus then told them that serpents and scorpions would not harm them, and He gave them authority "over all the power of the enemy" (Luke 10:19).

But He added: "Do not rejoice that the spirits are subject to you." He is not saying that it was wrong for His disciples to have joy in ministry. He wasn't even saying that they should not have joy in the delegated authority they were privileged to utilize in ministry. What He was saying is that there is something much more important, something which should cause much stronger and more lasting joy.[1]

Rejoice Because Your Names Are Written in Heaven

While we can have joy in ministry, a greater joy, the joy which must undergird all ministry if it is to be effective, is joy in our eternal security: "rejoice because your names are written in heaven." The Lord is speaking here of the Book of Life, which is the Book which lists the names of all who have everlasting life (cf. Phil 4:3; Rev 20:12, 15; 21:27).[2]

Bock comments:

> Yet Jesus keeps this work in balance when he tells the disciples not to be impressed with their power to cast out spirits, but that their names are written in heaven (10:18-20). That is, Jesus wants his disciples to focus on and to rejoice in their gracious *and secure standing before God*.[3]

Likewise, Morris says:

---

[1] This joy over the demons being subject to them only occurred when they cast out demons, which was rarely. In fact, it is likely that the Lord stopped allowing demon possession by AD 70 when the temple was destroyed. Demon possession is never reported in the OT. It first appears in the ministry of Jesus, and it continued for a time during the ministry of the apostles. It seems the Lord allowed demon possession for a short time to underscore the power and authority of Jesus and His apostles. There is no reference to demon possession, or to how to cast out demons, in the epistles, which there certainly would be if this were to be an ongoing ministry in the church age.

[2] This verse shows that during the ministry of Jesus, those who believed in Him were given everlasting life. Since Jesus' ministry was still under the OT dispensation, it shows that all OT believers had everlasting life. Regeneration did not wait until Pentecost to occur. All believers of all time have been regenerated, and all have their names permanently recorded in the Book of Life.

[3] Darrell L. Bock, *A Theology of Luke and Acts* (Grand Rapids, MI: Zondervan, 2012), 252, emphasis added. See also C. Marvin Pate, *Luke* (Chicago, IL: Moody Press, 1995), 232-33.

> Jesus goes on to teach that they must get their priorities right. Their real ground for rejoicing is not their victory over *the spirits*…Much more important is that their names *are written* (perfect tense pointing to what is permanent) *in heaven*…Jesus turns their attention to realities that will last.[4]

This is the only place in the Gospels where we learn of the seventy disciples[5] who were sent out. We do not know the identity of the seventy. While this group could include the twelve, it likely does not. Note the words "seventy *others* also" in v 1.

While the Lord does not mention in v 20 the reason why their names are written in heaven—because they are believers—He does allude to that fact in the verses that follow. He goes on to say that God "revealed" the truth about Him to them (v 21) and the Son "reveal(s)" the Father to them (v 22). The truth is revealed to someone when he believes it. It is "hidden…from the wise and prudent" and "revealed…to babes."

Another way in which we know the Lord is alluding to the faith-alone message is because the only way one can get into the Book of Life is by believing in the Lord Jesus Christ. Only those who believe in Christ have everlasting life (John 3:14-18; 11:25-26; 20:31; Acts 16:31; 1 John 5:9-13).

---

[4] Leon Morris, *Luke,* rev. ed. (Grand Rapids, MI: Eerdmans, 1974, 1988), 203.
[5] Some manuscripts read *seventy-two*.

SEVENTY-FIVE

Slay Those Enemies of Mine (Luke 19:24-27)

And he said to those who stood by, "Take the mina from him, and give it to him who has ten minas." (But they said to him, "Master, he has ten minas.") "For I say to you, that to everyone who has will be given; and from him who does not have, even what he has will be taken away from him. But bring here those enemies of mine, who did not want me to reign over them, and slay them before me."

The Servants and the Enemies in the Parable of the Minas

If space permitted, I would quote and discuss the entire parable, Luke 19:11-27. One obvious point is that the parable begins and ends with a discussion of both Christ's servants (Luke 19:13, 15-26) and His enemies (Luke 19:14, 27). The servants represent believers. The enemies represent unbelievers, those who do not want Jesus to reign over them (v 14), that is, who do not believe He is the Messiah/King of Israel but is instead an imposter.

The parable mentions ten servants, but only follows the judgment of three of them. Each of these servants is given the same amount of money, one mina, or about $10,000 today. They are each told, "Do business till I come" (v 13). Doing business refers to investing the money so that the Master would receive a return on His investment (cf. Luke 19:22-23). It does not refer to believing in Him. The fact that they are His servants shows that they believe in Him. The issue for the servants in this parable is their eternal reward. Will they rule with Christ in the life to come, and if so, over how many cities?

The first servant maximizes his potential and brings a return of ten minas. As a result, the Lord says to him after He returns (at the Judgment Seat of Christ), "Well done, good servant; because you were faithful in a very little, have authority over ten cities" (Luke 19:17).

The second servant is half-hearted in his service and only nets five minas. The Lord does not praise him. He did not say, "Well done, good servant," as He said to the first servant. Instead He simply says, "You also be over five cities" (Luke 19:19). The number of cities over which the servants will rule in the life to come is related to their faithfulness in their use of time, talent, and treasure.

But the third servant failed to meet even the minimum expectations of the Lord.

The Unfaithful Servant Loses His Opportunity to Reign with Christ

Verses 20-26 discuss the judgment of the third servant. He brings zero return on the Lord's investment. He was given one mina, and he returns one mina. He tries to justify himself by saying that he knew the Lord expected much of him, and he was afraid of doing something wrong. So, he did nothing with the mina. That is, he disobeyed the command, "Do business till I come."

Rather than disagreeing with His unfaithful servant ("you wicked servant," v 22), the Lord acknowledges that He indeed had high expectations for each of His servants. At the very least, the man could have put the mina in the bank[1] and earned some interest (v 23).

---

[1] The Greek word translated as *bank* (*trapeza*) means *table* and is always translated that way in its other NT uses. It probably refers to the tables of those who loaned money. After discussing the translation issue, Morris adds, "It would have been possible to put the money to use, but the frightened servant did nothing" (Leon Morris, *Luke*, rev. ed. [Grand Rapids, MI: Eerdmans, 1974, 1988], 301).

In the verses quoted above, the Lord makes it clear that this man's mina will be taken from him and given to the man who has ten. The minas correspond with cities to be ruled over. The faithful servant is now given a bonus city, an eleventh city to rule over. The unfaithful, wicked servant loses his opportunity to reign in Christ's kingdom. He won't even rule over one small city.

But will the unfaithful servant be in Christ's kingdom? The final verse (v 27) makes it clear that he will.

Christ's Enemies, by Contrast, Experience the Second Death

Verse 27 begins with a contrast word, *but* (*plēn*): "But bring here those enemies of mine, who did not want me to reign over them, and slay them before me." The third servant is not in that group. Indeed, the servants are all judged before and apart from the enemies. The enemies must be brought to the Lord to be slain.

The Great White Throne Judgment of Rev 20:11-15 is pictured in v 27. In both Luke 19:27 and Rev 20:15, those not in the Book of Life are slain (Luke 19:27), that is, experience the second death (Rev 20:14-15) of being cast into the lake of fire. While slaying and death are different words in Greek and English, they convey the same idea, separation from Jesus' life and kingdom forever.

While the enemies are not called *unbelievers*, that they do not believe that Jesus is the Messiah is evident since they "did not want [Him] to reign over them."

Pate comments on the last verse of the parable:

> Even though the action taken toward the disobedient servant was severe (even as it will be on Judgment Day for the unfaithful Christian), there is no hint in the text that the salvation of the faithless servant of the Lord was in jeopardy...The strong adversative (*plēn*) seems to contrast the punishment of the unprofitable servant with

that of the master's enemies (cf. v. 14) who did not want him to rule over them."[2]

Likewise, Morris also sees a distinction between the way in which Jesus deals with "his trading servants" and with "*these enemies of mine.*"[3]

While the servants are not called believers, they *did want Jesus to reign over them*,[4] and they did get into His kingdom, in contrast to the enemies who do not.[5] Therefore, while faith-alone is not directly mentioned in this parable, it is implicit.

---

[2] C. Marvin Pate, *Luke* (Chicago, IL: Moody, 1995), 358.
[3] Morris, *Luke*, 302.
[4] That is, they wanted Him *to reign over them forever in His kingdom*. The issue was not a desire for Him to reign over their lives *now*, although the first two sentences certainly illustrate such an attitude.
[5] So, Pate, *Luke,* 358; Morris, *Luke*, 302.

SEVENTY-SIX

John the Baptist Led People to Believe in Christ (John 1:7)

This man came for a witness, to bear witness of the Light, that all through him might believe.

John the Baptist Came to Bear Witness of the Light

This man refers to John the Baptist (cf. John 1:6, "whose name was John"). *The Light* refers to Jesus Christ (cf. John 1:1-5, 15-18). John, as the forerunner of Jesus, was to prepare people for His coming (Mal 3:1; Matt 11:10; Mark 1:2; Luke 7:27).

In John's Gospel, John the Baptist is the prime example of one who openly bears witness of Jesus (see John 3:22-36).

Brown comments, "Ordinarily light can be seen and there is no need for someone to testify to it; but in [John 1:] 19ff. it is a question of testifying before those who are hostile and who have not yet seen Jesus."[1] Of course, even after the Jewish people saw Jesus perform miracles and speak with an authority never seen among them, they, for the most part still did not believe (John 1:11). The OT indicated that a legal matter needed to be confirmed by two or three witnesses. After referring to John the Baptist's witness (John 5:33-35), Jesus then adds three other witnesses that He is the Messiah: "the very works that I do," "the Father Himself who sent me," and "the Scriptures" (John 5:36-40). While someone certainly should have come to faith in the Light simply by hearing Him and seeing the miracles He did, God gave an overabundance of proof that the Light is the Messiah.

---

[1] Raymond E. Brown, *The Gospel According to John I-XII* (New York, NY: Doubleday, 1966), 28.

The Aim of John's Witness Was That All
Through Him Might Believe in Christ

While John the Baptist performed a baptism of repentance (Mark 1:4; Luke 3:3; Acts 19:4), the Apostle John does not mention that in his Gospel. He does make a passing reference to John's baptism in John 4:1, where he mentions that John baptized people, but he says nothing about repentance. The reason for this is that the purpose of the Fourth Gospel is to lead people to believe in Jesus and thereby to have everlasting life (cf. John 20:30-31). Morris comments: "In the Synoptists [sic] John's preaching of repentance and his practice of baptism are noted. In this Gospel his one function is to bear witness to Jesus. We know him as 'John the Baptist' but in this Gospel the references to his baptism are incidental."[2]

John the Baptist's aim was that through him, that is, through his preaching, all might believe in the Light, Jesus Christ. Michaels is being overly cautious when he writes, "We are not yet told what, or in whom, people were to believe. A reasonable guess is that they were to believe in 'the light.'"[3] It is no guess. The Apostle said that John the Baptist came *to bear witness of the Light, that all through him might believe.* The intended object of faith is the Light to whom he bore witness.[4]

The aim of John's witness coincides with the purpose of the Gospel of John, which is why, of course, in his prologue the Apostle John brings up John the Baptist.

---

[2] Leon Morris, *The Gospel According to John* (Grand Rapids, MI: Eerdmans, 1971), 89-90.

[3] J. Ramsey Michaels, *The Gospel of John* (Grand Rapids, MI: Eerdmans, 2010), 60.

[4] Michaels does go on to say that "The statement that John 'came for a testimony, to testify about the light' (v. 7a) anticipates John's recorded testimonies in 1:19-34, while the intent 'that they all might believe through him' (v. 7b) comes to realization in 1:35-37" (*John,* 60).

Everlasting Life Is Present in the Context

The faith-alone message has three elements: 1) believing, 2) in Jesus Christ, 3) for everlasting life (or justification). John 1:7 has the first two of those elements, but not the third.

However, everlasting life is implied since it is present a few verses later in John 1:12-13, as well as throughout the Gospel of John (e.g., John 3:14-18, 36; 5:24; 6:35, 47; 11:25-27; 20:30-31). John the Baptist sought to lead people to faith in Jesus Christ for everlasting life (cf. John 3:36; Acts 19:4).

SEVENTY-SEVEN

Many Believed in His Name (John 2:23)

Now when He was in Jerusalem at the Passover, during the feast, many believed in His name when they saw the signs which He did.

Jesus Performed Miracles in Jerusalem during the Passover Feast

This was the first Passover of Jesus' ministry. He was there with His disciples. During that time, "they saw the signs which He did." John does not say what these miracles were.

According to John 20:30-31, the purpose of the signs was to lead people to believe that Jesus is the Christ, the Son of God, and that by believing, they would have everlasting life in His name. In the second half of John 2:23, John indicates the response that many had to the signs that first Passover.

Many Believed in His Name

The Apostle John tells us that "many believed in His name when they saw the signs which He did." The word *many* does not indicate a percentage of those present. By the end of three years of ministry, there were only about five hundred who believed in Jesus (1 Cor 15:6). Perhaps a dozen or more came to faith in Christ on this occasion.

Or did they?

There is only one other use of the expression *believing in His name* in John's Gospel. It is in John 1:12-13, which reads, "But as many as received Him, to them He gave the right to become children of God, to those who believe in His name: who were born, not of blood, nor of the will of the flesh, nor of the will of man, but of God." According to John, anyone who believes in His name has been born of God.

However, many commentators understand John 2:23 to refer to faith in Christ which is something less than saving faith. Under the heading "Inadequate faith," Carson explains, "To exercise faith on the grounds of having witnessed *miraculous signs* is precarious...Sadly, their faith was spurious, and Jesus knew it."[1] Tasker identifies their faith "as superficial."[2] Morris says, "It is not the deepest faith...It is no more than a beginning."[3]

However, Michaels seems to disagree, saying:

> Nothing in the text suggests that the faith of these Passover "believers" was anything but genuine...But are "those who believe in his name" *necessarily* given "authority to become children of God" simply because of their belief? It would be natural to assume so (on the basis of 1:12)...[4]

But then his very next words are: "but what immediately follows suggests that their faith, genuine though it may be, is not sufficient to identify them as those 'born of God' (see 1:13)."[5]

Michaels recognizes that John 1:12-13 naturally means that the people in John 2:23 who believed in His name were born of God. But he draws back from the obvious conclusion because the next verses say that Jesus did not commit or entrust Himself to them. A simple solution is that these new believers were like

---

[1] D. A. Carson, *The Gospel According to John* (Grand Rapids, MI: Eerdmans, 1991), 184.
[2] R. V. G. Tasker, *John* (Grand Rapids, MI: Eerdmans, 1960), 65.
[3] Leon Morris, *The Gospel According to John* (Grand Rapids, MI: Eerdmans, 1971), 206.
[4] J. Ramsey Michaels, *The Gospel of John* (Grand Rapids, MI: Eerdmans, 2010), 173.
[5] Ibid.

Nicodemus, unwilling to confess their faith in Christ.[6] As a result, Jesus was not ready to entrust more truth to them until they were ready to confess Him. The issue is not eternal destiny, but current ministry and privilege. After indicating that "these people obtained eternal life," Hodges comments concerning the fact that "Jesus did not commit Himself to them," saying, "This does not mean they were not really saved…But John's words do indicate that the level of their knowledge of Jesus remained rudimentary. He did not 'disclose' Himself to them more fully."[7]

It should be noted that it is the Apostle John who says in inspired Scripture that many believed in His name when they saw the miracles that He did. If Scripture tells us that someone believed in Jesus, then we know that person believed in Him.

While John 2:23 does not specifically mention everlasting life, it is included in our hundred faith-alone verses because the parallel text in John 1:12-13 shows that whoever believes in His name has been born of God.

---

[6] Most likely Nicodemus came to faith when he came to Jesus by night (John 3:1-18). However, Nicodemus is mentioned on two other occasions in John, and each time the reader is reminded that he is the one who "came to Jesus by night" (John 3:2; 7:50; 19:39). Nicodemus is an example of a secret believer, and so are the new believers of John 2:23 (compare the word *man,* which ends John 2:25 and which begins John 3:1).
[7] Zane C. Hodges, *Faith in His Name: Listening to the Gospel of John* (Corinth, TX: Grace Evangelical Society, 2015), 46-47.

SEVENTY-EIGHT

Believe in Him Whom He Sent (John 6:27-29)

"Do not labor for the food which perishes, but for the food which endures to everlasting life, which the Son of Man will give you, because God the Father has set His seal on Him." Then they said to Him, "What shall we do, that we may work the works of God?" Jesus answered and said to them, "This is the work of God, that you believe in Him whom He sent."

Jesus Gives Everlasting Life

What did Jesus mean when He said, "Do not labor for the food which perishes, but for the food which endures to everlasting life"? He might mean that we should labor, that is, strive, to find the bread of life, which is the food that, once received, results in everlasting life. But the phrase *which endures to everlasting life* sounds like it could refer to eternal rewards, fullness of life in the life to come.

When we consider what follows in the verse, the first understanding is suggested. Once one receives the bread of life, which Jesus identifies with Himself in John 6:36 ("I am the bread of life"), then that endures in him to everlasting life. That is the same as saying that when one drinks the water of life, it *springs up in him* to everlasting life.[1] Plummer says, "The discourse with the woman [at the well] should be compared throughout."[2] Michaels

---

[1] D. A. Carson, *The Gospel According to John* (Grand Rapids, MI: Eerdmans, 1991), 284.
[2] Alfred Plummer, *The Gospel According to St. John* (Grand Rapids, MI: Baker, 1882), 154.

writes, "The metaphor of food 'that remains to eternal life' recalls the spring rushing 'to eternal life' that Jesus promised the Samaritan woman (4:14)."[3]

Carson comments, "The continuing discourse shows that the 'food' is Jesus himself, but the idea is not so much that Jesus endures forever as that, because this food endures, the life it sustains goes on into eternity."[4]

Not by Works

Jesus' Jewish listeners are thinking in terms of acts of obedience that they must do to gain everlasting life: "What shall we do, that we may work the works of God?" They are thinking in terms of works, plural. Remember that Jesus was asked repeatedly about the two greatest commandments. The reason is that people wanted to know what they needed to do to gain everlasting life. Plummer writes, "They probably thought of works of the law, tithes, sacrifices, etc."[5]

But Jesus showed that the new birth is not by works when He said, "This is the work of God, that you believe in Him whom He sent." He spoke of "the work," singular. He is using the word *work* ironically here. The only *work*, or action, that one can take to gain everlasting life is to believe in Jesus, that is, "in Him whom He [God the Father] sent." This statement is similar to John 5:24 ("He who hears My words *and believes in Him who sent Me* has everlasting life…").

Morris comments, "Jesus replaces their 'works of God' with the singular, 'work of God.' But one thing is needful. And this one thing, He makes plain, is faith."[6]

---

[3] J. Ramsey Michaels, *The Gospel of John* (Grand Rapids, MI: Eerdmans, 2010), 365.
[4] Carson, *John*, 284.
[5] Plummer, *John*, 155.
[6] Leon Morris, *The Gospel According to John* (Grand Rapids, MI: Eerdmans, 1971), 360. Morris does, however, go on to say that "the present tense here denotes the continuing attitude, not the once-for-all decision" (p. 360). But one gains everlasting life the moment he partakes of the bread of life (or drinks the living water).

Calvin wrote, "[faith is] a passive work, for which no reward is given, and it gives people no other righteousness than what they receive from Christ."[7]

By Believing in Him Whom He Sent

The reception of everlasting life only comes to those who believe in Jesus for that life. Michaels comments, "A person does the 'work of God' by 'coming' to Jesus (see vv. 35, 37) in the sense of believing in him."[8] Ashton adds, "Jesus has already affirmed: 'This is the work of God, that you believe in him whom he has sent' (6:29)—and the reader already knows that belief in Jesus is what ensures life (cf. 3:16, 36, etc.)."[9]

This is another faith-alone verse.

---

[7] John Calvin, *John* (Wheaton, IL: Crossway Books, 1994), 156.
[8] Michaels, *John*, 67.
[9] John Ashton, *Understanding the Fourth Gospel* (Oxford: Clarendon Press, 1991), 186.

SEVENTY-NINE

If You Do Not Believe That I Am He (John 8:24)

"Therefore I said to you that you will die in your sins; for if you do not believe that I am He, you will die in your sins."

If You Do Not Believe That I Am He

What does the Lord mean when He says, "If you do not believe *that I am He*"? The expression *I am He* (or, *I am*) is not one we typically use today.

We find the same basic construction in John 4:26, "I who speak to you am *He*." In both cases the word *He* is supplied by the translators and is not in the Greek.

Some see these "I am" statements as statements of deity (cf. Exod 3:14). However, it is clear in John 4:26 that *egō eimi* means *I am He* or *I am the Messiah*.[1] The woman had just said, "I know that Messiah is coming" (who is called Christ). "When He comes, He will tell us all things." Jesus was affirming that He is the Messiah. The same is true in John 8:24, though He might mean that and more.

Many commentators suggest that *egō eimi* here has a more comprehensive meaning.[2] Hendriksen writes, "The meaning is:

---

[1] See also John 9:9. The expression *egō eimi* was used by the man born blind when he indicated that he was indeed born blind: "Some said, 'This is he.' Others said, 'He is like him.' He said, 'I am he.'" While it could be a statement of deity when Jesus says *egō eimi* (though I think it is not in John 8:24, but probably is in John 8:58), it is clearly not when a mere man says it.

[2] For example, C. K. Barrett in *The Gospel According to St. John* (Philadelphia, PA: The Westminster Press, 1955, 1978), 342, writes, "*egō eimi*

that I am all that I claim to be; the One sent by the Father, the One who is from above, the Son of man...the bread of life, the light of the world, etc."[3] Westcott says it means "that in me is the spring of life and light and strength; that I present to you the invisible majesty of God."[4]

You Will Die in Your Sins

The Lord does not mean that they will die *because of their sins*, though that is certainly true. Everyone dies *because of his or her sins*, believers and unbelievers. The wages of sin is death (Gen 2:17; Rom 6:23). Believers are not immune to death (John 11:25), unless, of course, they are alive at the time of the Rapture.

To die "in your sins" means to be a slave of sin all the way to the grave, and presumably beyond.[5] Believers are no longer slaves of sin in our position (Rom 6:17, 18, 20, 22). And we need not be slaves of sin in our experience, either (John 8:30-32; Rom 6:6, 16). Unbelievers, by contrast, are enslaved to sin. Later in John 8 the Lord debates his Jewish listeners who claim they have never been enslaved to anyone or anything (John 8:33-59).

Admittedly, everlasting life is not explicitly mentioned in John 8:24. However, it is implied. The one who does not believe dies in his sins because he has never been born again. To be set free from sin's bondage, one must be born again. The new birth is the time when sin's bondage is broken (cf. John 8:30-32; Rom 6:22-23). Faith alone is the condition for escaping bondage to sin and being born again.

---

does not identify Jesus with God, but it draws attention to him in the strongest possible terms. 'I am the one—the one you must look at, and listen to, if you would know God.' This open form of words is better than 'I am the Christ, the one who can save you'...just because it is open."
[3] William Hendriksen, *Exposition on the Gospel According to John: Commentary on Chapters 7-21* (Grand Rapids, MI: Baker, 1953), 46.
[4] B. F. Westcott, *The Gospel According to St. John* (Grand Rapids, MI: Eerdmans, 1881, 1981), 131.
[5] See Manfred Gutzke, *Plain Talk on John* (Grand Rapids, MI: Zondervan, 1968), 99. He says that Jesus is talking about "their life pattern" and that unless they were born again, "there was no relief in sight for them."

EIGHTY

If You Abide in His Word, the Truth Shall Make You Free (John 8:30-32)

As He spoke these words, many believed in Him. Then Jesus said to those Jews who believed Him, "If you abide in My word, you are My disciples indeed. And you shall know the truth, and the truth shall make you free."

Many Believed in Him

Many commentators think that the words "many believed in Him" do not refer to saving faith (cf. John 2:23; chap. 77).[1] However, in John 3:16 the Lord Jesus said that "whoever believes in Him…has everlasting life." Since *whoever* is a comprehensive term, we know that these who "believed in Him" have everlasting life. After all, it is the Apostle John who tells us, in inspired Scripture, that they "believed in Him."

The reason why most commentators doubt that these people are regenerate is because of what Jesus says to them in the words which follow.

---

[1] See D. A. Carson, *The Gospel According to John* (Grand Rapids, MI: Eerdmans, 1991), 347-49; Leon Morris, *The Gospel According to John* (Grand Rapids, MI: Eerdmans, 1971), 454-57; J. Ramsey Michaels, *The Gospel of John* (Grand Rapids, MI: Eerdmans, 2010), 503-505; John Calvin, *John* (Wheaton, IL: Crossway Books, 1994), 216-18.

If You Abide in My Word, You Are My Disciples Indeed

If all born-again people are always disciples of Christ, then the Lord is either suggesting that these people are not born-again yet, or that they are, but that they can lose everlasting life if they fail to abide in His teachings. But we know that everlasting life cannot be lost (John 5:24; 11:26). For this reason, some commentators conclude that these people were not born again, although John says that they "believed in Him." Carson writes, "Holding to Jesus' teaching (v. 31) not only establishes the genuineness of faith, it also has its own authenticating power."[2]

However, if a believer is only a disciple if he is sitting under Christian instruction, then a born-again person might not be a disciple. In fact, that is precisely what the Lord Jesus is saying here.

Though Michaels suggests that the faith of these believers was less than saving faith, his comments concerning abiding in Jesus' word are very helpful (and, surprisingly, make it sound like he thinks they are genuine believers):

> To "dwell on" Jesus' word presupposes that they have in fact "believed him" (that is, believed in him on the basis of his spoken words, v. 31). Jesus is asking them, now that they have believed, to "follow" him (see v. 12) or "walk with him" (see 6:60)[3] in the sense of giving him their allegiance, finally even to "dwell in him" (6:56) or become united to him in their very being. To be "truly my disciples," he insists, requires nothing less.[4]

---

[2] Carson, *John*, 348.

[3] Michaels may have meant John 6:66, "From that time many of His disciples walked with Him no more." Verse 60 is merely the complaint by some of the disciples about the difficulty of understanding this "hard saying." Or possibly he intended us to understand the context starting in John 6:60 (e.g., John 6:60ff).

[4] Michaels, *John*, 505.

If you have believed in Jesus, and you followed Him for a time, but you no longer abide in His teachings, then you used to be a disciple of Christ, but you are not now. You could become a disciple again in the future if you get back into Christian instruction in a Bible-teaching church. However, once you believed in Christ, you were saved once and for all. Your born-again status cannot change. But your status as a disciple can change.

You Shall Know the Truth, and the Truth Shall Make You Free

These are some of the most famous words of the Lord Jesus. But they are much misunderstood. Without reading the words that follow, one may miss His point. He is not saying that if we know the truth, then we are born again. Nor is He saying that if we know the truth, then we are free from any difficulties in life.

Jesus is speaking about freedom *from sin's bondage*: "Jesus answered them, 'Most assuredly, I say to you, whoever commits sin is a slave of sin'" (John 8:34).[5] His point in John 8:31-32 is that a believer is not automatically free from slavery to sin *in his experience*. The believer must abide in order to be free. Once saved, always saved. But only by continuous abiding does one experience freedom from sin's bondage.

Once again, there is no direct statement concerning everlasting life and the new birth in these verses. However, it is implied. We know from many other verses in John that whoever believes in Him has everlasting life. And we know that only born-again people can experience freedom from sin's bondage (cf. John 8:24, chap. 79). So, John 8:30-32 is another faith-alone text.

---

[5] Barrett says, "It is clear (v. 34) that by [the truth shall make you free] John means to express primarily the Christian liberation from sin." C. K. Barrett, *The Gospel According to St. John*, 2nd ed. (Philadelphia, PA: Westminster, 1955, 1978), 345. However, his very next words are puzzling: "that is, being made free is nothing other than a synonym for salvation."

EIGHTY-ONE

I Am the Way, the Truth, and the Life (John 14:6)

Jesus said to him [Thomas], "I am the way, the truth, and the life. No one comes to the Father except through Me."

I Am the Way, the Truth, and the Life

There are seven distinct "I am" statements by the Lord Jesus recorded in John's Gospel: "I am the bread of life" (John 6:35, 41, 48, 51); "I am the light of the world" (John 8:12; 9:5); "I am the door of the sheep" (John 10:7, 9); "I am the good shepherd" (John 10:11, 14); "I am the resurrection and the life" (John 11:25); "I am the way, the truth, and the life" (John 14:6); and "I am the true vine" (John 15:1, 5).

Two of the seven "I am" statements are compound statements. That is, they have more than one predicate nominative. John 11:25 has two components: "I am the resurrection *and the life.*" And John 14:6 has three elements: "I am the way, the truth, *and the life.*" I have added emphasis to show the one component both of these compound "I am" statements have in common: "I am the life."

Jesus had said, "and if I go to prepare a place for you, I will come again and receive you to Myself; that where I am, there you may be also" (14:3). Then He added, "And where I go you know, and the way you know" (v 4). That led Thomas to ask: "How can we know the way?" (v 5). John 14:6 is the Lord's answer to that question.

The disciples still did not realize that Jesus was going to die and return to the Father in the third heaven. Jesus is the only way to the third heaven and ultimately to His kingdom when He returns.

He is the truth. That is, everything He said was true. He was incapable of lying. While all He said was true, His promise of everlasting life was especially in view here. He was telling the truth when He said that whoever believes in Him has everlasting life (John 3:14-18; 5:24; 6:35, 47).

And Jesus is "the life."[1] That is, He is everlasting life. John says that himself in 1 John 1:2; 5:20. He *is the life*. We who believe in Him *have the life*. We are not and never will be *the life*. We have the life. He is the life. That is why John can later say, "He who has the Son has [the] life; he who does not have the Son does not have [the] life" (1 John 5:12).[2]

No One Comes to the Father Except Through Me

The clause *no one comes to the Father except through Me* is a faith-alone reference. While the Lord does not explicitly mention *faith*, it is clear, when we consider what He is cited as saying throughout John's Gospel, that that is what He means. Blum writes, "Jesus stressed that salvation, contrary to what many people think, is not obtainable through many ways. Only one Way

---

[1] I have taken these three elements as distinct. Some, however, see the life as central and the way and truth leading to it. Brown says that "Most of the Greek Fathers... understood the way and the truth to lead to the life (eternal life in heaven)" (Raymond E. Brown, *The Gospel According to John*, vol. 2 [New Haven, CT: Yale University, 2008], 621). Brown concludes that the emphasis is on *the way*. Carson says, however, that "the three terms are syntactically co-ordinate, and Greek has other ways of expressing subordination" (D. A. Carson, *The Gospel According to John* [Grand Rapids, MI: Inter-Varsity, 1991], 491).

[2] The Greek contains the definite article before *life* on both occasions in 1 John 5:12. While it is not wrong to leave it out of an English translation of 1 John 5:12, it is better to include it because of what the Lord Jesus Himself said in John 14:6. Most English translations omit the word *the* before *life*. But the NASB and LEB include it, and the NET Bible has *this life*.

exists (cf. Acts 4:12; 1 Tim. 2:5). Jesus is the only access to the Father."[3]

The one who does not believe in Him is condemned already (John 3:18). But the one who believes in Him has *the life,* everlasting life, and will come to the Father when he dies.

Carson comments, "*No-one,* Jesus insists, *comes to the Father except through me.* That is the necessary stance behind all fervent evangelism."[4]

I came to faith in Christ at the start of my senior year in college, during the height of what was called *the Jesus movement.* We called ourselves *the Jesus people.* (Others called us *Jesus freaks.*) We had bumper stickers that said ONE WAY. When we saw each other, we'd put our index fingers up and say *One Way* to each other. There is no other way, as the children's song says: "One-way God said to get to heaven, Jesus is the only way." The one way is the faith-alone-in-Christ-alone way.

---

[3] Edward A Blum, "John" in *The Bible Knowledge Commentary*, New Testament Edition, ed. by John F. Walvoord and Roy B. Zuck (Wheaton, IL: Victor Books, 1985), 322.

[4] Carson, *John*, 492.

EIGHTY-TWO

No Other Name by Which We Must Be Saved (Acts 4:12)

"Nor is there salvation in any other, for there is no other name under heaven given among men by which we must be saved."

Nor Is There Salvation in Any Other

After Peter and John healed a man who had been lame from birth (Acts 3:1-11), Peter preached a sermon in which he re-offered the kingdom to Israel ("times of refreshing" [v 19] and "the times of restoration of all things," [v 21]. In order for the kingdom to come for that generation of Jews, they had to turn from their sins (Acts 3:19, 26) and to believe in the Lord Jesus Christ (Acts 3:13-18, 22-23; 4:4).

Then the Jewish authorities arrested Peter and John and the next day questioned them. Peter's words in v 12 are his bold witness to the Jewish religious leaders.

What does *salvation* mean in this context? Is Peter speaking of the new birth? No. The prior context suggests Peter is speaking of *the national salvation of Israel*, the coming of the kingdom. When Peter restated his point in the words which followed, he confirmed that understanding.

For There Is No Other Name by Which We Must Be Saved

Peter is still referring to the Lord Jesus when he speaks of "no other name under heaven given among men." Only "the name of Jesus Christ of Nazareth" saves.

Most commentators understand the words *by which we must be saved* as a straightforward proclamation of the faith-alone message for individual Gentiles and Jews.[1]

However, the words *by which we must be saved* are a bit odd. Why the words *we* and *must*? Peter could have said, "by which anyone may be saved."

We in this context refers to Jews. Peter and John were Jewish. So were the religious leaders who had arrested them. Peter is not discussing the regeneration of individual Gentiles or of individual Jews. He is talking about the national salvation of Israel (Zech 9:9-10; Matt 23:37-39; Rom 11:26). Israel will not be saved from Gentile domination and futility unless and until the entire nation believes in Jesus Christ and turns from its sins.

The salvation of which Peter speaks is broader than salvation from eternal condemnation. Peter and John were already born again. But they would not see the national salvation of Israel in the first century, apart from a revival breaking out.[2] It is now nearly two millennia later, and Israel still has not been saved. That will occur at the end of the seven-year Tribulation (Revelation 6–19).

Toussaint comments,

> **4:12.** The word **salvation** goes back to Psalm 118 which Peter had just quoted, for it is a prominent theme there. Verses 22-29 in that psalm anticipate millennial deliverance. In Acts 4:12 Peter was speaking not only

---

[1] See, for example, F. F. Bruce, *The Book of the Acts* (Grand Rapids, MI: Eerdmans, 1988), 94; Joseph A. Fitzmyer, *The Acts of the Apostles* (New Haven, CT: Yale University, 2008), 302; R. C. H. Lenski, *The Interpretation of the Acts of the Apostles* (Minneapolis, MN: Augsburg Publishing House, 1961), 167; John B. Polhill, *Acts* (Nashville, TN: Broadman & Holman, 1992), 144. While Polhill understands *we* to be "a direct appeal to the Sanhedrin," he does see the salvation Peter mentions as regeneration only, not the coming of the kingdom for Israel.

[2] Peter knew, of course, that he would die before the kingdom would come (John 21:18-23). But like the other apostles, he expected the kingdom to come in the first century (e.g., 1 Thess 4:16-17; Jas 5:9; 2 Pet 3:3, 10-13; 1 John 2:18).

of individual justification, but also of national salvation, predicted in Psalm 118.

The rulers were thus put on the defense! They had rejected the only Savior of Israel and they were preventing the completion of God's building. Thus no other way of salvation is available to people (cf. John 14:6; 1 Tim. 2:5).[3]

But, when the nation is saved collectively, every single adult Jew will be a born-again believer in Jesus Christ (and in fellowship with Him).[4]

Peter's re-offer of the kingdom includes the promise of everlasting life to all who simply believe in Jesus Christ (note Acts 3:15, "the Prince of life"). Therefore, this too is a faith-alone reference.

---

[3] Stanley D. Toussaint, "Acts" in *The Bible Knowledge Commentary*, New Testament Edition, ed. by John F. Walvoord and Roy B. Zuck (Wheaton, IL: Victor Books, 1983), 363.

[4] When the kingdom comes after the Tribulation ends, every Jewish child will be part of the salvation of the nation. While unbelieving children will not be born again, they will be *delivered* from the Gentile armies and will be part of the covenant nation during the Millennium. But any unbelieving Jewish adult will die before the end of the Tribulation (Matt 24:13, 22). Unbelieving Jewish (and Gentile) children that survive the Tribulation will go into the Millennium in natural bodies. Those unbelieving Jewish children who go from the Tribulation into the Millennium will be "saved" in the sense of taking part in Israel's national deliverance but will not yet be saved in the sense of having everlasting life. In order for them to be born again, they will need to believe in the Lord Jesus Christ during the Millennium.

EIGHTY-THREE

They Believed Concerning the Name of Jesus Christ (Acts 8:12-13)

But when they believed Philip as he preached the things concerning the kingdom of God and the name of Jesus Christ, both men and women were baptized. Then Simon himself also believed;[1] and when he was baptized, he continued with Philip, and was amazed, seeing the miracles and signs which were done.

They Believed Philip As He Preached Concerning the Name of Jesus Christ

Philip is the only person in the NT called "the evangelist" (Acts 21:8). Paul told Timothy to "do the work of an evangelist" (2 Tim 4:5), which is not the same as saying that Timothy was an evangelist. While there were many evangelists in the early church (Eph 4:11), the fact that Luke gives us an account of the ministry of one of them is telling.

In Acts 8, Philip first led a group of Samaritans to faith in Christ (Acts 8:1-25). Then he went into the desert and led an Ethiopian eunuch to faith in Christ (Acts 8:26-39).

---

[1] Simon believed in Christ, and hence he too was born again. Commentators who defend the salvation of Simon include R. C. H. Lenski, *The Interpretation of the Acts of the Apostles* (Minneapolis, MN: Augsburg Publishing House, 1961), 322; and Joseph A. Fitzmyer, *The Acts of the Apostles* (New Haven, CT: Yale University, 2008), 405. See also Jody Dillow, "Simon Magus: Believer or Unbeliever (Acts 8:12-24)," *Grace in Focus* (March–April 2001) and Michael Heiser, "Dumbledore Meets Philip & Peter," *Bible Study Magazine* (vol. 2 no. 2).

Luke, the author of Acts, tells us that the Samaritans "believed Philip...concerning the kingdom of God and the name of Jesus Christ." While Luke does not explicitly tell the reader that they were born again at that time, that is certainly understood for three reasons. First, Luke tells us that they believed in Christ. While someone might falsely profess to believe in Christ,[2] that is not the case here. Scripture tells us they believed. Second, other texts make it clear that all who believe in Jesus Christ have everlasting life (Acts 16:31; cf. John 1:12; 3:16; 5:24). Third, Philip had the gift of evangelism, and he exercised that gift in Samaria. He shared the true saving message, not a false works-salvation message (cf. Gal 1:6-9).

Some commentators think that Luke was giving two conditions for everlasting life: faith in Christ and Christian baptism.[3] However, while Luke does indicate that the new Samaritan believers were baptized, he does not say or imply that their baptism was a co-condition for the new birth.[4]

Verse 17 needs to be considered since some might think that the Samaritans were not born again until days later when Peter and John laid hands on them, and they received the Spirit.

---

[2] There are two main ways in which false professions occur. First, a person might sincerely say, "I believe in Jesus as my Savior" and yet not believe the faith-alone message. There are untold millions who claim Jesus as their Savior, yet who do not believe that faith in Him is the sole condition of everlasting life. Second, a person might insincerely say, "I believe in Jesus for the free gift of everlasting life, apart from any works that I have done or will do." If you share your faith with a panhandler, you should be aware that he or she may indicate he agrees with you to get money.

[3] See, for example, Lenski, *Acts*, 322; and Fitzmyer, *Acts,* 405.

[4] Baptism is the first step in discipleship, in following Christ (Matt 28:18-20). If baptism were a condition of everlasting life, Paul would have said so when asked, "What must I do to be saved?" (cf. Acts 16:30). His response was simply, "Believe on the Lord Jesus Christ, and you shall be saved" (Acts 16:31). For more information, see Robert N. Wilkin, *Confident in Christ*, 2nd ed. (Denton, TX: Grace Evangelical Society, 1999, 2015), Appendix 2, "Baptism and Salvation," 197-208.

Then…They Received the Holy Spirit (v 17)

While today the Holy Spirit is received when one believes in Christ (Acts 10:43-48; 1 Cor 12:13), that was not the case in the very early Church. Jewish believers at Pentecost were born again when they believed in Christ (Acts 2:36-37), but they did not receive the Spirit until they repented and were baptized (Acts 2:38). It is not until the first group of Gentiles is born again in Acts 10:43-48 that the Holy Spirit falls on people when they believe, apart from repentance or baptism.

In the case of the Samaritans, they did not receive the Spirit until Peter and John laid hands on them. Why this unusual procedure? While Luke does not tell us directly, it is reasonable to conclude that Luke was suggesting that the reason was to prove to the Jewish believers that Samaritans were now fully accepted into the Body of Christ.[5]

The sole condition of the Samaritans being born again is the same as for Jews or Gentiles. There is but one condition, which is faith in Christ. For the Samaritans to receive the Spirit, however, they had to submit to Christian baptism and to an apostle laying hands on them.

Therefore, while this is an unusual text (since it deals with a transitional time), it does proclaim the faith-alone message.

---

[5] After Peter was used by God to be the first to bring the message of Christ to a group of Gentiles, he was grilled about that incident by Jewish believers back in Jerusalem (Acts 11:1-18). He won them over when he said, "If therefore God gave them the same gift as He gave us when we believed on the Lord Jesus Christ [i.e., the Holy Spirit; compare Acts 10:45, "the gift of the Holy Spirit"], who was I that I could withstand God?" The same argument applies to the Samaritans in Acts 8.

EIGHTY-FOUR

Words by Which You Will Be Saved (Acts 11:14)

"And he told us how he had seen an angel standing in his house, who said to him, 'Send men to Joppa, and call for Simon whose surname is Peter, who will tell you words by which you and all your household will be saved'" (Acts 11:13-14).

Cornelius Sought God

Cornelius was "a devout man and one who feared God with all his household, who gave alms generously to the people, and prayed to God always" (Acts 10:2). Luke tells us that the Lord sent an angel to Cornelius. "And when he [Cornelius] observed him [the angel], he was afraid, and said, 'What is it, lord?' So he said to him, 'Your prayers and your alms have come up for a memorial before God'" (Acts 10:4). This was before Cornelius sent for Simon Peter, before he heard the saving message, and before he was born again. Bruce comments, "salvation did not enter Cornelius's house until Peter came there with the gospel."[1] A. T. Robertson likewise says, "Clearly Cornelius was unsaved in spite of his interest in Jewish worship. Clearly also the household of Cornelius would likewise be won to Christ by the words of Simon Peter. This is household conversion before the household baptism (10:48; 11:17)."[2]

---

[1] F. F. Bruce, *The Book of the Acts* (Grand Rapids, MI: Eerdmans, 1988), 222.
[2] A. T. Robertson, *Word Pictures in the New Testament* (Nashville, TN: Broadman, 1933), s.v. Acts 11:14.

The Calvinist idea that unregenerate people cannot seek God (in response to Him seeking them) is contradicted by Acts 10–11.

God Told Cornelius to Send for Simon Peter

Luke reports this twice, in Acts 10:5-6 and Acts 11:13-14. The repetition shows its importance. Luke wants his reader, Theophilus, to know that Gentiles are not second-class citizens in the Body of Christ. There is no special condition of everlasting life for Gentiles, as Peter went on to say in Acts 10:34-43. Though he intended to say more, Peter's last words before the Spirit fell upon Cornelius and his household were, "To Him all the prophets witness that, through His name, whoever believes in Him will receive remission of sins." How did Cornelius and his household know that Peter was talking about what they had to do *to be saved*? They knew because of what the angel had told Cornelius, as reported in the last part of Acts 11:14.

Words by Which You Will Be Saved

The angel did not merely tell Cornelius to send for Simon Peter. He told Cornelius that "Peter...will tell you words by which you and all your household will be saved." Because of those words, when Cornelius and his household heard Peter say, "To Him all the prophets witness that, through His name, whoever believes in Him will receive remission of sins" (Acts 10:43), they knew that whoever believes in Him is not only forgiven, but also saved. (See chap. 23 for a discussion of Acts 10:43.)

Cornelius and his household had been told in advance that they would be saved *by responding properly to Peter's words*. His words as cited in Acts 10:43 made it clear that the response needed was to "believe in Him [Christ]." The issue was not doing good works, committing their lives, submitting to Christian baptism, or anything other than believing. Lenski comments,

"Shall be saved" is passive and implies the Savior as the agent. Despite his connection with the synagogue, Cornelius had not yet found salvation as is clear from 4:12. What Peter says brings out the very thing all these Jewish Christians must realize, namely that they were not saved by circumcision or legal ordinances of Moses but solely and also completely by the utterances which contain the gospel and are connected with the Savior. And these utterances were sufficient to save any man, be he Jew or Gentile.[3]

When Peter later reported on this incident before the Jerusalem Council in Acts 15:7-11, he stressed that faith in Christ is the sole condition of everlasting life for all, Jews and Gentiles. See chaps. 26, 27, and 87.

Polhill exclaims, "Certainly for Peter it was a Gentile Pentecost. He could hardly make more explicit comparisons!"[4]

---

[3] R. C. H. Lenski, *The Interpretation of the Acts of the Apostles* (Minneapolis, MN: Augsburg Publishing House, 1961), 444.
[4] John B. Polhill, *Acts* (Nashville, TN: Broadman & Holman Publishers, 1992), 267.

EIGHTY-FIVE

Rejecting the Words of Everlasting Life (Acts 13:46)

Then Paul and Barnabas grew bold and said, "It was necessary that the word of God should be spoken to you first; but since you reject it, and judge yourselves unworthy of everlasting life, behold, we turn to the Gentiles."

Rejecting the Word of God

On their first missionary journey, Paul and Barnabas arrived in Antioch in Pisidia and went to the synagogue there on the Sabbath. Being given an opportunity to speak, Paul preached Christ to the Jews and God-fearing Gentiles who were present. After saying, "by Him everyone who believes is justified from all things from which you could not be justified by the law of Moses" (v 39; see chap. 25), he warned them of the danger of rejecting Christ (vv 40-41).

The following Sabbath, Paul and Barnabas came again to the synagogue. This time the crowd was much larger when "almost the whole city came together to hear the word of God" (v 44). But some of the Jews "opposed the things spoken by Paul" (v 45). Then Paul and Barnabas said, "It was necessary that the word of God should be spoken to you first; but since you reject it, and judge yourselves unworthy of everlasting life, behold, we turn to the Gentiles" (v 46).

Most of the Jews in Pisidian Antioch rejected Jesus Christ. But when they rejected Christ, they were rejecting the very Word of God. They were wrong when they thought that they were upholding God's Word. Whenever anyone rejects Christ, he is rejecting the revelation from God the Father as well.

Lenski comments,

> Argument against this blasphemous passion was useless. The rupture had come. Paul and Barnabas accept it. It is for this reason that Luke gives such prominence to the story of Pisidian Antioch. Here for the first time in Paul's missionary experience the open breach with the synagogue occurred. Paul was to have this experience again and again. It was to become typical of his work.[1]

Judging Yourselves Unworthy of Everlasting Life

The reaction of Paul and Barnabas shows that people are responsible for how they respond to the Word of God. If people hear the message of life in Christ and reject it, then they are in effect "judging [themselves] unworthy of everlasting life." Ouch.

Paul does not say *that God judged them unworthy of everlasting life*. God sent His missionaries to bring them the promise of everlasting life in Christ to all who believe in Him. God wanted all the people in Antioch to come to faith and to gain everlasting life (1 Tim 2:4). But they rejected the message. They should have prayed about this message during the week between the two sermons. They should have searched the Scriptures to see if what Paul had said was true (Acts 17:11). Luke does tell us that after the first Sabbath message, "many of the Jews and devout proselytes [Gentiles] followed Paul and Barnabas, who, speaking to them, persuaded them to continue in the grace of God" (v 43).

---

[1] R. C. H. Lenski, *The Interpretation of the Acts of the Apostles* (Minneapolis, MN: Augsburg Publishing House, 1961), 549.

Anyone who was not persuaded after that first sermon could have prayed, searched the Scriptures, and followed Paul and Barnabas to learn more about Jesus Christ. But most of the Jews of the city did none of those things. They came the next Sabbath "filled with envy; and contradicting and blaspheming, they opposed the things spoken by Paul" (v 45).

The faith-alone message is evident in the solemn words of Acts 13:46. To reject the word of God concerning Jesus Christ is synonymous with not believing it. To not believe in Christ is to cut oneself off from the only Source of everlasting life. Those who believe in Him have everlasting life. Those who reject Him judge themselves unworthy of everlasting life.

Bruce comments:

> The life of the age to come had been brought near to them here and now as God's free gift in Christ; if they showed themselves unworthy of the gift by declining to accept it, there were others who would appreciate it: it would be offered direct [sic] to the Gentiles.[2]

Fitzmyer adds, "Lucan irony comes forth. 'Eternal life' is closely linked to acceptance of 'the word of God' in faith."[3] Polhill simply says, "But the Jews in Antioch had rejected the eternal life that is to be found in Jesus."[4]

---

[2] F. F. Bruce, *The Book of the Acts* (Grand Rapids, MI: Eerdmans, 1988), 266.

[3] Joseph A. Fitzmyer, *The Acts of the Apostles* (New Haven, CT: Yale University, 2008), 520. His words *closely linked* are understated. Eternal life is only for those who believe in Jesus Christ.

[4] John B. Polhill, *Acts* (Nashville, TN: Broadman & Holman, 1992), 308.

EIGHTY-SIX

As Many as Had Been Attracted to Eternal Life Believed (Acts 13:48)

Now when the Gentiles heard this, they were glad and glorified the word of the Lord. And as many as had been appointed to eternal life believed.

The Gentiles Glorified the Word of the Lord

Luke is not suggesting here that *all* the Gentiles in Antioch "were glad and glorified the word of the Lord." To be glad and to glorify the word of the Lord is another way of saying that they believed in Christ. The second part of v 48 is parallel to the first: "And as many as had been appointed [or *as had been attracted to*] eternal life believed." Lenski comments,

> What angered the Jews delighted the Gentiles, namely to hear that the gospel was intended also for them, for them directly without the necessity of first becoming Jews and submitting to all the Jewish regulations. Happy to hear it, they glorified "the Word of God," meaning the Word in the sense in which Luke has continually been using it, the gospel of Jesus, the Savior. It is always so: whereas some spurn that Word, others receive it joyfully. So these Gentiles "believed," the aorist stating the fact.[1]

---

[1] R. C. H. Lenski, *The Interpretation of the Acts of the Apostles* (Minneapolis, MN: Augsburg Publishing House, 1961), 552.

As Many as Had Been Attracted to Eternal Life Believed

The expression *eternal life* is only found twice in Acts. Both are in Acts 13, the first in v 46 (see chap. 85)[2] and the second just two verses later.

Most English translations render the Greek verb *tetagmenoi* (from *tassō*) as *had been appointed*. Calvinists see in this word confirmation of their understanding of individual pre-temporal election to everlasting life.

However, the context and the meaning of the verb suggest a different translation. Just two verses prior, Luke quoted Paul as saying to the Jews who opposed his preaching: "you judge yourselves unworthy of everlasting life." By willingly rejecting the message concerning Jesus Christ, they were rejecting everlasting life.

The verb *tassō* means 1) "to arrange, put in place" and 2) "to order, fix, determine, appoint."[3] In the middle voice (used here), it can refer *to preparing oneself for* something, in this case, preparing oneself for everlasting life.[4]

Robertson comments,

> The Jews here had voluntarily rejected the word of God. On the other side were those Gentiles *who gladly accepted what the Jews had rejected* [emphasis added]...Why these Gentiles here *ranged themselves on God's side* [emphasis added] as opposed to the Jews, Luke does not

---

[2] In the NKJV the same Greek words, in reverse order (and different cases), *aiōniou zōēs* and *zōēn aiōnion*, are unfortunately translated *everlasting life* in v 46 and *eternal life* in v 48. Most translations render that expression as "eternal life" in both places (e.g., NASB, NIV, HCSB, NET, LEB, ESV, MEV, NRSV). Elsewhere in Acts the words *justified* (Acts 13:39), *saved* (Acts 15:11; 16:31), and *purified* (Acts 15:9) are used.

[3] Bauer, Danker, Arndt, and Gingrich, *A Greek-English Lexicon of the New Testament and Other Early Christian Literature*, 3rd ed. (Chicago, IL: University of Chicago Press, 2000), s.v. *tassō*, 991.

[4] See Bob Wilkin, "A New View on Acts 13:48 'As Many as Were Prepared for Eternal Life Believed,'" at https://faithalone.org/grace-in-focus-articles/a-new-view-on-acts-13-48/.

tell us. This verse does not solve the vexed problem of divine sovereignty and human free agency. There is no evidence that Luke had in mind an *absolutum decretum* of personal salvation. Paul had shown that God's plan extended to and included Gentiles. Certainly the Spirit of God does move upon the human heart *to which some respond* [emphasis added], as here, while others push him away.[5]

Often lost in the study of Acts 13:48 is that it is a strong faith-alone verse. Everlasting life is for those who believe in Jesus Christ for it. In contrast to those who reject the Word of God and the life it promises (Acts 13:46), those who accept the Word get the life by faith alone (Acts 13:48).

---

[5] A. T. Robertson, *Word Pictures in the New Testament* (Nashville, TN: Broadman, 1933), s.v. Acts 13:48.

EIGHTY-SEVEN

Hearing the Gospel and Believing in Christ for Salvation (Acts 15:7)

And when there had been much dispute, Peter rose up and said to them: "Men and brethren, you know that a good while ago God chose among us, that by my mouth the Gentiles should hear the word of the gospel and believe."

The Context Is the Jerusalem Council

Controversy arose among the Jewish people who heard Paul and Barnabas as to what Gentiles had to do to be saved. As a result, the church in Jerusalem convened a council to settle the matter.

Two issues were under consideration. First, while Paul and Barnabas were back in Syrian Antioch, some Jews came and said: "'Unless you are circumcised according to the custom of Moses, you cannot be saved'" (Acts 15:1). Second, after Paul and Silas came to the church in Jerusalem to clear up this matter, "Some of the sect of the Pharisees who believed rose up, saying, 'It is necessary to circumcise them, and to command them to keep the law of Moses'" (Acts 15:5). *Their concern was sanctification.*

Luke calls the first group, "certain men." By contrast, he calls the second group "some of the sect of the Pharisees *who believed*" (emphasis added). The strong implication is the first objectors were unbelieving Jews, unlike the second objectors who were specifically identified as believing Jews.

The foremost issue to be considered at the Jerusalem Council was whether Gentiles had to become Jews in order to be saved.[1]

Peter Is Talking about the Time He Evangelized Cornelius and His Household

Not surprisingly, after "much dispute," the first to speak was the Apostle Peter, the leading Apostle to the Jews (Acts 15:6-7a). Peter represented the view of all the apostles.

When Peter said, "you know that a good while ago God chose among us, that by my mouth the Gentiles should hear the word of the gospel and believe," he was referring to the time he was in Joppa, and God sent him to lead Cornelius and his household to faith in Christ (Acts 9–10).

Lenski comments,

> The work of Paul and of Barnabas was not an innovation and did not present a new question. Far back in those days God "made choice for himself," elected of his own accord (middle voice), "for the Gentiles to hear (effectively, aorist) through my mouth the Word of the gospel and to believe (effectively, aorist)." At that time God made Peter the medium as he had now made Paul and Barnabas his media...God was the great agent in bringing Peter to Cornelius by using a vision and an angel.[2]

Hearing the Gospel and Believing in Christ for Salvation

Peter is summarizing the message he proclaimed to Cornelius and his household, the message that resulted in their salvation (Acts 10:43-48; 11:14). Peter preached the good news of Jesus' death and resurrection:

---

[1] The issue of the sanctification of Gentile believers was considered at the end of the Jerusalem Council. See Acts 15:28-29.
[2] R. C. H. Lenski, *The Interpretation of the Acts of the Apostles* (Minneapolis, MN: Augsburg Publishing House, 1961), 602.

> *"...how God anointed Jesus of Nazareth with the Holy Spirit and with power, who went about doing good and healing all who were oppressed by the devil, for God was with Him. And we are witnesses of all things which He did both in the land of the Jews and in Jerusalem, whom they killed by hanging on a tree. Him God raised up on the third day..."(Acts 10:38-40).*

Peter followed with the words cited in Acts 10:43 (see chap. 23): "To Him all the prophets witness that, through His name, whoever believes in Him will receive remission of sins."[3] Considering Acts 11:14 ("Send men to Joppa, and call for Simon whose surname is Peter, who will tell you words by which you and all your household will be saved"), Cornelius and his household believed in Jesus for their salvation, even though Peter had not yet mentioned that in his sermon.

Fitzmyer writes, "*and come to believe in it.* The reaction expected of human beings to the 'gospel' is faith, which Luke expresses by the infinitive of purpose *pisteusai.*"[4]

The faith-alone message, which Paul and Barnabas proclaimed to the Gentiles, was powerfully defended by Peter, the Apostle to the Jews.

---

[3] Believing in Jesus for the forgiveness of sins is not the same as believing in Him for everlasting life. However, if a person is convinced that he is eternally secure because his sins have been forgiven, then it would essentially mean he was believing the same thing. Unfortunately, many people today believe that by faith in Jesus their sins are forgiven, and they think that they are starting on a path that can lead to "final salvation" if they persevere in faith and good works until death.

[4] Joseph A. Fitzmyer, *The Acts of the Apostles* (New Haven, CT: Yale University Press, 2008), 547.

EIGHTY-EIGHT

The Gift of God Is Eternal Life in Christ (Romans 6:23)

For the wages of sin is death, but the gift of God is eternal life in Christ Jesus our Lord.

The Wages of Sin Is Death

Romans 6:23 is in the sanctification section of the letter, Romans 5–8. Therefore, it would be surprising if Rom 6:23 were a verse about justification, or, in this case, regeneration (i.e., eternal life). It is not.

"The wages of sin is death" refers to the deadly consequences of sin *in this life*. Paul is not talking about "the second death" (Rev 20:14) here. From the beginning, death reigned because of the sin of Adam and Eve (cf. Genesis 5; Rom 5:12-21). If a believer lets sin reign in him (Rom 6:12-14, 21-22), then he will experience the death-dealing consequences of sin (Rom 8:6).

Morris favorably quotes Smart: "'Death here is the negation or absence of a life that is truly life. Sin robs life of its meaning, purpose, fulfillment' (Smart, p. 91)."[1] While Morris goes on to apply that to the unbeliever, Paul is applying that to the believer. Sin *robs the believer's life* of its meaning, purpose, and fulfillment.

Fitzmyer succinctly says, "The more one serves sin, the more pay in the form of death one earns."[2]

---

[1] Leon Morris, *The Epistle to the Romans* (Grand Rapids, MI: Eerdmans, 1988), 267.
[2] Joseph A. Fitzmyer, *Romans* (New Haven, CT: Yale University, 2008), 452.

The Gift of God Is Eternal Life

Note the clear contrasts here. Wages are contrasted with the gift. Sin is contrasted with eternal life.

Everlasting life is God's gift (cf. John 4:14; Eph 2:8-9).

Now what we do with the life of God in us determines our present experience, which is what Paul is talking about. If we yield ourselves to sin, then we will reap the experience of death (temporal judgment that potentially results in premature death). If we yield ourselves to righteousness, then we will reap an abundant experience of everlasting life (cf. John 10:10b).

Morris notes, "As in the previous verse, eternal life seems to be used to include both the present possession and the glorious consummation at the end of the age."[3] In terms of the present life, its fullness is dependent on doing what Paul says in Romans 6–8 (considering yourself dead to sin, yielding your members to God, and having your mind set on the things of the Spirit).

Hodges comments, "Eternal life is an *unearned* experience because at its core *eternal life* is the gift of God that is given in Christ Jesus our Lord...When we produce holiness, we are living out *the gift* that God gave us when we were justified by faith."[4]

Eternal Life Is in Christ

The last part of v 23 brings in the faith-alone element. Though faith is not stated explicitly, it is there implicitly. Eternal life is by faith "in Christ Jesus our Lord."

Mounce comments, "believers...receive a gift—the gift of eternal life, which comes by faith through Jesus Christ their Lord."[5]

---

[3] Morris, *Romans*, 267.

[4] Zane C. Hodges, *Romans: Deliverance from Wrath* (Denton, TX: Grace Evangelical Society, 2013), 181.

[5] Robert. H. Mounce, *Romans* (Nashville, TN: Broadman & Holman, 1995), 159.

EIGHTY-NINE

If It Is by Grace, It Is No Longer of Works (Romans 11:6)

Even so then, at the present time there is a remnant according to the election of grace. And if by grace, then it is no longer of works; otherwise grace is no longer grace. But if it is of works, it is no longer grace; otherwise work is no longer work (vv 5–6).

If It Is by Grace, It Is No Longer of Works

Grace and works are typically contrasted in Paul's writings. Compare Rom 4:4-5; Eph 2:8-9; 2 Tim 1:9; and Titus 3:5.

Romans 9–11 concern the future of Israel. God has not forgotten His chosen people: "Even so then, at this present time there is a remnant according to the election of grace" (Rom 11:5).

Witmer comments,

> Paul was only one of many in his generation elected to faith from the people of Israel. In every generation of the church 'a remnant chosen by grace' has been called from among the Jews. Paul added that this choice is totally by God's grace (cf. Eph. 2:8–9) and he emphasized the antithesis between grace and works (cf. Rom. 4:4–5; 9:30–32).[1]

---

[1] John A. Witmer, "Romans" in *The Bible Knowledge Commentary*, New Testament Edition, ed. by John F. Walvoord and Roy B. Zuck (Wheaton, IL: Victor Books, 1985), 482-83.

Witmer's "elected to faith" reflects his understanding of "the election of grace" in v 5. However, grace and faith are not synonymous concepts. "The election of grace" does not refer to some pre-temporal election of individuals to everlasting life. Instead, *the election of grace* could well refer to God's choosing of *the nation of Israel* as His chosen people.[2] From within the chosen people, any who believe in Christ are part of the remnant.

Lenski has a slightly different and more literal understanding, seeing grace as personified by Paul and as choosing a remnant:

> Grace (see 3:24) which asks for nothing on the sinner's part, which gratuitously bestows God's righteousness through Christ to be accepted by faith (trust) alone, *this grace makes an election in accord with its nature by taking for itself all those whom it wins for faith* and for the acceptance of this gift of God's righteousness. This is its *eklogē*. It operated thus in Paul's time (as in every other), and we see this "remnant," Jewish believers all; all the rest of Judaism despised grace and would not let it work faith in them.[3]

Grace is God's favor. His favor in salvation is seen in the substitutionary death of Messiah on behalf of all, Jews and Gentiles. It is also seen in the fact that God's Spirit is drawing all toward Christ (John 12:32; 16:7-11). The very ministry of Paul was an expression of God's grace to the Jew first and also to the Greeks.

While faith in Christ is not explicitly mentioned here, it is understood. Salvation is by grace "through faith" (Eph 2:8).

Otherwise Grace Is No Longer Grace

If being part of the remnant of Jews who are born again were a matter of works, then it would not be a matter of grace, because

---

[2] René A. López, "The Epistle of Paul the Apostle to the Romans" in *The Grace New Testament Commentary*, ed. by Robert N. Wilkin (Denton, TX: Grace Evangelical Society, 2010), 680.

[3] R. C. H. Lenski, *The Interpretation of St. Paul's Epistle to the Romans* (Columbus, OH: Lutheran Book Concern, 1936), 683, emphasis added.

"otherwise grace is no longer grace." God is not bestowing His favor on someone if He gives that person what he has earned.

Moo says, "if human beings could by their works secure the blessing of God (as Paul points out in the second part of the verse), grace would 'no longer' be grace. For grace demands that God be perfectly free to bestow his favor on whomever he chooses."[4]

If It Is of Works, It Is No Longer Grace

If salvation were a matter of works, then it would no longer be grace. Grace and works are mutually exclusive in the reception of everlasting life.

Morris comments, "If works come into salvation at all, and the end result is called grace, then Paul has misunderstood what grace is; the meaning of the term would have been drastically altered."[5]

Otherwise Work Is No Longer Work

Paul completes his thought by saying that if salvation were "of works, it is not longer grace; otherwise work is no longer work." Morris says, "It is important to take grace seriously and not to let works creep in by some back door."[6]

---

[4] Douglas Moo, *The Epistle to the Romans* (Grand Rapids, MI: Eerdmans, 1996), 678.
[5] Leon Morris, *The Epistle to the Romans* (Grand Rapids, MI: Eerdmans, 1988), 402.
[6] Ibid.

NINETY

Now Our Salvation Is Nearer Than When We First Believed (Romans 13:11)

And do this, knowing the time, that now it is high time to awake out of sleep; for now our salvation is nearer than when we first believed.

It Is High Time to Awake out of Sleep

Moral lethargy should have no place in a believer's life. Morris says, "Slumber will denote a lethargic Christian life."[1] Believers should "know the time." We are living in the last days. Christ's return is imminent. Our actions should reflect our understanding of the times in which we live.

Mounce comments,

> The world lives as though human history were destined to continue forever. The Christian knows that God is in control...and is directing history to a predetermined end. Since the end is near, we are to arouse ourselves from sleep, to "wake up to reality" (Phillips).[2]

---

[1] Leon Morris, *The Epistle to the Romans* (Grand Rapids, MI: Eerdmans, 1988), 471.
[2] Robert Mounce, *Romans* (Nashville, TN: Broadman & Holman, 1995), 247.

Osborne rightly sees an allusion to the Judgment Seat of Christ: "Christians will be delivered and vindicated, but they will also be accountable for their conduct."[3]

Now Our Salvation Is Nearer

In Romans the words *save* (Rom 5:9, 10; 8:24; 9:27; 10:9, 13; 11:14, 26) and *salvation* (1:16; 10:1, 10; 11:11; 13:11) are used in reference to deliverance from God's wrath in this life, not to salvation from eternal condemnation.[4]

López comments, "The connection of v 16 with v 18 becomes vitally important since *salvation* and *wrath* are linked in this way. From the beginning of his letter, Paul defines *salvation* as *deliverance from God's present wrath brought about by sins*."[5] Concerning Rom 13:11 he says, "*Salvation* here parallels the 'salvation' in 1 Thess 5:9. Both contexts are similar. Therefore, in light of the believer's deliverance from impending Tribulation wrath, Paul commands them to live in a holy manner."[6]

Moo says,

> The text now before us shifts the perspective, encouraging Christians to look at the present in light of the future. For, while transferred by God's grace into the new realm of righteousness and life, Christians still await full and final salvation (cf. 5:9-10), 'the redemption of the body' (cf. 8:23).[7]

---

[3] Grant R. Osborne, *Romans* (Downers Grove, IL: InterVarsity, 2004), 352.
[4] For a discussion of the various uses in Romans, see Robert N. Wilkin, *The Ten Most Misunderstood Words in the Bible* (Denton, TX: Grace Evangelical Society, 2012), 41-43.
[5] René A. López, "The Epistle of Paul the Apostle to the Romans" in *The Grace New Testament Commentary*, ed. by Robert N. Wilkin (Denton, TX: Grace Evangelical Society, 2010), 626.
[6] Ibid., 694.
[7] Douglas Moo, *The Epistle to the Romans* (Grand Rapids, MI: Eerdmans, 1996), 818.

Similarly, Morris writes, "Paul writes elsewhere, 'We eagerly await a Savior from there (i.e., heaven)' (Phil. 3:20), and it is something like that that he is saying here. There is the thought of eager expectation and the thought that the fulness of all that salvation...is yet to come."[8]

Believers will be saved from the Tribulation wrath (cf. 1 Thess 5:8-10). Our salvation via the Rapture (1 Thess 4:13-18) is nearer every day. When that occurs, we will have glorified bodies and a fullness of everlasting life that we've not yet experienced.

Than When We First Believed

Once a person is born again, his salvation from eternal condemnation is a done deal. That salvation never gets *nearer than when we first believed*. We are as eternally secure when we first believe in Christ for everlasting life as when we've been in the faith for forty years.

While it is true that the Lord did not return in Paul's day—or in nearly two thousand years since then—He could have. The expectation was always there, as it is today. He is coming back soon for His church. The phrase *when we first believed* does not refer to when we twenty-first century believers first believed (though we can apply it in that way). It refers to the time when Paul and the believers in Rome first believed. Their salvation from the Tribulation was nearer than when they first believed. And our salvation from the Tribulation is nearer than when they first believed.

Paul mentions *when we first believed* because he was writing to believers[9] and because only believers in Jesus Christ have everlasting life and will be saved from the Tribulation. Paul is alluding to the faith-alone message here.

---

[8] Morris, *Romans*, 471.
[9] Simeon writes, "It was to 'believers' that St. Paul addressed the words before us" (Charles Simeon, *Romans* [London: Holdsworth and Ball, 1833], 510).

NINETY-ONE

Whose Names Are in the Book of Life (Philippians 4:3)

And I urge you also, true companion, help these women who labored with me in the gospel, with Clement also, and the rest of my fellow workers, whose names are in the Book of Life.

Euodia, Syntyche, and Clement Labored with Paul

Paul often praised those who labored with him (e.g., Eph 6:21; Phil 4:3; Col 4:12-14; 1 Tim 5:17; Philem 24).

Evidently Euodia and Syntyche were involved in some sort of disagreement ("I implore Euodia and Syntyche to be of the same mind in the Lord," Phil 4:2). Lightner comments, "At one time Euodia and Syntyche contended at Paul's side in the cause of the gospel. But as he wrote they were not in harmony with each other. They were contentious, rather than content."[1]

But that does not stop Paul from asking his "true companion [*suzugos*]" in Philippi (identity unknown, unless *Suzugos* is a proper name) to "help these women." The exact nature of this help is not stated. Lightner suggests that it could refer to "bring[ing] them back into fellowship with each other."[2] Melick takes a more cautious approach, saying, "Many scholars have attempted to identify them [the women and their dispute], but the

---

[1] Robert P. Lightner, "Philippians" in *The Bible Knowledge Commentary*, New Testament Edition, ed. by John F. Walvoord and Roy B. Zuck (Wheaton, IL: Victor Books, 1985), 663.
[2] Ibid.

conclusions are all conjecture, and the best course of action is to stay within the bounds of Scripture."[3]

It is not clear whether Paul is asking his true companion to also help Clement and the rest of Paul's co-workers (in some unspecified way) or whether he is asking Clement and his other co-workers to lend a hand in helping Euodia and Syntyche. Lenski strongly rejects the latter option: "The idea that all these people are to help the two women in minding the same thing (even if some of them were women) is untenable. Too many cooks spoil the broth; nor does this assistance need such a host of assistants."[4]

Their Names Are in the Book of Life

Philippians 4:3 is quite like Luke 10:20 (see chap. 74). Both refer to those who labored for the Lord and whose names are "recorded in heaven" (Luke 10:20) and "whose names are in the Book of Life" (Phil 4:3).

According to Rev 20:15, anyone whose name is in the Book of Life will not be cast into the lake of fire. In other words, all those in the Book of Life have everlasting life and are eternally secure.

While Paul does not state *why* the names of these women and Clement and Paul's other co-workers are in the Book of Life,[5] the reason is clear in light of Paul's teachings on justification by faith alone (e.g., Acts 13:39; Rom 3:21-31; 4:1-8; Gal 2:16) and regeneration by faith alone (e.g., Acts 16:31; Eph 2:5, 8; 1 Tim 1:16).

Paul is not suggesting that these people were in the Book of Life because they labored with him. They were in the Book of Life because they believed in the Lord Jesus Christ for everlasting life.

---

[3] Richard R. Melick, Jr., *Philippians, Colossians, Philemon* (Nashville, TN: Broadman & Holman, 1991), 146.

[4] R. C. H. Lenski, *The Interpretation of St. Paul's Epistles to the Galatians, to the Ephesians and to the Philippians* (Columbus, OH: Lutheran Book Concern, 1937), 873.

[5] Paul might simply be saying that these women's names are in the Book of Life, since the emphasis in these verses is on them. But even if so, the implication is clear that Clement and Paul's other co-workers are also in the Book of Life.

Two others who labored with Paul illustrate that their eternal destiny was based on faith alone, but their value in ministry was based on their actions.

John Mark labored with Paul and Barnabas for a time as their assistant on their first missionary journey (Acts 13:5) and then left—"departing from them, [John Mark] returned to Jerusalem" (Acts 13:13). Later, there was a rift between Paul and Barnabas since Paul was determined not to take John Mark again, while Barnabas insisted that he be taken (Acts 15:37-38). The result is that Paul and Barnabas split up (Acts 15:39). Of course, John Mark's eternal salvation was not dependent on whether he remained in the ministry or not.[6]

Another of Paul's co-workers was Demas. He is mentioned positively in the closings of two of Paul's letters (Col 4:14; Philem 24). Yet near the end of 2 Timothy, Paul uses Demas as an example of one who did not continue in the work, saying, "Demas has forsaken me, having loved the present world, and has departed for Thessalonica" (2 Tim 4:10). We are never told whether Demas later got back into ministry. But his eternal destiny was not in doubt. What was in doubt, as the verses before 2 Tim 4:10 show, was his eternal rewards (cf. 1 Cor 9:27; 2 Tim 4:6-8).

---

[6] Paul later changed his opinion of John Mark and found him once again helpful for ministry. See Col 4:10; 2 Tim 4:11; and Philem 24.

NINETY-TWO

Eternal Security for All Believers Who Have Died (1 Thessalonians 4:14)

For if we believe that Jesus died and rose again, even so God will bring with Him those who sleep in Jesus.

We Believe That Jesus Died and Rose Again

First Thessalonians 4:13-18 is the greatest single NT passage on the Rapture. Evidently some in the church of Thessalonica thought that their believing loved ones who had died would miss out on the millennial kingdom because they would not be alive at the time of the Rapture.

Paul starts out by saying, "But I do not want you to be ignorant, brethren, concerning those who have fallen asleep, lest you sorrow as others who have no hope." While believers rightly grieve, our grief should be far different from that of unbelievers who lose loved ones.

Those who sleep (*tōn kekoimēmenōn*, from *koimaomai*), whenever used figuratively, refers to the death *of believers* (Matt 27:52; John 11:11; 1 Cor 11:30; 15:6, 18, 20, 51; 1 Thess 4:14, 15).[1]

Paul bases his discussion of believers who have died by referring to the gospel. Jesus' death and resurrection are fundamental truths of the Christian faith. Our knowledge of what will happen to believers who have died is sourced in our knowledge that Jesus died on the cross for our sins and rose bodily from the dead.

---

[1] There are two references that might simply refer to the death of anyone—1 Cor 7:39 and 2 Pet 3:4—but both probably refer to the death of believers as well.

Shenton writes,

> The logical conclusion of the death and resurrection of Jesus is that all those who believe in him, whether dead or alive, will rise again to eternal life. The Thessalonians had to realize that not even death severs the union of a believer with Christ, which is the foundation of the Christian's hope: "Christ has indeed been raised from the dead, the firstfruits of those who have fallen asleep" (1 Cor. 15:20).[2]

We Also Believe God Will Bring with Him Those Who Sleep in Jesus

Jesus Himself made it clear that not only do believers have everlasting life right now as a present possession (John 11:26), but they are guaranteed that on the last day of this age, He will raise them bodily from the dead so that they can take part in His kingdom (John 11:25). Paul might have been alluding to Jesus' words, "He who believes in Me, though he may die, he shall live" (John 11:25b). This is the promise of bodily resurrection.

If the dead in Christ were to miss out on the Millennium, as some of the believers in Thessalonica evidently believed,[3] Jesus would have lied in John 11:25b. The idea that believers who are alive at the time of the Rapture would be raised one thousand years before believers who have died is absurd.[4]

---

[2] Tim Shenton, *Opening Up 1 Thessalonians* (Leominster: Day One Publications, 2006), 88-89.

[3] Beale writes, "On the other hand, there was also apparently the belief that those living at the time of the *parousia* would be translated bodily and gloriously but would not be bodily reunited with their dead fellow-Christians" (G. K. Beale, *1–2 Thessalonians* [Downers Grove, IL: InterVarsity, 2003], 133).

[4] Beale additionally suggests, "Some also denied that there would be a final, physical resurrection of all God's people (1 Cor 15:12; 2 Tim 2:18)" (*1–2 Thessalonians*, 132).

Green comments, "Upon this foundation [Jesus' death and resurrection] was built the hope in the resurrection of the dead. Over and again in the apostolic teaching, *the resurrection of Jesus is put forward as the guarantee of the resurrection of believers.*"[5]

Because He rose from the dead, all who have died in Him will be raised from the dead when He returns. Those who have died in Him are believers. All who believe in Him are guaranteed future bodily resurrection.

Paul ends this section by saying, "Therefore comfort one another with these words" (1 Thess 4:18). He states no exceptions. Paul does not say that the dead in Christ *who persevered in faith and good works* will rise first. Faith in Christ guarantees that the believers who died before the Rapture will be the first ones raised. There would be no comfort if we had to analyze the lives of our departed loved ones and hope to figure out if they likely had enough good works to justify their being part of Christ's kingdom.

Here too is the faith-alone message.

---

[5] Gene L. Green, *The Letters to the Thessalonians* (Grand Rapids, MI: Eerdmans, 2002), 220, emphasis added.

NINETY-THREE

Even Morally Lethargic Believers Will Live Forever with Him (1 Thessalonians 5:10)

But let us who are of the day be sober, putting on the breastplate of faith and love, and as a helmet the hope of salvation. For God did not appoint us to wrath, but to obtain salvation through our Lord Jesus Christ, who died for us, that whether we wake or sleep, we should live together with Him (1 Thess 5:8-10).

God Did Not Appoint Us to Wrath

The wrath of 1 Thess 5:9 does not refer to the lake of fire and eternal condemnation. In this context, Paul is speaking of the wrath that will be poured out on earth during the seven-year Tribulation. In vv 1-10 Paul distinguishes between "them," the unbelievers, and "we," the believers. Concerning unbelievers, he says, "When *they* say, 'peace and safety!' then sudden destruction comes upon *them*" (v 3, emphasis added). Of the believers, Paul says, "God did not appoint *us* to wrath," that is, the sudden destruction which is the Tribulation (v 10, emphasis added).

God Appointed Us to Obtain Salvation Through Our Lord Jesus Christ

The *salvation* of v 9 concerns deliverance from the Tribulation. God appointed the Church to escape the Tribulation. When Paul says "through our Lord Jesus Christ," he is referring to Jesus being the agent of deliverance for all who believe in Him. In the words which follow, Paul makes it clear that faith alone is the condition.

Whether We Wake [Watch] or Sleep

The NKJV reads "whether we *wake* or sleep" (emphasis mine). However, the Greek literally says *whether we **watch** or sleep*. The word in question is *grēgoreō*. That same word was used four verses earlier by Paul: "Therefore let us not sleep, as others do, but let us *watch* and be sober" (emphasis mine).

Whether believers are watching and alert for Christ's soon return or are morally asleep,[1] they retain everlasting life and future participation in His coming kingdom. Wiersbe says, "'Wake' and 'sleep' here do not mean 'alive' and 'dead' as in 4:13–18; they mean respectively 'alert' and 'careless.' Christians should be living clean, dedicated lives when Jesus comes."[2]

The final words of v 10 make it clear that Paul is stressing the security of the believer.

We Should Live Together with Him

The expression *we should live together with Him* is a statement about eternal security. Some translations say, "we *should live* together with Him (NKJV, KJV; NIV has *may live* and ESV has *might live*). Others say, "we *will live* together with him" (NASB, HCSB, LEB, NET). Green comments, "He died for believers so that they in turn might live together with him. This exchange touches the heart of the gospel of God."[3]

---

[1] The word used here for *sleep* (*katheudō*) is a different word than the one used in 1 Thess 4:13-15 (*koimaomai*) to refer to believers who have died. Some commentators suggest that Paul is talking about whether believers are alive or dead (e.g., Lenski, Beale, *The New Bible Commentary*, and *FaithLife Study Bible*), but that is inconsistent both with the context and with the changed word for *sleep* used here.

[2] Warren W. Wiersbe, *Wiersbe's Expository Outlines on the New Testament* (Wheaton, IL: Victor Books, 1992), 604.

[3] Gene L. Green, *The Letters to the Thessalonians* (Grand Rapids, MI: Eerdmans, 2002), 243.

Constable writes,

> **5:10.** What did Paul mean by **whether we are awake or asleep?** Did he mean "whether we are alive or dead," or "whether we are spiritually alert or lethargic"? It seems that he meant the latter because he used the same words for "awake" (*grēgorōmen*) and "asleep" (*katheudōmen*) as he used in verse 6, where they clearly mean spiritually alert and spiritually lethargic. If so, then Paul's point is that Christians are assured of life **together with Him,** whether they are spiritually watchful or not. That they might live with Christ was His purpose in dying for them. They *will* escape God's wrath whether they are watchful or not (cf. 1:10). This is a powerful argument for a pretribulational Rapture.[4]

The point is clear: all believers will spend eternity with Jesus in His kingdom. None will be excluded. Faith alone is the condition for inclusion in Christ's kingdom.

---

[4] Thomas L. Constable, "1 Thessalonians" in *The Bible Knowledge Commentary*, New Testament Edition, ed. by John F. Walvoord and Roy B. Zuck (Wheaton, IL: Victor Books, 1985), 707.

NINETY-FOUR

Sanctified by Faith Once for All (Hebrews 10:10)

By that will we have been sanctified through the offering of the body of Jesus Christ once for all.

By That Will We Have Been Sanctified

The expression *by that will* looks back to the previous verses, which spoke of the inadequacy of animal sacrifices, culminating with Jesus saying, "'Behold, I have come to do Your will, O God'" (Heb 10:9). The Lord Jesus willingly died on the cross for our sins. "By that will," by Jesus' willing self sacrifice, "we have been sanctified."

The word *sanctified* means *set apart*. There are three types of sanctification. *Past sanctification*, being set apart into God's family, is the same as justification. *Present sanctification*, which is also called *progressive sanctification*, refers to the fact that the Holy Spirit is seeking to move believers toward ever-increasing holiness. *Future sanctification*, also called *glorification*, points to the return of Christ when all believers will gain glorified bodies, will lose the ability to sin, and will become immortal and pain-free.

The author of Hebrews always uses the word *sanctification* to refer to past sanctification (Heb 2:11; 10:10, 14, 29; 13:12). Essentially, when Hebrews refers to sanctification, it is talking about justification before God.

Hodges comments:

> The words rendered "made holy" involve a single Greek word (*hēgiasmenoi*) often rendered "sanctify" (cf. 10:14,

29). Here it occurs in a tense that makes it plain, along with the rest of the statement, that the sanctification is an accomplished fact. Nowhere in Hebrews does the writer refer to the "progressive sanctification" of a believer's life. Instead sanctification is for him a functional equivalent of the Pauline concept of justification. By this sanctification, which is accomplished through the death of Christ, New-Covenant worshipers are perfected for guilt-free service to God (cf. 2:11).[1]

Bruce adds,

> The sanctification which his people receive in consequence is their inward cleansing from sin and their being made fit for the presence of God, so that henceforth they can offer him acceptable worship. It is a sanctification which has taken place once for all; in this sense it is as unrepeatable as the sacrifice which effects it.[2]

Through the Offering of the Body of Jesus Christ

The author now makes it clear that in the first part of v 10, he was speaking of the death of Christ. The blood of bulls and goats could never do what the blood of Jesus Christ could and would do when He offered up His own body at Calvary (Heb 10:4).

Past sanctification was "through the offering of the body of Jesus Christ." While the author does not explicitly mention faith in Christ, it is clear from the entire letter that he viewed faith as the means by which one was sanctified (cf. Heb 4:2; 11:6, 31; 12:2; 13:7). Stedman comments, "It is a holiness obtained by faith, not by self-righteous effort…"[3]

---

[1] Zane C. Hodges, "Hebrews" in *The Bible Knowledge Commentary*, New Testament Edition, ed. by John F. Walvoord and Roy B. Zuck (Wheaton, IL: Victor Books, 1985), 804.
[2] F. F. Bruce, *The Epistle to the Hebrews,* rev. ed. (Grand Rapids, MI: Eerdmans, 1990), 243.
[3] Ray C. Stedman, *Hebrews* (Westmont, IL: IVP Academic, 1992), s.v.

Once for All

The Greek word *ephapax,* the last word in the Greek sentence, means "taking place once and to the exclusion of any further occurrence, *once for all, once and never again.*"[4] Lenski says, "The periphrastic perfect 'we have been sanctified' is modified by the adverb 'once for all,' which is placed emphatically at the end."[5] He later adds, "We see at once that this sanctification = our permanent justification, which 'once for all' sets us apart for God."[6]

The author of Hebrews is stressing the eternal security *of the believer.*

Heb 10:1-10. See also, "Believers have been separated from their sins and set apart to God…" (*The Nelson Study Bible*, ed. by Radmacher, Allen, and House [Nashville, TN: Thomas Nelson, 1997], s.v. Heb 10:10).
[4] Bauer, Danker, Arndt, and Gingrich, *A Greek-English Lexicon of the New Testament and Other Early Christian Literature*, 3rd ed. (Chicago, IL: University of Chicago, 2000), s.v. "*ephapax,*" 417.
[5] R. C. H. Lenski, *The Interpretation of the Epistle to the Hebrews and of the Epistle of James* (Columbus, OH: Lutheran Book Concern, 1938), 331. Some commentators suggest that the author is referring instead to the death of Christ being "once for all." However, the author already stated that in Heb 7:27 and 9:28, and here the syntax suggests that it is sanctification that is once for all.
[6] Ibid., 332.

NINETY-FIVE

Perfected Forever (Hebrews 10:14)

For by one offering He has perfected forever those who are being sanctified.

By One Offering

The death of Christ was a *once for all* offering (Heb 7:27; 9:28). The author now repeats that theme to start v 14.

He Has Perfected Forever

The problem with animal sacrifices is that they could never make anyone perfect (Heb 7:11, 19; 10:1). But the Son of God, the God-Man, by His one offering, could and did perfect people forever. The author identifies those people with another reference to past sanctification.

Bruce comments, "emphasis is being laid on the fact that by that same sacrifice those who have been cleansed and 'perfected' are now *eternally constituted* God's holy people."[1]

Those Who Are Sanctified

The NKJV translation, "those who are being sanctified," gives the impression that progressive sanctification is in view. However, a better translation is *those who are set apart:* "Hence Christians are *hēgiasmenoi* [i.e., sanctified ones] (cp.... Hb 10:14; Ac 20:32;

---

[1] F. F. Bruce, *The Epistle to the Hebrews*, rev. ed. (Grand Rapids, MI: Eerdmans, 1990), 247, emphasis added.

26:18)."[2] Acts 20:32 and Acts 26:18 say, "among all those who are sanctified."

Those who are in the position of being sanctified, that is, those who have been sanctified once for all (v 10), have been perfected forever. Once again, this is a powerful statement of eternal security. Hindson and Kroll comment,

> Three factors within this verse make perfected absolute, suggesting the eternal security of the believer. The word itself (Gr *teleioō*) involves completion, the bringing of something to its end. Second, the use of the Greek perfect tense suggests that the perfection has been accomplished and its effects are continuing. Third, the modifier, for ever, expresses security for the believer.[3]

Commentators, of course, are divided about what the present participle means here. Some see it, as I do, as a restatement of the perfect tense in v 10. Some see it as referring to progressive sanctification. Lenski takes the view that it emphasizes that this sanctification refers to a completed and eternally abiding justification:

> The main point is that we should not think merely of being sanctified in the narrow sense of the term, sanctified in holy living, but in the wide sense, namely *being cleansed from sin by justification through Christ's sacrifice, a justification that is entirely complete and abides forever*, of which holy living is only the fruit.[4]

While faith in Christ is not explicitly mentioned as the means by which past sanctification occurred, it is understood.

---

[2] Bauer, Danker, Arndt, and Gingrich, *A Greek-English Lexicon of the New Testament and Other Early Christian Literature*, 3rd ed. (Chicago, IL: University of Chicago, 2000), s.v. "*hagiazō*," 10.

[3] Edward E. Hindson and Woodrow Michael Kroll, eds., *The KJV Bible Commentary* (Nashville, TN: Thomas Nelson, 1994), 2564.

[4] R. C. H. Lenski, *The Interpretation of the Epistle to the Hebrews and of the Epistle of James* (Columbus, OH: Lutheran Book Concern, 1938), 338, emphasis added. He does not explain whether he thinks holy living is the expected or guaranteed fruit. That is his final comment on v 14.

NINETY-SIX

He Brought Us Forth by the Word of Truth (James 1:18)

Of His own will He brought us forth by the word of truth, that we might be a kind of firstfruits of His creatures.

Of His Own Will

God desired that humans might gain everlasting life and spend eternity with Him in His kingdom. When James wishes to talk about being *brought forth*—the next phrase in v 18—he introduces it with the prepositional phrase "of His own will."

He Brought Us Forth

The words "He brought us forth" refer to the new birth. The word translated "He brought us forth," *apokueō*, is used one other time in the NT. In Jas 1:15 it refers to sin *giving birth* to death. The Lord taught Nicodemus in John 3:3, 7 the idea of being born again by God, though He used different wording (*gennēthē* [from *gennaō*] + *anōthen* = born again). Peter also spoke of being born again (*anagegennēmenoi*, from *anagennaō*, 1 Pet 1:23). To be born again is to be brought forth by God. The means by which this new birth occurs is now explained.

By the Word of Truth

He brought us forth "by the word of truth."[1] That is, the means by which He regenerates people is by their believing the word of truth regarding Christ. Blue comments, "In stark contrast with the morbid scene of death that descends from unbridled lust is the bright scene of new life that emanates from the Word of truth (v. 18; cf. Eph. 1:13; Col. 1:5)."[2]

Admittedly, James does not use the word *believe*, and he does not mention the Lord Jesus by name. But it is obvious when he says they were brought forth "by the word of truth" that James is speaking of being born again *by faith in the word of truth concerning the Lord Jesus.*

James calls the readers *brethren* fifteen times in the letter. Only believers are brothers and sisters in Christ. And he refers to their faith in Christ (Jas 1:3; 2:1) and to justification by faith alone (Jas 2:23).

Davids comments,

> ...in the NT, however, while never becoming a univocally [sic] technical term, *the word of truth* does frequently mean the gospel (2 Cor. 6:7; Eph. 1:13; Col. 1:5; 2 Tim. 2:15; 1 Pet. 1:25...), and in 2 Cor. 6:7 it appears with this meaning without the article...only Christian and post-Christian sources provide real parallels to James's "bringing forth by the word of truth." This fact secures the reference to the gospel and regeneration.[3]

Richardson says, "God gives birth to believers by means of his truthful word. The word of truth here is virtually synonymous

---

[1] In John 3 the new birth is by faith in Christ (vv 14-18). In 1 Pet 1:23, as in Jas 1:18, it is by the Word of God.
[2] J. Ron Blue, "James" in *The Bible Knowledge Commentary*, New Testament Edition, ed. by John F. Walvoord and Roy B. Zuck (Wheaton, IL: Victor Books, 1985), 822.
[3] Peter H. Davids, *The Epistle of James* (Grand Rapids, MI: Eerdmans, 1982), 89.

with the gospel…The word of truth is the instrument by which God implants new life in the believer."[4]

That We Might Be Firstfruits of His Creatures

Those whom God brings forth by the Word of truth become the "firstfruits of His creatures." While the fullness of everlasting life is yet future, believers already have that life once and for all.

Richardson rejects the idea that being brought forth by the Word of truth refers to the original creation (a view of some commentators). Nonetheless, he suggests that James intended a connection between regeneration and the creation:

> The Word of truth by which God gives birth to new creatures produces a harvest that he had intended since the moment of his first creating. Here is a wonderful uniting of first and second creation. What God brings about in salvation was contained in the original purpose of his creation.[5]

In Jas 1:18 we find the faith-alone message. While James does not specifically say in this single verse that the new birth is *by faith* in the word of truth *concerning Jesus*, faith in Christ is understood when we consider the entire letter.

---

[4] Kurt A. Richardson, *James* (Nashville, TN: Broadman & Holman, 1997), 87.
[5] Ibid.

NINETY-SEVEN

Faith Was Accounted to Abraham for Righteousness (James 2:23)

And the Scripture was fulfilled which says, "Abraham believed God, and it was accounted to him for righteousness." And he was called the friend of God.

The Scripture Was Fulfilled

The word translated *fulfilled* (from *plēroō*) is commonly used to refer to fulfilled prophecy. When Abraham offered up Isaac, he was fulfilling Gen 15:6 (Jas 2:21) *in some sense*. But what sense does James have in mind?

Adamson suggests that Gen 15:6 was fulfilled in the offering up of Isaac because Abraham had "promise[d] to believe."[1] But Moses does not say that Abraham *promised to believe.* He says that *Abraham believed God.*

Davids comments, "It would be incorrect to see *eplērōthē* simply functioning in the form of prophecy-fulfilment (contra Mayor, 104; Ropes, 221), but rather in the sense that the scripture in Gn. 15:6 says the same thing that James has been arguing."[2] But Gen 15:6 does not say that Abraham would offer up his promised son.

Hodges, by contrast, sees in Abraham's faith, as recorded in Gen 15:6, something which "could develop and undergird a life of obedience."[3] He continues, "Simple and uncomplicated though

---

[1] James B. Adamson, *The Epistle of James* (Grand Rapids, MI: Eerdmans, 1976), 131.
[2] Peter H. Davids, *The Epistle of James* (Grand Rapids, MI: Eerdmans, 1982), 129.
[3] Zane C. Hodges, *The Epistle of James* (Denton, TX: Grace Evangelical Society, 1994, 2010), 69.

it was at first, Abraham's justifying faith had potential ramifications which only his works, built on it, could disclose."[4]

Abraham's Faith Was Accounted for Righteousness

God has a simple accounting method. He determines that anyone who believes in His Son is righteous. Faith in Christ was accounted to Abraham for righteousness (see chapter 37).

Lenski makes this excellent comment:

> Although he was not righteous but a sinner, God counted, reckoned, pronounced him righteous, and did that not because of the worth and merit of his act of believing but because of the value of what he embraced by believing. Abraham embraced the promised Messiah and the perfect righteousness of this Messiah (John 8:56) as it was offered to him in God's promise. That is the substitution which is involved in God's reckoning of faith as righteousness, acquitting the believer and pronouncing him righteous.[5]

He Was Called the Friend of God

The "fulfillment" of Abraham's initial faith in Messiah resulted in his being called "the friend of God." He was called God's friend by the Jewish people (e.g., Jub 19:8; 30:20; Philo, *On Abraham*, 273). And he was called God's friend by God Himself (Isa 41:8; 2 Chron 20:7).

Adamson comments, "The key to James's idea of justification appears to be the covenant relationship, a relationship *which for Abraham at least ripened into friendship*, for he was called 'the friend of God'…"[6]

---

[4] Ibid.
[5] R. C. H. Lenski, *The Interpretation of the Epistle to the Hebrews and of the Epistle of James* (Columbus, OH: Lutheran Book Concern, 1938), 594–95.
[6] Adamson, *James*, 132, emphasis added.

After discussing how Abraham is called God's friend in the OT and in Jewish writings, Johnson makes this excellent statement: "More significant is the way that James 2:23 connects to the key verse in 4:4. *Abraham stands for James as the supreme example of what it means to have 'friendship with God' rather than 'friendship with the world.'*"[7]

The faith we exercise in daily living is not foreign to the initial faith we had in Christ when we were justified. All subsequent actions which are applications of our ongoing faith in Christ are a fulfillment of the potential held in our initial faith.

Justification by faith alone has great potential to produce godly men and women who will be called friends of God.

---

[7] Luke Timothy Johnson, *The Letter of James* (New Haven, CT: Yale University, 2008), 244, emphasis added.

NINETY-EIGHT

Born Again Through the Word of God (1 Peter 1:23)

...having been born again, not of corruptible seed but incorruptible, through the word of God which lives and abides forever...

Having Been Born Again

Peter is reminding his readers about the new birth (cf. John 3:3, 5, 7), which is the same as speaking of someone receiving everlasting life (cf. John 3:14-18, 36; 5:24; 6:35, 47; 11:25-27; 20:31; 1 Tim 1:16). The words *having been born again* translate a Greek perfect passive participle (*anagegennēmenoi*). We did not regenerate ourselves. God regenerates us. In the words that follow, Peter uses the analogy of two types of seeds.

Of Incorruptible Seed

Plant (and animal) seeds[1] are corruptible. They decay over time. By contrast, the spiritual seed that results in regeneration is incorruptible. It never decays. Nearly two millennia after the death, resurrection, and ascension of the Lord Jesus, that seed remains totally viable.

The *Faithlife Study Bible* sees a reference to eternal security: "The new birth is completely distinct from human birth and life;

---

[1] The Greek word for *seed* used by Peter is *spora*. A related Greek word for *seed* is *sperma*, from which we get our word *sperm*. While *spora* suggests plant seed, the context suggests that procreation may be in view.

it involves supernatural birth and is secure because God handles the process."[2]

What is this incorruptible seed? Peter goes on to tell us.

Through the Word of God

The incorruptible seed is "the word of God which lives and abides forever." While Peter does not explicitly refer to *faith* in the Word of God *concerning Jesus Christ*, faith in Christ is implicit. (See chap. 96. James uses similar language in Jas 1:18.)

Elliott says, "the equation of 'seed' (*hē spora*) with the word of God would parallel a similar equation of 'seed' (*ho sporos*) and the word of God in the parable of the sower (Luke 8:11; cf. Mark 4:14)."[3]

---

[2] *Faithlife Study Bible*, ed. by Barry, Brown, Heiser, Curtis, Ritzema, and Bomar (Bellingham, WA: Lexham, 2012, 2016), s.v. 1 Pet 1:23.

[3] John H. Elliott, *1 Peter* (New Haven, CT: Yale University, 2008), 389. This observation is outstanding. Note how in Luke 8:12, "the devil comes and takes away the word out of their hearts, *lest they should believe and be saved*" (emphasis added). See chap. 2.

NINETY-NINE

The Promise of Life (1 John 2:25)

And this is the promise that He has promised us—eternal life.

The Promise That He Has Promised Us

The English translation and the underlying Greek words are a bit redundant. John could have said it more simply: *This is what He has promised us*...or *What He promised us is*...or *His promise to us is*...

The redundancy produces emphasis both in Greek and English. John is emphatic about this promise. In Greek when an author uses a noun (*hē epangelia*) followed by its corresponding verb (*epēngeilato*), the resulting expression can be translated by repeating the word in question (*the promise He has promised*) or by emphasizing the word (e.g., *the profound promise*). I could not find a translation that gave that second type of translation. What many others did instead was to simply leave out the emphasis: "this is the promise that He Himself made to us" (HCSB, NET, NASB, CSB; see also RSV); "The Son has promised us eternal life" (CEV; see also NCV); and "this is what he promised us" (NIV).

Is Eternal Life

The promise is not the chance to win everlasting life by faithfulness. It is not the promise of probationary life. It is the promise of everlasting life, which is both life that cannot be lost and life which is full of potential (John 6:35; 10:10; 11:26).[1]

Verse 25 is part of a context dealing with false teachers (2:18-27). The false teachers wanted to strip the readers of assurance of their eternal destiny (v 26). John is countering their efforts by emphasizing the promise of everlasting life.

The Promise of Life in the New Testament

Marshall gets started in the right direction:

> Elsewhere in the New Testament, especially in the Pastoral Epistles, we hear of the promise of life (1 Tim. 4:8; 2 Tim. 1:1), and this is said to have been promised by God (Tit. 1:2; Jas. 1:12). The thought is of the eternal life of heaven which is promised by God to those who serve him faithfully in this life. Here, however, the promise is probably traced back to Jesus himself (Jn. 10:10, 28).[2]

---

[1] Some commentators understand John to be speaking about the promise of fullness of everlasting life in the future when believers gain glorified bodies and will sin no more. While that is indeed promised to believers and is sometimes called *everlasting life* (e.g., Titus 1:2), the context here makes it clear that this is the promise that the believer *has everlasting life right now*.

[2] I. Howard Marshall, *The Epistles of John* (Grand Rapids, MI: Eerdmans, 1978), 161. Two comments are warranted for two of the verses he cites. First, 1 Tim 4:8 uses the word *promise* not in the sense of something guaranteed to be done, but in the sense of providing a basis for expectation. Bodily exercise *has promise* both for this life (in terms of enhancing and extending it) and godliness has promise for the life to come (in terms of laying up eternal rewards). Second, Jas 1:12 speaks of "the crown of life which the Lord has promised to those who love Him." That might refer to eternal rewards in the life to come. However, more likely it refers to rewards in this present life. Either way, it does not refer to the promise of everlasting life to the believer. The crown of life is for those who love Him, which is not the same as everlasting life for those who believe in Him.

He is right that "the promise" is "the promise of life."[3] But the promise of everlasting life is not "to those who serve him faithfully in this life." It is to *those who believe in Him for that life*. Akin comments, "This promise echoes the promises of life that Jesus makes in the Gospel (John 3:14–15, 36; 4:14; 5:24; 6:40, 47; 8:51; 17:2; 20:31)."[4]

Of course, Marshall's explanation is a very popular one in Evangelicalism today. People say that the promise of everlasting life is for those who serve faithfully, who persevere in faith and good works, who follow Christ till the end of their lives, etc. While those explanations are well intentioned, they are quite like those of the false teachers "who [tried] to deceive" the readers (v 26; compare 5:9-13).

Everlasting life is promised to all who believe in the Lord Jesus for it. The faith-alone message was under attack in John's day. And it is under attack in our day. But the promise of everlasting life really is by faith alone, apart from works.

---

[3] Verses that use the term *promise*, or the related terms *word* or *message*, and that deal with the promise of everlasting life, include Rom 4:16, 20, 21; Gal 3:21-22; Eph 3:6; 2 Tim 1:1; 1 John 1:1; 2:25. See also Acts 5:20, which speaks of "the words of this life."

[4] Daniel L. Akin, *1, 2, 3 John* (Nashville, TN: Broadman & Holman, 2001), 124. N.B.: Some commentators quibble, pointing out that the word *promise* is not found in John's Gospel. However, the Lord Jesus repeatedly said that the person who believes in Him has everlasting life. Akin is right. That is the promise of life.

ONE-HUNDRED

Having One's Name in the Book of Life (Revelation 20:15)

The sea gave up the dead who were in it, and Death and Hades delivered up the dead who were in them. And they were judged, each one according to his works. Then Death and Hades were cast into the lake of fire. This is the second death. And anyone not found written in the Book of Life was cast into the lake of fire *(Rev 20:13-15, emphasis added).*

The Great White Throne Judgment

Verse 15 concludes Revelation 20, which deals with the Millennium, the rebellion at its end, and the Great White Throne Judgment where all the unbelieving dead[1] of all time will be judged (after first having been resurrected).[2]

---

[1] At least some natural-body believers will die during the Millennium (Isa 65:20; Matt 5:22). Most likely they will be judged by Christ in a separate unnamed judgment after the Millennium. But Rev 20:15 is flexible enough that it might suggest that some are present whose names are in the Book of Life. Of course, if all believers of all time are present to act as witnesses, then v 15 might simply refer to the security of the witnesses, those who are in the Book of Life.

[2] Ford says that the words *Death and Hades delivered up the dead who were in them* "suggests that there will be a resurrection of the wicked." See J. Massyngberde Ford, *Revelation* (New Haven, CT: Yale University, 2008), 359. Robertson concurs, "In Dan. 12:2 there is a resurrection to death as well as to life and so in John 5:29; Acts 24:15" (A. T. Robertson, *Word Pictures in the New Testament* [Nashville, TN: Broadman, 1933], s.v. Rev 20:15).

The judgment of believers will occur *before the Millennium* at the Judgment Seat of Christ (2 Cor 5:9-10; cf. 1 Thess 4:16-17). The purpose of the Bema will be to determine what eternal rewards each believer will receive.

The purpose of the Great White Throne Judgment, while not stated directly, is indicated by the nature of the judgment.

The Books of Works and the Book of Life

Those present will first be judged by books of works (Rev 20:12). In light of the principle that whatever a man sows he will also reap (Matt 16:27; Luke 19:11-27; Gal 6:7), the purpose of judging the works will be to determine degrees of torment in eternity for the unbelievers. A possible secondary purpose will be to show that none of those present were sinless.

Completely different will be the examination of what is in "the Book of Life." That Book contains a list of all those who have everlasting life. People in that Book will spend eternity in Jesus' kingdom. Hence none in the Book of Life will be eternally condemned.

One gets everlasting life by believing in the Lord Jesus Christ for that life (John 3:16; 5:24; 6:35; 11:25-27; Acts 16:31; 1 Tim 1:16). Therefore, one gets into the Book of Life by believing in Christ during this life (John 11:26, "*He who lives and believes in Me* shall never die," emphasis added). Though faith is not explicitly mentioned, it is understood. Here is another powerful faith-alone verse.

The Lake of Fire

Unbelievers will not spend eternity in Hades, also called hell. Instead, "Death and Hades were cast into the lake of fire" (Rev 20:14). The lake of fire will be the eternal abode of unbelievers.

Vacendak writes, "All who die without faith in Christ alone for eternal life (anyone not found written in the Book of Life) will experience the second death—the lake of fire—forever."[3]

---

[3] Robert Vacendak, "The Revelation of Jesus Christ," in *The Grace New*

Possibly the lake of fire will be a planet with oceans of fire (e.g., molten rock with fire shooting up) surrounding the land masses. Oceanfront property will definitely not be desirable.

Walvoord comments,

> Though many have attempted to find some scriptural way to avoid the doctrine of eternal punishment, as far as biblical revelation is concerned there are only two destinies for human souls; one is to be with the Lord and the other is to be forever separated from God in the lake of fire. This solemn fact is motivation for carrying the gospel to the ends of the earth whatever the cost and doing everything possible to inform and challenge people to receive Christ before it is too late.[4]

All who believe in Christ are in the Book of Life and will not be cast into the lake of fire. The only condition for escaping the second death (v 14) is faith in the Lord Jesus Christ.

Testament Commentary, ed. by Robert N. Wilkin (Denton, TX: Grace Evangelical Society, 2010), 1326.

[4] John F. Walvoord, "Revelation," in *The Bible Knowledge Commentary*, New Testament Edition, ed. by John F. Walvoord and Roy B. Zuck (Wheaton, IL: Victor Books, 1983), 983.

Epilogue

I came to believe the faith-alone message through Eph 2:8-9: "By grace you have been saved through faith, and that not of yourselves; it is the gift of God, not of works, lest anyone should boast." That was the only faith-alone text I knew at the time. But it was enough.

No one needs a hundred verses in the Bible to know that the only condition of everlasting life that can never be lost is believing in the Lord Jesus Christ for that life. One is enough. But it helps to believe the one verse you have heard if you discover that there are dozens more just like it.

When you share your faith, keep it simple, saint. Do not overload your family members or friends with dozens of verses. One does fine. If they remain unconvinced and are still open, then you might share another. But avoid bruising the fruit. When the fruit is ripe, it will be ready to pick.

The faith-alone message is an excellent way to talk with someone who lacks assurance of everlasting life. You might express your desire that your friend or loved one knows for sure he will be with Christ forever. That is a positive message. You are showing that you know he believes the Bible and that he believes in the coming kingdom. Very few people are offended when you say you would like them to have assurance of their eternal destiny. That is something people want.

The sole condition of everlasting life that can never be lost is faith-alone in the Lord Jesus Christ. Apart from works. Faith-alone. That is good news. May that promise produce in you an attitude of gratitude that stays with you the rest of this life. Forty-eight years later, I still can't get over it.

Subject Index

abide, 6, 65-67, 195, 221-223

abiding, 171, 177, 194, 222-223, 266

Abraham, 4-7, 11-13, 20, 22, 90, 101, 106-110, 112-126, 147, 154-163, 169, 270-272

accounted, 5, 7, 11, 106, 108-110, 112-113, 121, 124, 154-155, 270-271

antinomianism, 135

approval, 74

ashamed, 5, 133-135, 179

assurance, 88, 173, 177, 183, 192-195, 276, 281

assurance of salvation, 173, 183

atonement, 163

authority, 44, 65, 203-204, 207, 210, 214

believe, 4-6, 8, 14-15, 17, 21-29, 31, 35-39, 41, 43-47, 49, 51-53, 55-60, 62-66, 68-70, 74, 77, 80-86, 88, 90, 92-94, 97-98, 100-103, 107, 109, 112-116, 119-120, 124-126, 131, 134, 137-142, 147, 149, 155-164, 166-167, 169, 173, 176-180, 184, 186-187, 190-198, 200, 205-206, 208, 210-211, 213-214, 216-220, 225-227, 229, 231-232, 234, 237-238, 241-244, 248, 252, 256-259, 268, 270, 274, 276-277, 280-281

believed, 4, 6-7, 11-16, 18, 24, 34-38, 41, 43, 47, 49, 51, 58, 60-61, 72-75, 81, 85, 88, 93, 96, 106-107, 120, 122, 125-126, 139, 142, 148-149, 152, 154, 160, 164, 168-170, 179-181, 184, 186, 190, 194, 204, 213-215, 221-223, 230-232, 239-240, 242, 244, 250, 252, 254, 257, 270

believing, 5-7, 15, 22, 25, 28-29, 42, 45, 47, 49, 52-53, 56, 58, 61, 64, 66, 68-70, 75-76, 78, 80, 84-85, 93, 104, 107, 109, 121, 125, 130, 133-134, 139-140, 142-143, 145, 149, 151, 161-162, 168, 176-177, 186-187, 194-195, 197-199, 203, 205-206, 212-213, 218, 234, 238, 242-244, 256, 268, 271, 279, 281

birth, 18, 41, 44, 58, 112, 121, 123, 156, 169, 171, 188, 217, 220, 223, 227, 231, 267-269, 273-274

blood, 17, 94-96, 128, 214, 263

Book of Life, 7, 198, 204-205, 208, 253-254, 278-280

born again, 7, 14, 16, 45, 49, 58-59, 70, 75, 82, 142, 163, 171, 173, 177, 185, 187, 189, 220,

222-223, 228-233, 248, 252, 267-268, 273
born of God, 6, 18, 187-188, 214-215
bread, 46-47, 216-217, 220, 224
bread of life, 46-47, 216-217, 220, 224
bride, 199
Campus Crusade for Christ, 44, 50
certainty, 177, 181
cheap grace, 135, 187
children, 4, 17-18, 46, 64, 67, 157, 189, 214, 226, 229
chosen, 247-248
church, 72-76, 88, 106, 112, 123, 140, 168-169, 173, 177, 183, 185, 189, 199, 204, 223, 230, 232, 242, 247, 252, 256, 259
commitment, 15, 37, 42, 47, 49, 64, 142, 187
condemn, 22, 65
condemnation, 14-15, 22, 24-26, 29, 66, 84, 101, 138-139, 228, 251-252, 259
confess, 24, 138-140, 215
confession, 27, 47, 61, 138-140
confidence, 125
continuous, 142, 223
conversion, 233
cross, 20, 22, 44, 73, 85, 94-97, 141-143, 256, 262
death, 20, 22, 25, 37-41, 44, 55, 57-59, 85, 91, 125, 133, 142-143, 146-147, 149, 164, 169, 179, 182, 198, 200, 208, 220, 243-246, 248, 256-258, 263-265, 267-268, 273, 278-280
death of Christ, 263-265
decision, 217
deity, 186-187, 219

die, 4, 22, 40, 51, 54-55, 57-59, 61, 68-69, 91, 94, 97, 125, 143-144, 146-147, 219-220, 225, 228-229, 257, 278-279
dikaioō, 89-90, 174
dikaiosunē, 89-90, 92, 115, 174
disciple, 36, 188, 222-223
discipleship, 53, 63, 231
discipline, 73
disobedience, 28, 29
doubt, 48, 52, 65, 121, 144, 181, 194, 221, 255
drink, 30, 32, 172, 197
earthly, 96, 144
easy believism, 134, 187
election, 240, 247-248
essence, 41
eternal, 4, 6-8, 14-15, 19-24, 26-29, 31, 40-41, 43, 45-47, 51-54, 61, 66, 84-85, 88, 100-101, 107, 118-120, 126, 138-139, 141-142, 144-145, 154, 157, 161, 169, 171, 173, 175, 177, 179-181, 184-185, 190-191, 193-195, 198, 200, 204, 207, 215-217, 225, 228, 238-240, 245-246, 251-252, 255-257, 259-260, 264, 266, 273, 275-276, 279-281
eternal life, 4, 6-7, 19-22, 27-29, 31, 40-41, 43, 45, 51-53, 61, 66, 84, 177, 184-185, 190-191, 193-195, 200, 215, 217, 225, 238-240, 245-246, 257, 275-276, 279
eternal rewards, 40, 179-181, 216, 255, 276, 279
eternal security, 7, 46-47, 53-54, 204, 256, 260, 264, 266, 273
evangelism, 30, 85, 226, 231

everlasting, 4-8, 12, 18, 20-22, 24-36, 38-43, 45-51, 55, 58, 60-61, 63-66, 69-70, 73, 75-76, 78, 82, 84, 87, 96, 100, 105, 141-143, 145, 147, 152, 164, 169-173, 176-181, 186-188, 190-200, 204-205, 211-213, 215-218, 220-223, 225-226, 229, 231, 234-238, 240-241, 244, 246, 248-249, 252, 254, 257, 260, 267, 269, 273, 275-277, 279, 281

everlasting life, 4-8, 12, 18, 20-22, 24-36, 38-43, 45-51, 55, 58, 60-61, 63-66, 69-70, 73, 75-76, 78, 82, 84, 87, 96, 100, 105, 141-143, 145, 147, 152, 164, 169-173, 176-181, 186-188, 190-200, 204-205, 211-213, 215-218, 220-223, 225-226, 229, 231, 234-238, 240-241, 244, 246, 248-249, 252, 254, 257, 260, 267, 269, 273, 275-277, 279, 281

faith, 1-2, 5-8, 11-15, 18-20, 24, 26-27, 31-32, 34, 37-45, 47, 49-51, 53-55, 58-63, 69-71, 73-75, 77-83, 85-115, 117-127, 129-135, 137, 139-140, 142-158, 160-168, 171-175, 177, 179, 181-185, 187-191, 195, 197, 199, 203, 210-215, 217-218, 220-222, 225-226, 230-232, 235, 237-238, 241, 243-244, 246-248, 252, 254-256, 258-263, 266, 268-272, 274, 277, 279-281

faith alone, 1-2, 5, 8, 12, 15, 17, 28-29, 31, 35, 37-38, 42-45, 56, 58, 71, 81, 86, 91, 93, 101-103, 106, 110-114, 122-124, 127, 129, 134-135, 137, 139-140, 142, 147, 149, 153-155, 157-158, 160-163, 165, 167, 170, 173, 180, 181, 183, 195, 203, 205, 209, 212, 215, 218, 220, 223, 225, 228-229, 231-232, 238, 241, 244, 246, 252, 254-255, 258, 260-261, 268, 269, 272, 277, 279, 281

faithful, 40, 123, 162, 184, 188, 207-208

faithfulness, 16, 157, 207, 275

faithless, 208

fall away, 15-16, 88

false professor, 140

fellowship, 73, 140, 149, 188, 192-193, 229, 253

final judgment, 40

finished, 72

fire, 41, 57-58, 198, 200, 208, 254, 259, 278-280

flesh, 17, 91, 93, 105, 148, 214

follow, 22, 52-54, 63, 139, 155, 162, 171, 176-178, 180, 191, 197, 205, 221-223, 260, 273, 277

free gift, 134, 200, 231, 238

fruit, 16, 189, 192, 266, 281

gift of God, 7, 30, 171-172, 245-246, 248, 281

gift of salvation, 5, 74, 76

glorification, 49, 56, 60-61, 88, 262

glorified bodies, 41, 58, 69, 144-145, 185, 252, 262, 276

gospel, 7, 13, 15-16, 18, 20-22, 25, 27-29, 31-32, 34, 36-41, 44-49, 51-56, 58-61, 64, 68-70, 73, 80, 82, 131, 149, 151, 153, 158-160, 168-169, 179-180, 192,

210-221, 223-225, 233, 235, 239, 242 244, 253, 256, 260, 268-269, 277, 280
grace, 1-2, 5-7, 13, 64, 81-83, 90-91, 94-96, 99-100, 105, 107-109, 112, 115, 118-120, 122, 125, 127-128, 131, 133, 135, 137-138, 148, 171-173, 179, 184-185, 187-189, 191-192, 194, 200, 215, 230-231, 237, 246-249, 251, 270, 279-281
Great White Throne Judgment, 40, 49, 139, 208, 278-279
growth, 103
holiness, 110, 173, 246, 262-263
Holy Spirit, 72, 74-75, 77, 80, 105, 150, 152, 164, 166, 168-169, 178, 184, 199, 232, 244, 262
humility, 103
"I am" statements, 46, 55, 219, 224
inheritance, 87, 117-118, 185
in His name, 4-6, 17-18, 25, 68, 70, 213-215
Isaiah, 72
John the Baptist, 6, 27-29, 36, 123, 157, 164, 210-212
judge, 25, 65, 128, 236-238, 240
judgment, 25, 28, 39-40, 49, 66, 84, 139, 180, 206-208, 246, 251, 278-279
Judgment Seat of Christ, 40, 180, 207, 251, 279
justification, 5-6, 11-12, 43, 51, 77-78, 80, 90-91, 93, 95-107, 109-116, 118-119, 122-128, 132, 134, 137-140, 148-150, 153-155, 157-158, 160-167, 172, 174-175, 178, 184-185, 212, 229, 245, 254, 262-264, 266, 268, 271-272

justified, 5-6, 77-79, 81-82, 89-95, 98, 100-105, 108, 110, 112, 114-115, 117, 119, 122-123, 125, 127-130, 132-134, 139-140, 148-151, 153-155, 157-158, 160, 162-163, 165, 175, 184-185, 236, 240, 246, 272
law, 2, 5, 43, 77-79, 81-83, 92-93, 98-103, 105-106, 117, 119-120, 123, 130-134, 136-137, 148-153, 157, 160-161, 163, 166, 174, 189-190, 217, 236, 242
law of faith, 5, 99-100
legalism, 109
life, 4-8, 12, 15, 18-22, 24-58, 60-61, 63-66, 68-70, 73-76, 78, 82, 84, 87, 89-91, 96, 98, 100, 104-105, 125-126, 137-138, 140-143, 145, 147, 152, 157, 164, 169-174, 176-181, 184-188, 190-200, 204-205, 207-208, 211-213, 215-218, 220-226, 229, 231, 234-241, 244-246, 248-254, 257, 260-261, 263, 267-270, 273, 275-281
lifelong faith, 142
light, 5, 12, 20, 32, 63-67, 87, 90, 107, 147, 160, 164, 179, 210-211, 220, 224, 251, 254, 279
living water, 4, 30-31, 33-34, 37, 47, 172, 196-197, 200, 217
Lord, 4-6, 8, 11-16, 18-22, 24-25, 28-33, 37, 39-42, 44-53, 55-58, 60-67, 69, 71, 73-75, 77, 79, 81-89, 92-93, 99, 101, 103, 107, 112, 119-120, 124-125, 127-128, 135, 138, 141, 145-148, 156-157, 159-160, 163, 169, 172, 175, 178-179, 185-186, 189, 192-193, 196,

198-199, 203-205, 207-208, 219-225, 227, 229, 231-233, 239, 245-246, 252-254, 259, 262, 267-268, 273, 276-277, 279-281
Lordship, 139
Lord's Supper, 148
lost, 8, 11, 20, 32, 38, 51, 171, 187, 194, 196, 222, 241, 276, 281
love, 21-22, 98, 103, 127, 186, 188-189, 259, 276
mature, 193
maturity, 16
Messiah, 6, 11-12, 20, 30-31, 33-34, 38-39, 44, 52, 61, 69, 82, 107, 118-120, 122, 125-126, 130, 133, 154-155, 158, 160-161, 169, 182, 187-188, 206, 208, 210, 219, 248, 271
ministry, 14, 27-28, 50, 63, 71, 75, 96, 152, 164, 176, 178, 203-204, 213, 215, 230, 248, 255
Moses, 12, 19-20, 77-79, 81, 117, 146, 148, 150, 158, 160, 189, 235-236, 242, 270
neighbor, 189
not by works, 6, 151-152, 184, 217
obedience, 15, 42, 47, 49, 137, 182, 187, 192, 217, 270
parable, 14-15, 206, 208-209, 274
parousia, 257
past sanctification, 87, 262-263, 265-266
perish, 4, 19-22, 52-53
perseverance, 42, 47, 61-62, 147
pisteuō, 69, 93, 149, 155
pistis, 93, 120, 155, 172
Positional Sanctification, 5, 87-88
prayer, 37, 85, 103, 195

pride, 99
promise, 5-7, 11, 23, 26, 40-42, 48, 51, 53-56, 73-74, 82, 85-86, 107, 117, 119-122, 141-142, 144-145, 147, 159, 163-164, 166-168, 170, 173, 178, 180, 193, 195-199, 225, 229, 237, 257, 270-271, 275-277, 281
punishment, 72, 208, 280
Rapture, 146, 220, 252, 256-258, 261
redemption, 94-95, 251
Reformers, 106
regeneration, 75, 77-79, 96, 106, 139, 150, 152-153, 164, 167, 169, 172, 178, 183-185, 195, 204, 228, 245, 254, 268-269, 273
religion, 34, 99-100, 106, 120
remission of sins, 5, 71-72, 234, 244
repentance, 15, 64, 103, 211, 232
rest, 56, 86, 193, 248, 253-254, 263, 281
reward, 111, 180, 207, 218
righteous, 11, 49, 77, 89-90, 92, 94, 97-98, 102, 104, 108-109, 113, 128, 130-131, 137, 141, 155, 157, 175, 271
righteousness, 4-7, 11, 77, 89-90, 92-94, 97-98, 106, 108-118, 120-122, 124-126, 130-133, 136-140, 154-155, 167, 174-175, 184, 186, 189, 218, 246, 248, 251, 270-271
righteousness of faith, 5, 114, 117-118, 130-132
ruling with Christ, 180
sacrifice, 97-98, 262-263, 265-266

salvation, 5-8, 14-15, 20, 22, 24, 37, 39, 43, 51, 53, 61-62, 65, 72-74, 76, 81-85, 89, 99-100, 138-140, 142-143, 157, 167-169, 171-173, 181-186, 195, 203, 208, 223, 225, 227-231, 233, 235, 241-244, 248-252, 255, 259, 269

sanctification, 5, 87-88, 127-128, 130, 242-243, 245, 262-266

satisfaction, 98-99

save, 6, 43, 65, 83-84, 141-142, 169, 176-177, 180, 220, 235, 251

saved, 4-8, 14-15, 22, 25, 38-39, 51, 65-66, 71, 81-86, 99, 101, 119, 123, 130, 138, 140, 142-143, 165, 168, 170-173, 178-179, 182, 184-186, 189-190, 215, 223, 227-229, 231, 233-235, 240, 242-244, 252, 274, 281

saving faith, 50, 61, 103, 168, 177, 183, 214, 221-222

Savior, 36-38, 122, 128, 141, 179, 184, 229, 231, 235, 239, 252

sealed, 6, 74-75, 168-170

sealing, 169

secret believer, 215

secure, 4, 39-40, 46, 61, 69, 73, 77, 88, 139, 145, 204, 244, 249, 252, 254, 274

seek, 41, 43, 45, 133-134, 164, 234

seeking, 131-132, 136, 163, 234, 262

service, 16, 207, 263

shame, 133-134

sign, 114

signs, 68, 213-214, 230

sin, 39, 78, 88, 93, 95, 97-98, 103, 110, 112, 125, 166, 169, 198, 220, 223, 245-246, 262-263, 266-267, 276

sinners, 127, 167, 176, 192

slave, 76, 220, 223

soil, 15-16

sons of Abraham, 6, 156-157, 160

sons of light, 5, 63-64

submit, 232

suffering, 72, 144, 179, 181

surrender, 47, 64, 187

temporal, 170, 180, 246

the Christ, 5-6, 34, 36-38, 44, 46, 52, 56, 60-61, 68-70, 187-188, 196, 200, 213, 220

the Christ, the Son of God, 5, 38, 46, 60-61, 68-70, 213

the Son of God, 5, 28, 38, 46, 60-61, 68-70, 183, 190-191, 193-195, 213, 265

thirst, 4, 30-32, 37, 45-47, 147, 196-198

transformation, 146

treasure, 207

true faith, 103

trustworthy, 26, 162

truth, 6-7, 23, 31, 39, 43-44, 58, 63, 90, 110, 114, 123, 141, 149, 168-169, 197, 205, 215, 221, 223-225, 267-269

unfaithful, 207-208

verbal, 143

vindication, 174

vine, 224

walking in the light, 64

water of life, 6, 47, 196-197, 199-200, 216

wisdom, 141

witness, 29, 35-37, 52, 61, 71-72, 123, 190-193, 210-211, 227, 234, 244

Word of God, 7, 14, 16, 88, 123, 151, 183, 236-241, 268, 273-274

word of truth, 7, 168, 267-269

works, 6-8, 11, 14, 20, 37, 42-43, 45, 52, 60-62, 82, 90, 92-93, 96, 99-103, 106, 108-112, 114, 123, 126-127, 132-134, 137, 139, 142, 147-153, 155, 160, 163-165, 171-173, 179-181, 183-184, 186, 188-189, 210, 216-217, 231, 234, 244, 247-249, 258, 271, 277-279, 281

works salvation, 34, 43, 138, 142, 153, 231

worship, 33, 139-140, 233, 263

Scripture Index

Genesis
2:17 220
3:15 169
12:1-3 12
12:3 107, 159-160, 163
15:1-5 107
15:1-6 12, 107, 154, 160
15:6 11, 98, 107, 109, 110, 113, 114, 122-126, 155, 159, 160, 161, 270
17:1-14 114
17:11 114
22:1-14 169
22:1-19 155

Exodus
3:14 219

Numbers
21:6 19

Deuteronomy
18:15-18 34
21:23 163
27:26 163
32:4 97
34:5-6 146

2 Chronicles
20:7 155, 271

Psalms
9:7-8 97
32:1-2 112
118 228

Isaiah
8:14 133
28:16 133
33:24 72
41:8 155, 271
52:13 169
53:11 72
53:4-6 72
65:20 278

Jeremiah
31:34 72

Daniel
9:24 72

Joel
2:32 140

Habakkuk
2:4 90

Zechariah
9:9-10 228

Malachi
3:1 210

Matthew

3:9 157
5:22 278
9:6 194
10:8 197
10:15 40
11:10 210
11:22, 24 40
12:36 40
16:21 169
16:21-28 38
16:24-27 40
16:27 279
17:1-13 146
17:4 146
23:37-39 228
27:52 256

Mark

1:2 210
1:4 211
2:10 194
4:14 274
6:11 40

Luke

2:34-35 169
3:3 211
5:24 194
7:27 210
8:11 274
8:11-12 14
8:13-15 15
10:14 40
10:20 254
10:27 189
10:29 189
11:31 40
16:19-31 146
16:23-31 147
16:24 147
19:11-27 206, 279
19:13, 15-26 206
19:14, 27 206
19:16-26 40
19:17 207
19:22-23 206
19:24-27 206
19:27 208

John

1:1-5, 15-18 210
1:1-18 17
1:4, 5, 7, 9 63
1:6 210
1:7 36, 210
1:11 17, 39, 130, 210
1:12 17, 18, 39, 231
1:12-13 212-215
1:13 18, 188
1:29 95, 98, 141, 143
1:49 69
2:23 213-215, 221
3:1-18 215
3:2 24, 215
3:3 188
3:3, 5, 7 273
3:3, 7 267
3:14 24
3:14-15 277
3:14-18 28-29, 96, 205
3:14-18; 5:24; 6:35, 47 225
3:14-18, 36 212, 273
3:15 20
3:16 21-24, 45, 65, 71, 77, 88, 105, 218, 221, 231, 279
3:17 22, 24, 65
3:18 24, 26
3:19-21 24
3:22-36 27, 210
3:27 28
3:36 27, 29, 212
4:1 27
4:1-42 187
4:7-26 30

290

4:10 30, 94
4:10, 13-14 200
4:10-14 31, 47, 196, 200
4:10-26 38
4:13-14 30, 47
4:14 31, 196, 246
4:14, 26 46
4:15 31
4:17 33
4:18 33
4:25 33
4:25-26 33
4:26 34, 219
4:27-29 34
4:39 36
4:39-42 36
4:41 36
4:42 37
5:22 40
5:24 25, 28, 39, 45-46, 125, 186, 191, 199, 212, 217, 222, 231, 273
5:29 49, 56
5:31-47 29
5:32-36 29
5:33-35 210
5:36-40 210
5:39-40 43, 79, 197
6:27-29 216
6:28-29 79, 125
6:29 93, 100, 218
6:35 31, 45-47, 197, 276
6:35, 37, 39, 40 50
6:35, 41, 48, 51 224
6:35, 47 28, 45, 212, 273
6:36 200, 216
6:40 48, 49
6:47 50, 51, 88
6:68-69 52
6:69 61, 68
7:50 24, 215
8:12 63, 224
8:24 198, 219-220

8:24, 34 166
8:30-32 220-221
8:31-32 223
8:33-59 156, 220
8:34 223
8:41 156
8:45-47, 56, 58 157
8:48, 52 156
8:56 12, 107, 125
8:58 219
9:5 63, 224
9:9 219
9:33-47 157
10:10 66, 178, 246, 276
10:10, 28 276
10:11, 14 224
10:27–29 191
11:11 256
11:24 61
11:25 56, 125, 144, 190, 224, 257
11:25-26 48, 205
11:25-27 28, 38, 52, 96, 187, 212, 273
11:26 46, 55, 58, 68, 145, 196, 222, 257, 276
11:27 60, 68-69
12:32 248
12:35, 46 63
12:36 63-64
12:44-50 65
13:1-17 73
13:10, 11 81
14:1-4 54
14:3 54
14:6 55, 190, 224, 229
15:1, 5 224
15:3 81
16:7-11 248
16:8-11 40
19:35 36
19:39 24, 215
20:29 49

20:30-31 38, 52, 61, 68, 187, 211, 212, 213
20:31 17, 46, 70, 205, 273

Acts

2:1-13, 38 74
2:4 80
2:33 164
2:36-37 232
2:38 232
3:1-11 227
3:13-18 227
3:15 229
3:19, 26 227
4:4 227
4:12 226-228
8:1-25 230
8:4-13 71
8:12-13 230
8:14-17 74, 75
8:26-39 71, 230
10:2 233
10:4 233
10:5-6 234
10:15 81
10:34-43 234
10:43 71-72, 81, 234, 244
10:43-48 232, 243
10:44–46 80
10:47 164
10:48 233
11:1-18 232
11:13-14 234
11:14 71, 73, 233-234, 243-244
11:15 80
11:17 233
13:5 255
13:13 255
13:16-38 77
13:39 77, 254
13:46 78, 142, 236, 238, 241
13:48 239, 241
15:1 81, 153, 242
15:1-6 80
15:5 242
15:6-7 243
15:7 71, 81, 242
15:7-11 73, 235
15:9 240
15:9-10 82
15:11 82
15:37-38 255
15:39 255
16:14 85
16:25 84
16:27-28 84, 85
16:30-31 142
16:31 84, 205, 231, 254
16:32 85
17:11 43-44, 237
17:31 97
19:4 211-212
20:32 266
21:8 230
26:18 87, 266

Romans

1:16 134, 251
1:17 89-91
1:18-32 138
2:13 110
3:9-20 98
3:21-27 101
3:21-29 104
3:21-31 142, 254
3:21–4:25 91, 127
3:22 92
3:23 93, 95, 98, 110, 132, 136, 166, 192
3:24 197
3:25 128
3:26 95, 97
3:27 99
3:28 101, 175
3:30 104-105, 175
4:1-3, 9, 12, 13, 16 154

4:1-8 11, 148, 254
4:2 90
4:3 11, 98, 106, 122, 154
4:4-5 119, 142, 200, 247
4:4-5, 6-8, 9-12, 13-21 122
4:5 109
4:9 112
4:11 114
4:13-14 119
4:19-21 121
4:23-24 124-125
5:1 127, 129, 175
5:1-11 127
5:2 175
5:9-10 138, 251
5:12-21 245
6:1 110
6:4 91
6:6, 16 220
6:6, 17, 18, 20, 22 166
6:12-14, 21-22 245
6:17, 18, 20, 22 220
6:22-23 220
6:23 200, 220, 245
8:6 91, 178, 245
8:13 91
8:17 166
8:24 251
8:33-34 128
9:27 251
9:30 130
9:31 130
9:32 175
9:32-33 133
10:1, 10 251
10:2 136
10:4 136-137
10:9-10 134, 138
10:9, 13 251
10:10 139, 140
10:11 134
10:13 138-139
11:5 247
11:6 247
11:11 251
11:14, 26 251
11:20 175
11:26 130, 228
12:2 88
13:11 250-251
14:10-12 40

1 Corinthians

1:18 141
1:21 141-142
1:23 141
2:2 141
3:10-15 40
9:24-26 180
9:24-27 40
9:27 180, 255
11:30 256
12:13 232
15:3-4 44, 168
15:6 213
15:6, 18, 20, 51 256
15:52 88

2 Corinthians

1:24 175
3:18 88
5:1, 7 144
5:2, 4 144
5:7 175
5:8 146, 147
5:9-10 144, 279
5:9-11 40
11:7 197
11:22 156

Galatians

1:6-9 42, 231
1:8-9 153
2:14 149
2:16 78, 93, 102, 142, 148, 175, 184, 254

2:20 175
2:21 197
3:1 150
3:1-2 153
3:2 150
3:5 152, 161
3:5-9 155
3:6 11, 154-155
3:6-14 11
3:7 156, 160
3:7, 8, 9, 14 154
3:7-14 155
3:8 107, 160
3:8-9 163
3:8, 11, 22, 24 175
3:9 107, 161-162
3:10-14 155
3:14 163-164
3:21 137
3:22 166-167
3:28 76
5:4 153
5:5 175
5:6 115
6:7 279
6:7-9 40

Ephesians

1:13 164, 168, 268
2:5 126
2:5, 8 169, 254
2:5, 8-9 142
2:8 165, 248
2:8-9 8, 94, 99, 184, 191, 246-247, 281
3:6 168
5:8 64
5:9 174
6:15 168
6:17 169
6:19 169
6:21 194, 253

Philippians

1:11 174
3:5 156
3:9 115, 174
3:12-14 174
3:20 252
4:2 253
4:3 204, 253-254

Colossians

1:5 268
2:13-14 73
3:25 97
4:12-14 253
4:14 255

1 Thessalonians

4:13-18 252
4:14 256
4:14, 15 256
4:16 56
4:16-17 145, 279
4:17 88
5:5 64
5:8-10 252
5:9 251, 259
5:10 259

2 Thessalonians

3:8 197

1 Timothy

1:13 176
1:15 176
1:16 51, 100, 142, 176-177, 196, 254, 273, 279
2:4 237
2:5 226, 229
4:8 41, 276
5:17 253
6:11 174

2 Timothy

1:1 276
1:8 134
1:9 247
1:12 179
2:22 174
3:15 182
3:16 174
4:5 230
4:6 179
4:6-8 40, 180, 255
4:7 135
4:10 255

Titus

1:2 276
2:14 81
3:5 247
3:5-8 184

Philemon

24 253, 255

Hebrews

2:11 262
4:2 263
7:11, 19 265
7:27 265
9:28 265
10:1 265
10:1-10 264
10:2 81
10:4 263
10:9 262
10:10, 14 87, 174
10:10, 14, 29 262
10:14 265
10:23-25 88
11:6 263
11:9, 19 125
11:10 12, 154
11:10, 16 107
11:33 174
12:2 263
12:11 174
13:7 263
13:12 262

James

1:3 268
1:12 276
1:15 267
1:18 267, 269, 274
2:1 268
2:13 40
2:21 270
2:23 155, 268, 270, 272
3:1 40
4:4 128
5:9 40

1 Peter

1:22 81
1:23 267, 273
2:24 174

2 Peter

2:21 174

1 John

1:2 190, 225
1:3-4 193
1:8, 10 174
1:9 73
2:2 141, 143
2:12-14 193
2:18, 22; 4:3 193
2:24-25 195
2:24-26 193-195
2:25 275
2:28 40
2:29 174, 194
3:7 174
4:17-19 40

4:20–5:3 188
5:1 38, 187, 196
5:6-13 193
5:9-12 190
5:9-13 205
5:10 193
5:12 225
5:13 193-195
5:20 191, 225
5:21 190

Revelation

20:11-15 25, 40, 49, 208
20:12 279
20:12-13 56
20:12, 15 204
20:13-15 278
20:14 57, 245, 279
20:14-15 208
20:15 198, 254, 278
21:6 196, 197, 200
21:27 204
22:12-14 40
22:12-17 200
22:14 200
22:17 197, 199, 200

www.ingramcontent.com/pod-product-compliance
Lightning Source LLC
Chambersburg PA
CBHW071207090426
42736CB00014B/2737